Arc[illegible]iors

Recollections of Royal Signals Soldiers serving with AMF(L)

Arctic Warriors

Recollections of Royal Signals Soldiers serving with AMF(L)

Jim Hindle

Author: Jim Hindle
Cover design: Jim Hindle
ISBN:

CONTENTS

INTRODUCTION

The years from 1960 until 1980 were probably the height of the 'Cold War' between the USSR and the Western nations, divided by Churchill's famous 'Iron Curtain'. The threat to world peace felt real and the West, in the form of NATO, needed a high-profile quick reaction force to address this threat to any NATO country with a common border with the USSR. The result was the formation, in 1960 of a new Force, the Allied Command Europe (ACE) Multinational Force, Land or AMF(L). In 1967, the Royal Corps of Signals added its first permanent unit to this force and this commitment continued until the disbandment of AMF(L) in 2002.

AMF(L) was intended as a multinational, brigade-sized quick reaction force that could be quickly despatched to any part of ACE's command area - from North Norway, to Germany, to eastern Turkey and Greece to demonstrate the solidarity of the alliance and its ability to resist all forms of aggression from the USSR against any member state. The AMF(L) formation consisted of a Headquarters at Heidelberg, Germany, with combat, combat support and combat service support units assigned to it by several NATO nations. For over four decades AMF(L) supported a wide variety of NATO exercises including frequent deployments to Norway, Turkey, Greece, Denmark and other areas. The most specialist theatre of operations was the frozen arctic waste of Northern Norway, with its common border with the USSR. To survive and fight in this hostile environment, British forces required specialist training in arctic warfare and survival. In 1967 we didn't have these skills and relied heavily on training provided by Norwegian Army Liaison Officers. All British AMF(L) units were rotated through this winter warfare and survival training in Norway at the start of each year. This was known as Exercise Hardfall. Training was usually based in the area of Voss. In the early years

Tvildemoen camp and Bømoen camp were used as bases for training. As the size of the contingent grew over the next few years other accommodation had to be found outside Voss and small hotels and hostels were occupied by single units. Exercise Hardfall was repeated annually until the final years of AMF(L). Soldiers gaining these winter warfare and survival skills became known as 'Arctic Warriors' and were widely regarded as specialist troops in this area. Deployments also took place to the NATO Southern flanks of Turkey and Greece with occasional deployments to Germany and Denmark.

This book is principally a collection of individual experiences and recollections of Royal Corps of Signals soldiers who served with AMF(L) over this period, rather than a formal work on AMF(L), and should be read in this context. The main Units involved with AMF(L) were 30 Signal Regiment, 244 Signal Squadron (AS) and 249 Signal Squadron AMF(L).

Producing this book has been a collaboration and I would like to thank Mick Fitzpatrick for allowing me access to the material on his 249 Signal Squadron website, The Wire Magazine and the Royal Signals Journal for allowing me to include articles from both publications and the contributions from those who served with AMF(L) units throughout the period. The views expressed are of the individuals themselves, in their own words, reflecting their personal experiences, which may not reflect official military views at the time.

From the 1960's to the late 1980's, most photographs were taken on small, affordable, plastic Instamatic or 'cassette' style cameras where the camera came with the film pre-loaded in its own cassette, which you then loaded into your camera. There was little scope for making adjustment to exposures with these simple cameras which were mainly of the 'point and shoot' variety. The picture definition quality varied quite a lot. The majority of photos in this book were taken in extreme climates, in operational conditions, by non-professional photographers. Additionally, at that time, photographs tended to be printed out, put into an album or box, and would gradually deteriorate over time. Many of the photographs in this book have been scanned and have lost some of their definition in the process. This is the type of photograph that I have had to work with, predominantly, throughout this book and I ask for your understanding regarding quality and definition. My view was that it is better to have a poor photo than no photo at all!

The book follows the timeline of AMF(L). Hopefully, this should show how the role, equipment and training methods developed and changed over the years. I hope you enjoy this insight into what was a unique way of service in the Royal Corps of Signals.

THE EARLY DAYS 1967 TO 1976

1967 to 1974 - Jim Hindle - Battalion Signal Troop AMF(L)

My first posting in the summer of 1967, after recruit and trade training in Catterick, was to 30th Signal Regiment in Blandford Forum. I travelled by train on a Sunday from Manchester to Salisbury on the 'Milk' train, which seemed to stop at every station along the way. In those days duty rail travel was by the most cost effective (cheapest!) route, regardless of how long it took. Going via London or the fastest route was not an option then. I struggled with all my kit, packed into a large army suitcase and army kit bag, from the rail station to the bus station in Salisbury and caught a bus to Blandford Forum, eating my stale, curled up British Rail cheese sandwich. The driver knew where I was going by my kit so dropped me off at a place known as 'Engineers Corner' on the way into Blandford Forum. I had to walk the couple of miles alongside fields to the Regimental Lines, known as 'Swan Lines'. It was a dark evening and I could just make out the dim lights from the guardroom as I approached. The camp consisted of old wooden Spider blocks spaced along a central road running through the small

Blandford Camp 'Swan Lines' in the 1960's

camp. During WW1 it was a training base for the Royal Navy Division, and it was here that poet Rupert Brooke, penned his renowned poem 'The Soldier'. It was also used as a US Army Hospital after D Day in WW2 and had changed little since. It was a depressing, cold and uninviting place.

After a week in transit, I was allocated to a newly formed Troop and issued with 1958 Pattern Webbing which was a big improvement on

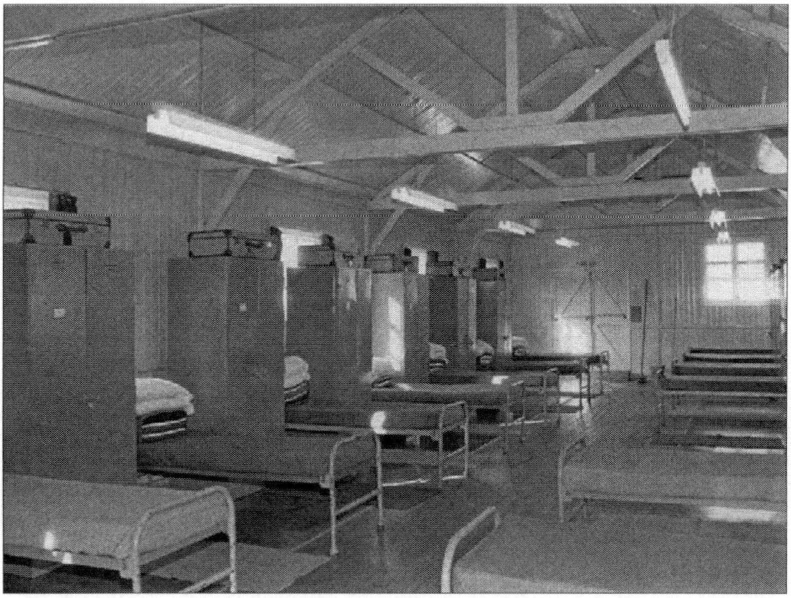

Typical barrack room in a Spider

the old 1937 pattern – no more 'blancoing'! I moved out of transit accommodation and into the spider leg that the troop occupied. All the troop, except for a couple of married pads, lived in this sixteen-man room which meant that you were with them twenty-four hours a day. You soon got to know everyone, what their likes and dislikes were, what their good and bad habits were. We bonded very quickly into a tight team and socialised together most of the time. Another benefit of living in a sixteen-man room is that there is always someone to talk to, to annoy or do something with. I remember one guy who joined the troop for a short while straight from Netley. Netley hospital was not far from Southampton and provided military psychological services at that time. He maintained that he was sane and had a 'certificate' from Netley to prove it! One night shortly after his arrival we were all woken up abruptly. In the dark, you could just make him out, standing on a 6ft GS table, wearing an army blanket and reciting Shakespeare's Richard the Third at the top of his voice. We never saw him again after the following day.

The Troop was just forming in 1967 and its role was to provide RCP, Echelon and Liaison Officer communications to the UK Infantry battalion in the multinational force, Allied Command Europe Mobile Force (Land) (AMF(L)). The Troop Cpl was 'Scouse' Connor and the Troop Sgt was Fred Mackay, replaced later by Dave Coultish. Both were good men and didn't take any hassle from the 'newbies' in the Troop. At this time, the troop had no vehicles or equipment, so we spent each day in tracksuits road running and undergoing fitness training and practising trade skills in preparation for winter warfare training in Norway in the coming February.

RAF Argosy Transport Plane 1968

In February 1968 it was time for us to leave for Norway on Exercise Hardfall 2. Luckily, by this time we had been issued with our arctic clothing, which was a combination of UK, Norwegian and Canadian kit. You can see some of this kit in a later Chapter. This was to be my first time flying and my first time out of the UK! We flew from RAF Lyneham on a RAF Argosy cargo plane to Bergen. The Argosy had two tail fins and a main cargo section, where we sat along the sides in net seating. We then travelled by train to Voss, which was an up-market ski resort. The train route took us up over the

Norwegian mountains and was a beautiful journey. As we fell-in outside the train station the view was like a picture postcard. It was early evening and there was a thick layer of snow everywhere which sparkled in the glow of the street lighting. You could see your breath crystalize on contact with the cold night air. We were dressed in our full arctic uniform and carrying our Bergen's on our backs containing all our kit.

To the curious looks of the people of Voss, we marched from the station, through Voss town and on to Tvildemoen Camp, around two miles outside Voss, where we were to be based for the next three weeks. During this time, we were to be trained in infantry tactics and survival techniques in a hostile winter environment.

1968, Our first Winter training. L-R Mick Ryder, Dave Raybold, Jim Hindle, Ken Staniforth

Without vehicles, we moved everywhere on snowshoes pulling Pulks, which are a style of military toboggan for carrying equipment cross country on snow. It wasn't until the following year that we were issued our standard NATO Planks (ski's) and started to learn to ski.

The famous 'Tennant Girls'. It certainly gave us something to concentrate on at the NAAFI and on board the LSL's, having our two can daily ration!

In camp we lived in Norwegian bell tents which had a wood burner stove in the centre to keep the tent warm. During the night we had to take shifts on Fire Watch and keep the fire going until morning. There were few facilities in the camp. Mobile showers visited once a week and a small NAAFI had been set up in one of the buildings which also doubled up as a cookhouse for meals. On my first visit to the cookhouse I thought that I recognised the cook behind the serving counter. It turned out that we had both been in the same year in the same senior school. What a small world! When we were out training, we slept in lightweight Norwegian tents and cooked on 2 burner stoves fuelled by naphthalene, a liquid fuel with a very low freezing point. For water we would melt down snow using the pressure cooker. It

Living in Norwegian Tents

takes a lot of snow to make enough water for six men, so we used our fresh water sparingly.

The pressure cooker was a great piece of kit which saved lots of time and effort. We had to learn new techniques. Selecting an overnight camp place, pulling our pulk to the site, sending someone back to obliterate our tracks using branches cut from a fir tree, marking out the tent base by holding out a ski pole and turning 360 degrees to mark out a circle then shovelling out all the snow down to the hard ground or hard ice. Three men would put up the tent while others marked out a perimeter security track and mark out the naphthalene store and 'yellow ice' area with ski sticks so that we could find them if it snowed. The 'yellow ice' area was where you went to the toilet. Hence the phrase – 'never eat yellow ice!!'. Then it was down to sorting kit out in the tent. Blowing up the airbeds and lighting the stove. Melting snow and getting a meal on the stove was next while the first person went 'on stag' patrolling around the perimeter track, looking for any signs of footprints coming into the area. Stags lasted an hour outside followed by an hour on fire watch inside, watching the stove during the night. We got into the routine of washing and shaving at night using limited water. Then it was into our sleeping bags, putting your damp socks into your bag with you and your DMS boots between the two bags to stop them from freezing up. At this time, we were issued with standard rations, either 24-hour packs or 4-man packs.

We were also issued an 'Arctic Supplement' which consisted of sachets of muesli, packets of nuts and raisins, extra sugar, Dextrose tablets and chocolate bars. The idea was that you would use these to graze on through the day to help keep your calorie intake up. Some of us brought blocks of Kendal Mint cake with us as we were used to eating that when tabbing in the Lake District. During the night the guy on fire watch would melt snow to make hot water for our flasks so that we could have a hot drink next day without having to unpack the cooker and other kit.

In the morning it would be an early rise to eat and then pack up everything back into our bergens and pulk ready for the off. One thing that we did learn is that it is very difficult to move tactically pulling a pulk in the open! We also learned very quickly to use the layer system to keep cool and stop overheating, especially when pulling the pulk. Our Norwegian officer also showed us how to dig safe snow holes and build igloo's so that we could stay out overnight without tentage. The digging was hot work and we found that we had to dig several snow holes before we got our technique right, leaving enough depth of snow to prevent the roof from caving in. Constructing the 'cold trap' was also critical so that you didn't lose warm air. You also had to make sure that there was ventilation so that you didn't run out of air during the night. We did this by pushing a ski pole through a hole in the roof and would have to move it around every hour or so to keep the vent open. This also showed others where your snowhole was and stopped further snowfall from blocking the vent.

Cpl's Bob Geddes and Ray Cripps checking out the Voss slopes 1968

Our two-week infantry training culminated with us carrying out a full night attack, on snowshoes, carrying all kit and weapons. We were glad when that was over but also felt confident in our ability to survive and fight in the Arctic winter. This training became known as Exercise Hardfall.

Battalion Troop digging snow holes - Andy Baron at the front, Dave Parry digging

The following is an article that I wrote for 'The Wire' in 1968:

AMF (L) Signal Troop - a report on Winter Warfare Training Norway (Hindle, 1968)

Members of the Regiment do not always head for the tropics, as the following article, written by Signalman Hindle shows: Last November saw the resurrection of AMF(L) Signal Troop, here at Blandford, as part of 2 Squadron. The Troop provides rear-link and liaison communications for 1st Bn Somerset and Cornwall Light Infantry (SCLI) (the present UK AMF(L) Battalion) and has the Northern flank of NATO as its major stamping ground. Initial training, mainly concentrated on getting the Troop fit, ready for the winter warfare exercises, whilst Sergeant Mackey and two Corporals attended a winter warfare course run by 1 SCLI. In January, the Troop was fitted out with its winter warfare clothing, most of which had just arrived from Canada and Norway. Then members of the Troop went on an internal refresher driving course for three weeks, whilst the remainder continued with fitness and trade training. During the last three weeks of February the whole Troop went on Exercise "Hard Fall II" in Norway. The exercise was for sub-unit training in winter warfare and was held at Voss which is some 50 miles inland from Bergen. The Troop Commander,

Lieutenant Byrom, was fortunate enough to have been in Norway for the three weeks prior to the Troop's arrival and so training began immediately. Lieutenant Bengstom, of the Royal Norwegian Army, was assigned to the Troop as its instructor, and was virtually in command for the first two weeks of training. This initial training was mainly on basic Infantry subjects and we began by learning to pack sledges, erect tent, use the cooking equipment and walk on snowshoes (we found we had muscles we never knew we had). This part of the training culminated in a five-day exercise, which included all that had been practised previously, plus field-firing and night-patrolling in temperatures of down to -30 C. Thanks to 1 SCLI lending the Troop radios and vehicles, the last week was spent on a communications exercise in which each vehicle travelled 400 miles on snow or ice-covered roads. The views were always marvellous; communications somewhat difficult, and all agreed that both snow chains and studded tyres were needed. Only one vehicle went off the road (unfortunately being driven at the time by our only 'professional' driver, our ED, Lance Corporal Cummins), and everyone had cameras out to witness a 3-ton FFR Landrover being rescued by a passing dried fish lorry. Weekends in Voss were spent on the civilian ski-slopes under the watchful eye of Lieutenant Bengstom. Voss is a large civilian ski centre and has its fair share of off-duty attractions and, despite the limitations of having to wear uniform, a few of the Troop found pleasant "extra mural" activities, who they then proceeded to entertain in the NAAFI at duty-free prices. All good things come to an end, however, and we soon found ourselves back in Blandford.

Accommodation at Bømoen camp

The Troop took part in Exercise Hardfall each year thereafter and progressed to using winterised Landover's and BV202E Snow cats, which were all subsequently used in Norway and the Arctic and deployment onto NATO exercises. We tended to use Bømoen Camp as our base but would spend much of our time up on the Hardanger patrolling on skis, living in snow holes, in igloos or driving our snowcats. One piece of information that sticks in my mind is that there are 104 grease nipples on a BV202, which had to be greased every morning using a grease gun!

Up on the Hardanger, Tony Astle, Dave Parry, Jim Hindle, Ric our civvy mate

I remember freezing hands and grease going everywhere. Driving a Volvo cross country was enjoyable when you got used to some of the angles of lean. The sight of virgin snow and the scenery all around you was breath-taking at times and you were relatively warm and comfortable in the cab. The troubles usually started when you came to a halt. Getting out of the cab in the earlier Volvo's took some time. You had to raise the fold up roof door, stand up onto the seat and climb out. The natural instinct was to just jump down. It was then that you realised the benefit of wide tracks which sat on top of the snow. You quickly found yourself up to your chest in deep snow, eye to eye with the tracks, and had to clamber around to get yourself out and onto more solid snow. Seeing someone do this usually brightened up the crew's day.

Battalion Troop 1969 - L-R Jim Hindle, Geordie Foster, Don McLennan, Ched Chick, Tony Astle, Bob Geddes, Dave Raybold (kneeling), Phil Pearce, Ray Cripps, John Kelloway, Pete Cole

Traversing on mountain tracks was fraught with danger. At times, especially when it was snowing, you could hardly make out the edges of the tracks and had to make an educated guess. Quite often this would result in you sliding over the edge of the track. Where it was steep, you could end up sliding down the mountainside. I remember this happening one day when the whole of the Volvo slipped off the track and slid down the mountainside. Luckily, we were still in the tree line and eventually came to a stop against a couple of fir trees. I was a bit shaken when I looked down at the drop below and gingerly got out of the drivers cab and down into the deep snow. It took us a few hours to recover the Volvo. Using steel tow wires from the other vehicles, along with the 'D' clamps and a pulley around a tree, we were able to slowly drag the Volvo back up to the track and get on our way again.

Italian 'Alpini' Mountain Troops in the early 70's

One of the Troop roles was to provide two Liaison Officer detachments to flanking infantry units from other nations. Each detachment consisted of three troop members who lived alongside these units and integrated with them during the deployments. These were interesting days as we learned a lot about how the other military contingents worked. The Alpini are the Italian Army's specialist mountain infantry. They were classily dressed in ski pants, mountain boots, great fitting jacket and a flamboyant hat with a great feather in it. They were outstanding skiers and looked stylish in whatever kit they were wearing! The Alpini distinguished themselves in combat during World War I and World War II and were well respected mountain troops.

Everyone was keen to get onto the US detachment as that meant better food which was usually fresh, field showers and cigarettes from their ration packs. At their Battalion Headquarters you would usually find a full 'Chuck' wagon which seemed to be permanently open for food and coffee. The Belgian ration packs included a pack of 20 Gaulouise cigarettes and a small bottle of brandy, but very little that you could eat! Strangely, our English tea was a very tradable item with the other nationalities as was our main ration

Jim Hindle and Bo Ridley waiting to load onto the LSL at Marchwood

meals of chicken curry, steak pudding or 'babies heads' as we called them, and apple dumplings. We couldn't give our tins of Spam away to anyone, not even the Americans!

We also took part in full AMF(L) deployment exercises in the Arctic circle, both in winter and summer, and usually deployed by Landing Ship Logistic (LSL) Sir Galahad, Sir Lancelot, Sir Tristram or Sir Percival. These were usually three to five-day voyages from Marchwood, complete with all our vehicles and equipment. Sailing by LSL was an experience never to be forgotten. We would drive our vehicles down to Marchwood and await loading. This could often be

LSL Sir Galahad (sadly lost in the Falklands War)

Typical dormitory below the water line.

a long wait! Once cleared to load, we would drive our vehicles into the cavernous hold of the ship, park nose to tail with the other vehicles and then set about shackling our vehicles to the deck to stop them moving about in rough seas. By this stage you would be covered in rust and grease from the chains and shackles and have to take your weapons and personal kit off your vehicle as you wouldn't be allowed back onto the vehicle deck until the boat docked. You were allocated to large dormitories below the water line. These windowless dormitories had lines of bunks three high along each wall with around three feet between each row. You had around two feet from the top of one bunk to the bottom of the one above which meant there was little space to do anything on your bunk other than sleep or read. You also had to stow your kit in the dormitory somehow. Packed like sardines, we had to make ourselves as comfortable as we could. Each morning we had to prepare for 'Captains Rounds'. This involved cleaning the dormitory, gangways, and galley, including dusting all the myriad of pipework that passed through the ship. Cleaning the 'Heads' also had to be done, clearing up other people's sick wasn't the nicest job. After breakfast, we would all have to go on deck to our 'Muster Stations', wearing lifejackets, while the Captain, or a Ships Officer did his rounds. This usually took a couple of hours. Standing at our muster stations I can vividly remember the smell of the diesel smoke from the ship's engines mixed with the smell of paint, disinfectant, and ozone. Along with the motion of the ship, this smell made quite a few people queasy. Once the inspection was over, those not feeling too well retreated to their bunks for the rest of the day while the rest played cards, read books, or chatted. The Galley opened around 11am to serve tea from tea urns. The tea was already made up so there was no choice! You would then take your mug out onto the deck to drink as there was little space in the galley to sit down. Meals were served in rotation due to the limited size of the Galley which could seat around fifty people per sitting. The crew of the ship were mostly from the Far East and for the duration of the voyage we were on basic ration entitlement. The food didn't really stir up your appetite. Boiled white cabbage, boiled potatoes and dubious stew or tough meat was the usual fare of the day, all swimming in water from the vegetables. The greasy breakfast was a sight to behold and sent many a man rushing to the deck to be sick. Experienced travellers would bring extra treats to eat in the dormitory as well as food accumulated from ration packs over time. A lot of people were unable to eat due to being seasick and there was a constant flow of people to the 'Heads'. In the evenings you could buy a ration of two cans of 'Tennents' beer per person. Not everyone felt up to this but those who did could go to the Galley to buy their ration and could watch a film on the overhead TV monitors, providing you could find somewhere to sit. The problem was that with the movement of the ship, the rattling of equipment due to the vibration of the engines and the noise from the wind meant that you couldn't really hear the soundtrack to the film. We just put up with that in preference to going back down into the bowels of the ship listening to people being sick!

Good view of the Bridge and Antenna masts on the LSL

On some voyages the Troop would have to provide ship to shore radio communications for the military contingent on board. This meant that I could spend my time in the ships radio room. The radio room was located directly behind the bridge of the ship and I had access to the antennas via the ladder from the bridge wing. Above the bridge you had to climb the radio masts to get to your antenna which in rough seas was a bit challenging. Standing on the highest part of the ship was invigorating! You had great views of the surrounding seas and had a bird-eye view of the waves breaking on

Battalion Troop 1971: L-R (-), Tony Astle, Chris Woof, Sandy McLean, Ian Ireland, Slick Sharpe, Jim Hindle

the bow of the ship. The Captain or Duty Officer on the Bridge were usually good to us. They didn't often have 'Pongos' up on the Bridge so they would tell us what they were doing with the ship, what they could see on the radar etc. This place was also my escape from the tedium of Captains Rounds each morning. I would always set up the radio schedules to ensure that we needed to man the radios in the mornings. Sitting in the Radio Room was very pleasant. You could make a brew when you liked and relax at your radio station. When the sea was a little rough you certainly felt the movement of the ship a lot more, being so high up. It wasn't a place for those who got seasick very easily, so I never had much competition for the job.

Inside the Arctic Circle in Northern Norway in winter meant almost twenty-four-hour darkness and in summer, almost twenty-four hours daylight. Both extremes took some adjusting to. In winter, map reading was difficult in the darkness as it was difficult to make out features that you could see on the map, especially in heavy snow conditions. In both winter and summer your senses had to adjust to living in almost permanent darkness or daylight.

You had to be strict about your sleep patterns otherwise your body clock became badly disrupted. The infantry has long adopted 'stand to' at dawn and dusk when deployed in the field. This is to ensure that your defences are manned in the event of an enemy attack at that time. Being with the infantry, we still had to 'stand to' at dawn and dusk regardless of the fact that it was either dark or light. This helped to maintain a rhythm of routine in the day rather than for any tactical purposes. 'Stand to' in a snow trench, at six in the morning in mid-winter in the arctic, with temperatures being around -20c to -30c was not too popular as you can imagine. Watching the Aurora Borealis, or Northern Lights did provide a distraction while you were trying to keep warm, waiting for the RSM to do his rounds and stand you down.

Early days skijoring

In February 1969, 'A' Company the Coldstream Guards, were to go to Alberta in Canada for six weeks to train with the Canadian Army. Our Troop provided a radio detachment to provide rear link communications back to the Coldstream's home base of Tidworth in the UK. The detachment chosen consisted of Cpl Cyril Soaris, Andy McBain and myself. We flew from Brize Norton out to Edmonton Alberta, via Nova Scotia, by Hercules transport aircraft and then by road down to CFB Wainwright in Alberta, which was a Canadian Forces Training Camp on the vast Alberta prairie. Shortly after our arrival we deployed out on a full field exercise with the Coldstream Guards and Princess Patricia's Canadian Light Infantry. The training area was vast and wild. We were in the middle of an extreme Canadian winter and temperatures dropped at times to well below -40c. The snow was shimmering powder which didn't melt or thaw. Your nostrils and eyebrows froze up with ice very quickly and your cheeks and nose froze very quickly if you didn't pay attention. Luckily, we were arctic trained so knew how to look after ourselves in those kinds of temperatures. We had a 'buddy-buddy' system where you each checked each other every four or five minutes for signs of frostbite on exposed areas of the skin. At the end of the training period, we were taken on a visit to Banff to see the Indian Fort Museum which was a great experience. The views over the Rockies were a sight to be seen. We also went on a visit to Edmonton where we were given a tour of the city by members of the Canadian Legion and were treated very well, especially as we were in full No 2 dress uniform. We were entertained in the Canadian Legion Club in Edmonton and were very well looked after.

In the summer of 1969 AMF(L) deployed on a full NATO exercise to Denmark. Again, this was to practise defending a NATO country against an aggressor. This was a summer exercise, so we took our Landrovers by sea to Denmark. On this exercise I was on a detachment providing communications for a Danish Liaison Officer. This helped a lot travelling around Denmark as he obviously knew where he wanted to go and didn't have any language problems. This was when I first tasted Danish pastries. He would go to a local town each morning and find a baker to buy pastries from. I'm not sure that he took the exercise very seriously. On completion of the exercise the Troop had some down time in Copenhagen, where we stayed overnight in a Danish Army barracks. We spent a couple of days touring around Copenhagen and Tivoli Gardens. As we were in No 2 Dress, we were a little conspicuous and had to be on our best behaviour. We were well looked after by the other Danish soldiers during our stay.

In November 1969, AMF(L) Force Radio Troop of 80 men was formed under the Command of Captain Ian Crouch. It was to serve HQ AMF(L) using the latest SSB Radios and Winterised 3/4 Ton Land Rovers. In April 1970, AMF(L) Force Radio Troop and AMF(L)

Battalion Signal Troop amalgamated to form 3 Squadron 30 Signal Regiment, under the Command of Captain Ian Crouch.

Battalion Troop Norway 1972: R-L Jim Hindle, Dave Parry, Tony Astle, Stretch Stenner, Andy Baron, Taff Ormond, Colin Bland, Dave Leggett, Tom Wilkinson

Colin Bland joined Battalion Troop as a Staff Sergeant (YofS) Troop OC in 1970. Colin came to us from 22 SAS and he soon had us developing our fitness and soldiering skills nearer to the standard that he had been used to. We would spend a lot of our time running and tabbing out on Salisbury Plain, living in bashers and doing lots of map reading and climbing a lot of hills! Each year, in preparation for the Winter deployment to Norway, Colin would take the Troop for ten days in Wales followed by ten days in The Lakes training on the hills and mountains ready for Norway. We would do this in early January and sleep out under a basher, which was a simple poncho sheet hung over a central rope. We would carry all our kit in our Bergens and would feed ourselves with the standard army ration packs using hexamine cookers. In Wales we focused on the Welsh 3000 Competition route which started from the top of Snowden and covered all the peaks over 3,000 feet. This involved a lot of climbing up from sea level then back down again before climbing up the next peak. The route would usually be Snowden summit down the Knife Edge down to Crib Gogh then running down the scree slopes to sea level at Llanberis. Climb up to Elidir Fawr and onto Y Garn then to

Glyder Fawr and Glyder Fach then over the Tryfan mountain and down Devil's Kitchen to the road below at sea level. We would do this several times during our stay, sometimes in reverse. Coming down Devil's Kitchen at night was an experience never forgotten. I can also remember putting up my basher at the top of Snowdon on one visit, surrounded by freezing fog which lasted until we eventually decided to move off at 5.30am. It took a while to pack up and get warmed up ready for the run down the Knife Edge that morning.

In Wales we used a small farmers field in Llanberis Pass as our base when we were not out on the mountains. Colin Bland made sure that we had all the luxuries; sleeping in our bashers; drinking water

Jim Hindle and Ian Ireland in Little Langdale in the Lake District – Another 'balmy' day on the mountains ahead

from the stream and cooking our 24-hour rations on a Hexamine cooker. Once we had completed our training in Wales, we would drive up to the Lake District where we used a small basic campsite at Little Langdale as our base. From here we would climb up Bow fell, onto Skafell Pike, over Great End and onto Glaramara and then down Borrowdale Fells to Seathwaite. Again, we would carry all our kit and rations and sleep out under our basher at nights, cooking our rations on a hexamine cooker. The plus side of this part of the trip was that we occasionally got the opportunity to visit the walkers and climbers bar at the 'Old Dungeon Gill' hotel for a beer and a warm around the fire on the nights that we were in Little Langdale. Over the years that we did this training we often formed part of Search and Rescue parties that were assembled to search for walkers or climbers who had gone missing. We were well equipped and trained and fit for this role but were amazed at the lack of equipment and preparedness of some of the people that we searched for. People don't realise that North Wales and the Lake District in winter are hostile environments that need treating with respect.

In the autumn of 1970, Bn Troop members joined Force Troop detachments to support their deployment. We deployed by ferry and road to Mertzig in Germany to stay with the German infantry for a couple of weeks. I remember us watching a squad of German conscripts tackling their assault course. They just wandered along, smoking, and chatting and wandered around the obstacles that they didn't fancy doing. It was then that we noticed that some were wearing hairnets. Apparently if you had long hair (this was the 70's) you could keep it as long as you wore a hairnet. Can't understand why this didn't catch on in the British Army! I remember well the food that we were given in the German cookhouse, weak black tea without milk or sugar, horse meat, sauerkraut, boiled potatoes and for breakfast, cooked meat and bread. Most of us filled up with bratwurst and schnitzel from the local 'Imbiss' when we were hungry or broke into our compo rations. Other vehicles and equipment sailed from the UK to Istanbul by LSL. After a couple of weeks in Mertzig we flew to Istanbul with the US Air Force from Mannheim in Germany for a full AMF(L) deployment exercise to the Turkish border area with Bulgaria. The transport aircraft were massive load carriers. We drove our Landrovers and trailers into the cavernous fuselage, lashed down and made ourselves comfortable in the netting seats fixed along the side of the aircraft. This was a noisy, cold, and uncomfortable flight and we were glad to touch down in Istanbul.

Once we had landed, we were rushed off the aircraft and deployed straight out into the field to a holding area as Istanbul had been classed as a Cholera infected area. Our job on this deployment was to show the presence of a NATO force on the Turkish border with Bulgaria, then a Warsaw Pact country. Driving up to the holding area was a bit precarious. It was getting dark and we were all a little tired. What didn't help was the fact that there was no street lighting and most of the other traffic didn't have any lights on.

I was amazed to see horses and carts trotting along the road with the driver nonchalantly hanging over the side, holding the reins loosely. He didn't bat an eyelid as we overtook him. One of our vehicles, which arrived later that night, rounded a bend and ran into the back of a horse and cart killing the horse and injuring the driver. When the Turkish Police arrived, the driver was found guilty and fined on the spot! It was all a bit surreal really.

When we first arrived in the 'holding up' area we were told that the adjacent fields were full of water melon and that we were to keep clear. Well, who wouldn't fancy a nice bit of cold melon as the sun is going down! If this hadn't been mentioned we probably wouldn't have noticed but suffice to say there were lots of gaps in the lines of melons the following morning.

Holding area next to the water melon field

During the exercise I decided to park my detachment in a small square overnight and bedded down beside our vehicle. We were up early and stripped down to have a wash and shave only to find us surrounded by the villagers and kids watching us in silence. I was obviously too young and naive to understand how offensive this must have seemed to them.

On 5th June 1970 Princess Anne visited Blandford Camp. Part of her visit included her reviewing detachments from 264 (SAS) Signal Squadron, 216 Parachute Signal Squadron and an AMF(L) detachment. I was nominated to display a Snowcat along with a selection of our arctic equipment under snow camouflage nets. At the end of her visit Princess Anne was to drive my Snowcat a short distance. When she was ready, I helped her up the specially made steps so that she could climb into the cockpit of the Snowcat. She drove for around fifty meters and then I helped her out and down the steps. I was to meet her again some years later and she remembered the experience.

One 'non-operational' job that the Troop was given was to go down and help clean up the Fovant Badges. This involved weeding out the chalk badges, trimming the outlines and refilling with chalk. When the WW1 broke out, there was a need to find accommodation for

Fovant Badges

the New Army. Thousands of men from all parts of Britain and overseas lived for a while in the area, passed on to the Western Front and returning from it. Many never returned but gave their lives on the battlefields in France. Others died of their wounds in the hospital or from disease. Rows of silent War Graves in Fovant and other nearby churchyards are testimony to their presence. In remembrance of their colleagues, many of the regiments carved replicas of their cap badges into the hillside. Many of these no longer survive, but by the end of WW1 there were some twenty discernible badges. During WWII, the badges became overgrown to disguise landmarks, which might assist enemy aircraft. Weather and time, as well as the effects of grazing cattle, caused decay. It was in the period of 1948-51 that the two Wiltshire regimental badges were cut and in 1970 the Royal Signals badge was added.

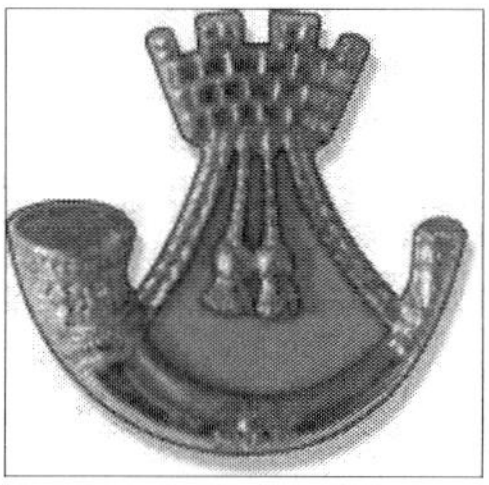

Over my time in Battalion Signal Troop, I worked closely with three infantry regiments. The Somerset and Cornwall Light Infantry, The 2nd Bn Coldstream Guards and the Royal Scots (First of Foot). Living and working alongside the infantry really opened my eyes. They were close knit units who didn't like outsiders and were fiercely proud of their regiments and traditions. The Royal Scots were very physical and aggressive soldiers, recruiting primarily from Glasgow. I remember my first day visiting the Signal Platoon where I was met by the Platoon Colour Sergeant, a big broad man with a broken nose and hands like shovels. Before I got chance to speak, he pinned me against the wall with my feet off the ground and said, *"If ye cause any trouble I'll shak 'ands wi ye windpipe"*. Needless to say, I towed the line! They were hard men who would fight at the drop of a hat and wouldn't back down to anyone. They were useful to have around when you went out into town! Learning to hold your own with these soldiers taught me a lot.

When I first visited the Coldstream Guards in their barracks in Tidworth, to meet the Signals Platoon, I had to park by the Guardroom as the daily guard mount was underway. I was amazed at how many people were involved. The guard, the Guard Commander and 2i/c Reliefs, the Orderly Sergeant, the Corporal in Waiting, the Orderly Officer and a Drummer-Bugler. The guard mounted to the beat of the drum and bugle calls without any commands. It was a spectacle to see. Behind the guard I could see a soldier dressed in full No2 dress, standing by his bed with all his kit laid out and his personal locker at the side, doors open displaying all his kit! Apparently, he had been picked up on the morning Platoon room inspection for a dirty bedspace and was to 'Show Bedspace' on that evenings 'Show Parade' during the Guard Mount. It was certainly different to what I had been used to. I quite liked serving with the Guards as you could hear anyone of importance coming well before they could see what you were up to. The noise of their crunching boots travelled quite a distance and their orders were 'barked' rather than spoken.

Working directly with the infantry meant that I had to extend my military vocabulary quite quickly. Staff Sergeants in the infantry are called Colour Sergeants and woe betide if you got it wrong. With the Guards, a Lance Sergeant wearing three stripes was equivalent to a corporal, but you had to call him Sergeant! A Corporal wore two stripes but was the equivalent to a Lance Corporal, which didn't please some of the corporals in the Troop. This was a result of Queen Victoria not wanting to see soldiers wearing one stripe in her Guards Regiments. Again, with the Guards, if you got picked up for anything on a parade or inspection you 'lost your name'. that meant that your name had been taken down for disciplinary action.

When we were deployed to Battalion Headquarters on exercise, we lived shoulder to shoulder with the HQ Defence Platoon. With the Royal Scots this consisted of the Pipes and Drums Platoon or P&D Pl. There were a lot of characters in the P&D and we had many a laugh with them. Even on exercise, they took their 'chanters' with them to practice and it was quite entertaining to listen to them. The drummers carried their drum sticks everywhere and would drum on anything that they could find to the constant irritation of everyone and the annoyance of the RSM! With the Guards, I came across guardsman trained as 'Tailor' who would sit cross legged on a bench working by hand on uniforms and could just about tailor anything!

By 1974 I was a Class 1 Radio Telegraphist, Class 3 Data Telegraphist, Crypto trained and held the rank of Corporal. My time in AMF(L) had made me into an experienced, confident and competent soldier and had given me the inner confidence that comes from surviving in hazardous conditions and meeting physical challenges. I later qualified as a Yeoman of Signals and went on to complete twenty-seven years' service in the UK, BAOR, Hong Kong and Belize, with time spent in Canada, Brunei, and Nepal, retiring as a Captain. Some of my fondest memories are of my time and experiences in AMF(L) and I'm still in touch with friends that I served alongside.

1968 to 1969 - Phil Pearce - Battalion Signal Troop AMF(L)

After three great years in Minden, I found myself posted back to the UK. Blandford was not too far from Bristol so hopefully able to get home at weekends and see the girlfriend. AMF(L) troop, 30 Signal Regiment was at that time part of 1 Squadron, but I had no idea what the role of the troop was or where we would be deployed.

I found myself part of a small troop, 19 in all, 14 chiefs and 5 Indians. The troop OC was Lt Baines who I had briefly known from 1 Division Signal Regiment in Verden. At that time he had been a corporal Technician, so seeing him in the new position was strange. The troop Sgt, Dave Coultish, was an NCO I remembered from my time at Denbury with the Junior Leaders Regiment Royal Signals. He was a SNCO who worked you hard but you had a lot of play time after. As this was in the October of 1968, the troop had not long returned from an exercise in Thetford with the Somerset and Cornwall Light Infantry (SCLI) and was in the process of winding down before Christmas. This was our last exercise with the SCLI as they handed over to 2nd Bn Coldstream Guards.

The troop was made up of a number of small detachments, based in Landrover FFR, quarter ton and three quarter ton models fitted with C11 R210 HF sets and C42 VHF sets and I found out that the role was to supply comms to the British infanty battalion of AMF(L), which at that time was the 2nd battalion of the Coldstream Guards, based in Tidworth, so we were often on route to them checking out winter warfare kit including white smocks, Mukluks boots, Army planks (ski's) and snow shoes.

I was a Det Commander and had three members as a crew. If I remember correctly the det consisted of Myself, Jim Hindle and Dave Raybold. Others in the troop at that time, that I can remember were Ray Cripps and John Kelloway who came from Exeter and were both techs, Ched Chick and Bob Geddes. Most days consisted of kit maintenance of one sort or another with not really a lot to do at that time of the year, except of course the customary guard duties.

After the Christmas break it was full speed ahead checking kit and preparing for Ex Hardfall in the late February of 1969. Frequent trips to the Guards in Tidworth to pick up ski's, winter kit and checking details etc ready for the off. We were, if I remember correctly, due to entrain at Luggershall to go by train to Newcastle and then board the troop ship Sir Galahad (later sunk in the Falklands) for Norway.

The trip North was to say the least very rough, wet and windy with much puking taking place below deck. On the second day at sea we had to go to muster stations, our's being in the Bow and with the rough weather it wasn't long before we were all soaking through. I recall the CO of the Coldstream's complaining to the Captain of the ship that he was taking too long to do his rounds and that troops were suffering from the cold and wet and that a number had to be taken to the sick bay for treatment.

We duly arrived in the port of Bergan in Norway and then by train to Voss, which was to be the troops main base, but a detachment did go to Bardufos further north.

Twildamoen camp was quite small and my memories are mainly of a very icy path up to the tents which caused many a slip, tumble and laugh. Every night we had one person on fire guard in the tent and the hot drink you made on the stove when you had your turn on-stag. Days were taken up with ski practise of one sort or another with cross country trips around the area and the Norwegian Officers instructing us in winter survival, including the cold snow bath to cool down after the trip out, followed of course by a sauna on return to camp.

On one training exercise we went with the Coldstreams up the local mountain and did a 20km cross country ski complete with packs, rifles and kit. Lots of laughs and knackered guys as many had never skied before. To get back down the mountain we had to ski down a steep slope about quarter of a mile to the ski lifts. What a sight it must have been to see all these Coldstream Guardsmen not being

Battalion Signal Troop 1969 L-R Jim Hindle, Pete Cole, Geordie Foster, Ched Chick, John Kelloway, Bob Geddes, Phil Pearce, Dave Raybold, Ray Cripps, Don McLennan

able to stop and just falling over at the bottom, with the locals and tourist's laughing and saying 'Gee British Ski troops' (if only they knew the truth).

The return trip to UK was on another LSL but we returned via Marchwood near Southampton. When all our kit had been returned to Tidworth the Troop went out on a Radio Exercise to various locations across the South of England. My detachment was to be based in Cornwall, just in time for the May 1st Helston Floral dance. We managed to talk a farmer into letting us use his barn on a farm outside the town, but I do remember that all three of us had a bottle each of Bacardi which, after getting some coca cola, we drank from our kidney mugs and it seemed to go down very smooth and fast.

During our time in Blandford we had many laughs. Wednesday was 'pay day' and the regular three card brag game in the centre barrack room, with much money changing hands. I managed a few games for the rugby team but once I bought a car most weekends were spent off home to Bristol.

John Kelloway had an old Triumph Herald car which was used to take us into Blandford for the pub, otherwise it was a few mile walk down to Blandford Forum and an uphill walk back. He always told us to mind the hole in the floor in the passenger footwell "don't put your feet through"! I remember him returning one Monday morning with a big dent and damage to his car. He had run into a deer on the way home..... opps.

L-R Rio McMahon, Jim Hindle, Ken Staniland, Phil Pearce - note the tans after the weeks in Cornwall

Summer 1969 came together with the summer exercise which was in Denmark. Having been there a number of times when in Verden with 1 Division Signal Regiment, I was looking forward to it.

We sailed this time from Marchwood and up the English Channel and then through the Keil canal to Denmark, which was a smooth trip and interesting. A lot of the time, the exercise was mainly non tactical so cam netting made a good bed when off duty. The exercise covered an area I had been to before and our job was to provide comms for the Danish Liason Officer. This was quite a nice job and we spent a lot of time touring around Denmark. After the exercise we went to a tented camp the other side from Copenhagen and were put up in 180 lb tents. The second night were had a very bad storm which required us to put the guy ropes onto the tow hitch of our land rovers to keep the tent up. The morning brought more problem in the shape of our troop Sgt who, because he kept getting duties from the RSM, picked on certain members who stayed in camp and one member, no names, pulled a bayonet on the guy and told him in no uncertain terms he had done more than his fair share and go pick on someone else. Nothing further was said. We had a few trips to different places while there and had many a laugh.

The return was not by ship this time but by Hercules into Brize Norton where we were turned over by the Customs, as usual, and many a bloke lost extra fags or drink. One Customs officer took delight in telling us to take our rolled sleeping bags off our bergens and throw them on the floor. As this was a popular place to carry your illicit bottle of spirits there was soon the sound of smashing and the smell of spilt whisky and brandy! In our vehicle, we had spent ages masking taping packets of cigarettes to the underside of the radio table in the back of the landrover. While we were waiting for the Customs Officer to get to us I quickly checked the back of the landrover, only to see that the masking tape holding the packs up had come loose and all the cigarettes were on full view. There wasn't time to do anything as the Customs officer had arrived. For some reason he didn't check the back of the landrover at all – our lucky day.

The following brochure and ski route map will give you a taste of what the ski slopes of Voss were like in 1969.

By this time we had been advised that a new Force Radio Troop was being formed. Both troops were moved into 3 Squadron under the new OC, Capt Dickinson. The OC was not allowing guys to go on course or training lest he lost them on return to postings, so with a sad heart I departed for Civi street in October 1969. If I knew then what I know now I would not have left. Certa Cito

1972 To 1976 - Ian (Larry) Little - 244 Signal Squadron (AS)

I was posted to 244 Signal Squadron in August 1972 from the Army Apprentices College in Harrogate. At that time, I was a Signalman, trained as a Radio Telegraphist. Throughout my time in the Corps, spanning 25 years, I was known as Larry, but our civilian population could not understand Larry from Ian so it was easier just to revert back to Ian, though any time I meet any military colleagues I would be called Larry.

There were two of us arrived at the same time, and were good friends at Harrogate. We both ended up in the same Troop so helped each other. Echo troop were a mixed bunch, some Para trained,others not. It had the most interesting role within the Squadron as there was so much variety in deployments supporting many other units in Air Support.

When we first arrived at RAF Benson there was not enough accommodation and around twenty of us were actually accommodated in a single block in RAF Abingdon. Getting to work involved getting on a Double Decker bus, after breakfast in Abingdon to RAF Benson. We would have an early evening meal in Benson so that we could get the bus back to Abingdon. There were personnel from all the different troops in the squadron based in Abingdon which led to a bit of a "skive" being played. It was "sheet exchange" every Monday in Abingdon so one member from each Troop would not bother going to Benson that day and change everyone's sheet. This ended up with four or five guys having nothing to do all day but to go on the piss in Abingdon. The social life was pretty good as some of the more senior corporals played darts for the Barley Mow pub and the locals, in the main, thought we were great. After about four months they managed to clear a block for us in Benson which put paid to any "Skives" – but it was much better to integrate with the rest of the Squadron guys.

The OC Squadron was a Major Phil Spooner, former Special Air Service, who chased us from our arrival right up until a year later when my good friend Geordie Knox and I got into a bit of bother and had to be disciplined by Major Spooner. He gave us a choice - we could either spend Christmas in jail or go to “P” Company. As it was only mid October it seemed to be a very harsh sentence but we had to call his bluff and both of us headed off to “P” Company which, thankfully, we both passed and spookily found ourselves back in RAF Abingdon for a month on the All Arms Parachute Course which was great as we knew so many people on the Station.

In June 1973 I deployed to Greece as part of the BASO team in Support of 19 Bde, who had an AMF(L) role at the time. They used to have the title 19 Airportable Brigade and they supported AMF(L) at times during this period.

BASO (Brigade Air Support Operations) provided the comminications between the Army unit we were in support of and whichever RAF Squadrons were being exercised. This could be either fast jets or helicopters under the guide of the MAOTs (Mobile Air Operations Teams) which were the forward element of 244 Signal Squadron. The BASO team sent the request to the MAOT’s to task the aircraft or the helicopters. There would be an RAF Liason Officer, which could range from a WIng Commander (Lt Col) down to a Flying Officer (Lieutenant), so these guys would be trained in the methodology of how a request for Air Support got turned into an aircraft or helicopter delivering on the request. 244 would operate HF/VHF/UHF radio’s and provide the BASO with the ability to talk directly to the pilots if necessary.

We flew to Thessaloniki Airport in RAF Hercules with the Land Rovers airportabalised, but the vehicles had to return via LSL which was good in one way as making Land rovers and equipment airportable was a mammoth task. We always had to go via the Air Mounting Centre in South Cerney to be checked, checked and checked again before we were allowed anywhere near an aircraft so we were quite happy not to have to do this. My detachment was a ¾ Ton FFR Land Rover and Trailer fitted with C15 HF Radio, C49 VHF Radio and A43 UHF Radio.

As this was my first time out of the UK I was like a fish out of water. Of course, the weather was scorching and we were in tents, apart from when we managed to get in the same area as the Americans when there was an abundance of air conditioning and ice cold cokes for which we paid a nominal sum for and just helped ourselves from the number of ice cold "bins" that the Coke's were placed in.

I remember seeing many fast jets flying past us and a lot of helicopter activity at certain times. I remember thinking – I sent the request for those to fly over.

Being a very young signalman, I got "jiffed" to sail back on the LSL Sir Galahad which the vehicles were being shipped back on. While we were docked in Thessaloniki harbour, beside a couple of guard duties, we used the LSL as a base to go on the beer in Thessaloniki for the rest of the time. The highlight of the return sailing was watching a Land Rover that had been written off in an accident being dumped over the side into the mediterranean sea. I wonder how the QM squared that one away?

This was my only time with AMF(L) as I went off and qualified as a parachutists and was "shoe horned" into the 16 Parachute Brigade's exercises which in those days were plentiful.

My short time with AMF(L) was thoroughly enjoyable and it was great to mix with the other nations, seeing the different standards of the different Army and Air Forces. I actually had a second tour with 244 from February1987 to July 1988 but by this time they had Alpha Troop, a dedicated AMF(L) Troop which I was not part of.

1975 to 1976 - David (Charlie) Rodgers - Force Radio Troop

I carried out two shortened tours with AMF(L), the first as a Cpl and the second some time later as a WO2 (YofS). My first tour was with Force Radio Troop AMF(L) with 3 Squadron, 30 Signal Regiment in Blandford Forum.

On my first tour I remember going to Norway and living in tents. We carried out more radio exercises than arctic warfare training. During our time off in Norway I remember (with others) "Knocking" on the Sgt's Mess tent and buying 200 fags and a bottle of brandy, this we sold at any of the bars down town, which gave us enough money for our night out in such an expensive country. We were also allowed to use the sauna's and after the first time we used them, enjoyed getting back to the tents and telling the others that it was a mixed sauna. Watching a load of men run, slip and slide to get to the sauna was funny, getting hassle from them when they got back was even funnier.

Honour Guard for the Commander of AMF(L) while we were in Turkey. I am far left

During my first tour we also went to Turkey where, one day we were sun bathing and the next we had our winter kit on taking part in an Honour Guard!

In September 1976 we deployed by road to Sardinia, we sailed from Haverford West to France and then drove in convoy all the way to Genoa where we got the ferry across to Sardinia. A couple of days before we got to the Italian Border there had been a big earthquake in the country and as we were waiting at the border a typical Squaddie sense of humour was not appreciated by some British Civilians. They pulled up next to the convoy and asked Bob Hill if we were going to Italy for the earthquake? His immediate reply was "No we couldn't get the tickets". We erupted in laughter but they drove off in disgust. During the ferry trip, the Officers and Seniors were at the Captain's Table for dinner and the rest of us were in the "cookhouse", we were all complaining about the food but would rather be together than sharing with "That lot upstairs", at that stage one of the Sgt's came in and said there are 2 places available on the Captains Table, who wants them? After much pushing, shoving and climbing over tables and chairs myself and Eric 'Cass' Cassidy got the seats.

Dave Turner and I enjoying some time off

During our time in Sardinia we had a bit of time off. However one of the funniest moments was when we were invited to the RAF Corporals Mess for a drink. We had 2 mini buses for transport and both were full. We had to take an officer with us so a very young Lt came with us (can't remember his name). We arrived at the mess and walked into the bar and all we could see was about 20 women, the only man in the room was the barman. Being Squaddies we immediately tried our luck with the women, however, after about an hour this other door opened and in came around 20 men (the husbands had been watching football in another room), the women had decided not to tell us they were married. At the end of the night the young Lt took one mini bus load back to our camp and I said I would bring the other lads back with me. A couple of hours later we left and got back to the camp. In the morning the young Lt asked why we were so late back, I saw a chance to have some fun, so told him I had got chatting with this couple and after a while they offered me the chance of a "Get Together" with them for the cost of 2 boxes of Compo. He obviously didn't believe me but the other lads played along, this went on all day. At around 5 that evening a RAF lad in uniform came in and said "Charlie, have you got those two boxes of compo". The face on the young Lt's face was fantastic. He believed this for the next few months until I eventually told him the truth, that I just told the RAF Guy that he could have some because he was off camping. I left 249 in late 1976 to AAC Harrogate, on promotion, to help prepare for my YofS Course.

The Wire Magazine 1968 to 1975

The following entries in The Wire magazine provide an insight into what was going on in AMF(L) units over this period. The role also involved deployment to the hotter climates of Greece and Turkey

June – July 1968

30 Signal Regiment

AMF(L) Signal Troop - a report on Winter Warfare Training in Norway

Members of the Regiment do not always head for the tropics, as the following article, written by Signalman Hindle shows:

Last November saw the resurrection of AMF(L) Signal Troop, here at Blandford, as part of 2 Squadron. The Troop provides rear-link and liaison communications for 1 SCLI (the present UK AMF(L) Battalion) and has the Northern flank of NATO as its major scamping ground.

Initial training, mainly concentrated on getting the Troop fit, ready for the winter warfare exercises, whilst Sergeant Mackey and two Corporals attended a winter warfare course run by 1 SCLI.

In January, the Troop was fitted out with its winter warfare clothing, most of which had just arrived from Canada and Norway. Then members of the Troop went on an internal refresher driving course for three weeks, whilst the remainder continued with fitness and trade training.

During the last three weeks of February the whole Troop went on Exercise 'Hard Fall II' in Norway. The exercise was for sub-unit training in winter warfare and was held at Voss which is some 50 miles inland from Bergen. The Troop Commander, Lieutenant Byrom, was fortunate enough to have been in Norway for the three weeks prior to the Troop's arrival and so training began immediately. Lieutenant Bengstom, of the Royal Norwegian Army, was assigned to the Troop as its instructor, and was virtually in command for the first two weeks of training. This initial training was mainly on basic Infantry subjects and we began by learning to pack sledges, erect tents, use the cooking equipment and walk on snowshoes (we found we had muscles we never knew we had). This part of the training culminated in a five-day exercise, which included all that had been practised previously, plus field-firing and night-patrolling in temperatures of down to -30 C.

Thanks to 1 SCLI, lending the Troop radios and vehicles, the last week was spent on a communications exercise in which each vehicle travelled 400 miles on snow or ice-covered roads. The views were always marvellous, communications somewhat difficult, and all agreed that both snow chains and studded tyres were needed. Only one vehicle went off the road (unfortunately being driven at the time by our only 'professional' driver, our ED, Lance-Corporal 'Slim' Cummins), and everyone had cameras out to witness a 3-ton FFR being rescued by a passing dried fish lorry.

Weekends in Voss were spent on the civilian ski-slopes under the watchful eye of Lieutenant Bengstom. Voss is a large civilian ski centre and has its fair share of off-duty attractions, and, despite the limitations of having to wear uniforms, a few of the Troop found pleasant "extra mural" activities, who they then proceeded to entertain in the NAAFI at duty-free prices. All good things come to an end, however, and we soon found ourselves back in Blandford. Perhaps we're the only people looking forward to next winter.

January – February 1969

30 Signal Regiment

The Ace Mobile Force (Land) Radio Troop

As part of new UK commitments to NATO we have now formed the Force Radio Troop to serve Headquarters Allied Command Europe Mobile Force (Land). HQ AMF(L) Force Radio Troop is as impressive as the title. It is superbly equipped with winterised ¾ ton Land Rovers, the most up to date SSB radio, a full scale of winter clothing/equipment for its Arctic role and over eighty professionals - Royal Signals NCO's and soldiers.

Exercise 'Deep Freeze '

This proved to be a well-chosen title and for a week the weather was at zero level temperatures during the Regimental exercise at Okehampton, Bovington and Tidworth. The AMF(L) Force Radio Troop detachments and UK Battalion Signal Troop were given a thorough test of their capability to work radio over extended ranges for both HF SSB and VHF, with the remainder of the Regiment providing representative DC and Battalion rear links. During the exercise we were visited by the Group Commander, Colonel EJ Winn. WOI (YofS) Tom Johnstone played his final role of 'enemy' for us and his imaginative flair for training will be well remembered, not least by the AMF(L) Force Troop rebroadcast detachments. YofS Johnstone leaves us in January for 32nd Regiment (V) and we offer our congratulations on being awarded a commission.

After returning from Exercise 'Deep Freeze' the AMF(L) Radio Troop and the Spearhead detachments were inspected at Blandford by CSO Army Strategic Command, Brigadier G Proudman MBE.

On 11th December the Regiment was honoured by a visit by General Sir Robert Bray, GBE, KCB, DSO, Deputy SACEUR, SHAPE, accompanied by CSO Army Strategic Command. After a visit to the Regimental mounting centre and a briefing by the Commanding Officer, Lieutenant-Colonel IM Rose, the visitors were given a demonstration layout of the AMF(L) Force Radio Troop and the UK Battalion Signal Troop. General Sir Robert Bray and Brigadier Proudman spent an hour talking informally to the officers, NCO's and soldiers of the troops on parade.

Visit of Deputy Supreme Allied Commander, Europe to 30 Signal Regiment

Lieutenant Bob Baynes explains some of the potentialities of the Volvo Toolkit to General Sir Robert Bray, CBE, KCB, DSO. Deputy SACEUR, SHAPE and Brigadier Proudman. In the photo also Major Cross and Captain Payne, Adjutant

Sergeant Cliff Coultish and Corporal Bob Geddes find General Bray particularly interested in the full-scale winter clothing equipment – suitable even for an Arctic role

February – March 1970

30 Signal Regiment

A vigorous start to the Seventies

The turn of the year has been a particularly busy time for the Regiment. Many weeks of preparation for the AFM(L) Force Radio Troop reached a climax when the complete Troop drove to Marchwood and embarked on LSL Sir Percivale on New Year's Day. The following morning, the Commanding Officer. Lieutenant-Colonel IM Rose, emplaned at Brize Norton to visit the Regiment's detachments in Anguilla and two days' later, Lieutenant Bob Baynes deplaned with the AMF(L) UK Battalion Signal Troop for Exercise 'Hardfall IV' in Norway. After a three-day voyage to Oslo, the AMF(L) Radio Troop are well established with the Norwegian School of Signal at Jorstamoen.

After weeks of preparation, AMF(L) Force Radio Troop of 30th Signal Regiment embark for Norway

1. L.S.L. Sir Percival prepares for embarkation of A.M.F.(L) Force Radio Troop at Marchwood
2. Sergeant Tuite, Troop M.T. sergeant glad to go aboard
3. A.M.F.(L) Force Radio Troop prepare for Norwegian snow conditions before embarking at Marchwood
4. Corporal Kay and Signalman Wise chain up one of the 190 troop tyres before A.M.F.(L) Force Radio Troop embark

March - April 1970

30 Signal Regiment

AMF(L) Force Radio Troop

With the return of Lieutenant-Colonel Rose, the Commanding Officer, from a five-day visit to Norway, came this report from AMF(L) Force Radio Troop:

After a stormy voyage, we arrived in Jorstadmoen, the home of the Norwegian Signals, for breakfast on Sunday 4th January. Captain Crouch, Staff Sergeant Gilder and Sergeant Watson, the advance party, had done all the ground work for us, and we were allotted rooms, which we immediately used to catch up on all our lost sleep from the journey.

The following day we were met and welcomed to Norway and Jorstadmoen by Major Steone, the Officer Commanding the Training Battalion, and we started learning to live and move in Artic conditions. The temperature when we arrived, - 32 °C which rose to a 'warm' - 15 °C., which made living easier. Under Norwegian Army instructors, we were taught the basics of skiing and survival, which we put inro practice the first week by camping out in our five-man tents. Sergeant West and Corporal Kynaston lead the field in the Skiing. We spent two days on cross-country skiing, setting off in the early morning in parties of twenty with a Norwegian instructor and covering sixteen kilometres across the mountains by dark. Notable events on these two days included Signalman Wilson (622) seeing Signalman Wilson (364) in a snowdrift overheard singing "Do you think I would leave you lying, when there's room on my skis for two" and Sergeant Wood, RAMC, was heard to say as he careered down a slope, "If you want medical assistance, stop me!"

Apart from skiing, we have done three exercises to try our radios and to practice operating in Arctic conditions. All three went very well; a lot of new problems were discovered and solved. We are leaving for Germany on 2nd February after a month's enjoyable and interesting stay in Jorstadmoen. All the Norwegian instructors have been most helpful and friendly, and we approach Exercise 'Arctic Express ' with confidence.'

May - June 1970

30 Signal Regiment

The Rovers Return

REPORT FROM NORWAY - Lance Corporal Mike Hunt tells Brigadier Proudman of his impression of Norway. Looking on is Lieutenant Jeremy Miller

Back from a highly successful Arctic exercise, AMF(L) Force Radio Troop and AMF(L) Battalion Signal Troop now amalgamate to form 3 Squadron, under the command of Captain Ian Crouch. They return from Norway with talk of Italian cooking, Canadian arctic clothing and American humour, but all seem to have enjoyed the experience despite the cold weather and the hard work involved.

Visit of CSO

On 23rd March, Brigadier G Proudman, the Chief Signal Officer, Army Strategic Command, and Major R Plant visited the Regiment for the annual fitness for role inspection. Fortunately, the weather stayed fairly bright as the Brigadier visited the new 3 Squadron who were set out as the AMF(L) headquarters employed during Exercise 'Arctic Express'.

Drive Past - 3 Squadron Landrovers with Pennants flying made an impressive drive past during Brigadier Proudman's inspection

October - November 1970

30 Signal Regiment

Visit of Commander AMF(L)

The Regiment has been honoured by the visit of General Li Gobbi, the Commander Allied Mobile Force (Land), on 10th September. Following a briefing in the Mounting Centre, General Li Gobbi was accompanied by the Commanding Officer on a helicopter visit to see the AMF(L) Force Radio Troop carry out training with detachments at Blandford, Bovington, Fovant and Larkhill.

The AMF(L) Force Radio Troop have already started their work-up exercises for Exercise 'Deep Express' in Turkey and will shortly depart for Germany to join their parent headquarters.

January - February 1971

30 Signal Regiment

AMF(L) Radio Troop - mobile once more By Corporal 'Scouse' Chapman

Tuesday, 22nd September, dawned bright and clear and found AMF(L) Force Radio Troop leaving Blandford Camp at normal AMF(L) convoy speed on the first part of their journey to Germany and Exercise 'Deep Test'. The night of the 22nd found us at our first staging camp at Shorncliffe, near Folkestone, three hours early. We were greeted at Shorncliffe with the news that the NAAFI was closing down the following day, and could we ease the manager's stock-taking problem. This was found to be no problem to Lance-Corporal Mooney and his friends, and it was a much-relieved manager that bid us goodnight and good morning with no beer left in his club.

We breakfasted on the 23rd on board a Townsend car ferry, and some caught up with sleep they had missed, due to the early start, and others due to their late finish. A military escort picked us up at Zeebrugge and escorted us to Emblem, in Belgium, which was our secondary staging camp. Our short stay in Emblem was long enough to beat the local basketball team and rehearse some of our songs for Germany in the NAAFI. We left Emblem enroute for Mertzig, our final destination.

On arrival at the German border the German customs officer at first refused to let us enter Germany, but after Corporal Dave Blackall had spoken to the customs, and movements control had produced a form, all was well, and we were once more speeding on our way. We arrived in Merzig at 20.00 hours on the 24th and were informed that a meal had been laid on for us. This turned out to be bread rolls and a mixture of German meats and green salad, which proved to be our staple diet over the weeks to come. The next day was spent cleaning and servicing our vehicles in preparation for the exercise, and also arranging recreational activities such as football, basketball and visits to places of local interest (Bierfest). The football match arranged by Lance-Corporal Pete Ryan and interpreted by Lance-Corporal 'Chippy' Wood (Pomfritte Holtz) turned out to be a mis-match, as we lost by 9-0, but if Lance-Corporal Les Rix had scored that penalty when the scores were 0--0, it could have been a different story. We had our revenge that night, as the losers challenged the winners to a drinking and singing match in the bier bar, and with the aid of two strikers, Lance-Corporal Alan Liddle and Corporal 'Scouse ' Chapman, we won trousers down. A visit was arranged to the local brewery, and the locals are still wondering how many people managed to get into one vehicle, especially as two of them were Sergeant 'Doug' Rogers and Sergeant 'Smudge' Smith. A more sedate party visited the steelworks, and after being shown around the works were provided with an excellent, meal and more liquid refreshment than the party at the brewery received!

The CPX in Germany was a great success, although some of the other nations that were with us must be wondering about the new drill movement performed by Sergeant 'Nobby' Clark, who was seen in the middle of the HQ area skipping, ably assisted on either end of the rope by SSM Roy Stark and Sergeant Paddy Tuite.

All too soon, our visit to Merzig came to an end, which coincided with the local Bierfest closing, and the last night saw FofS Terry Brabon, ably assisted by Sergeant 'Paddy' Tuite, on the stage, thanking all the local people for their hospitality, and his sentiments were echoed by the whole of the Troop.

And so, to Turkey - by Lieutenant Chris Johnson

Between 8th and 13th October, AMF(L) Force Radio Troop was airlifted from Frankfurt air base to Turkey to take part in Exercise 'Deep Express'. There was, of course, much speculation as to what it would be like in Turkey, opinions ranging from blazing hot weather and dry sandy conditions, to ten feet of snow. After all the glamorous speculation it was a let-down to find the weather no different to late summer in UK, in more ways than one. We were greeted by grey overcast skies, light rain and an RMP. Had it not been for the fact that the roads were straight, from the first impression we might easily have been back in UK. However, these ideas soon changed as daylight broke and things started to appear very un-English indeed. Gone were the rolling green hills and in their place a brown, treeless vista, interspersed with the odd wadi. The impression given was one of extreme poverty. The way of life of the people is such that a very high percentage make their living from the land. New houses seem to be very few and far between, and the majority of accommodation is poor by UK standards. In the European part of Turkey roads are bad. There are the only two metalled roads, both of which lead to Istanbul. In good weather the roads are usable, but even a small amount of rain turns these into treacherous skid-pans. At times they were so bad that four-wheel drive was no more effective than two!

This then, was the setting for the AMF(L) autumn manoeuvres in 1970. For the first stage of the exercise, we were located at Corlu, about 60 miles from Istanbul. At this stage, the headquarters was not tactical and was laid out over a vast area of barren plain. It was perhaps fortunate that there was no requirement to be tactical, as the nearest trees were about 70 miles away.

The exercise started and the detachments were deployed to their locations. Although life in the headquarters was still non-tactical, this was illustrated by a brass band and a quarter guard, which appeared with monotonous regularity. Life in the key Companies was tactical. The UK Reece Squadron also moved so regularly that it was difficult to find due to excellent camouflage. The exercise then moved to a location just outside Kesan, a few miles from the Greek border. The headquarters was carefully sited on top of a rubbish dump. I t was one of the few locations I have been in where used compo tins would have enhanced the scenery. However, it was decided that a policy of 'Keep Turkey Tidy ' should be initiated, and so the area was cleaned up. The exercise itself went very well and a lot was learnt by all. Considering the language problems, this was surprising, but evidently the policy of 'if you shout loud enough anyone can understand' was seen to work.

At the end of the exercise, we moved back to UK by air and sea. Those who went by air had the advantage not only of arriving home earlier, but also missing the opportunity of being violently ill on an LSL on the return journey! Those of us who came back on 31st October had the consolation of being able to sample the delights of Istanbul before we left, as the cholera scare was over, and the city was back in bounds.

As a result of this visit, Land Rovers were loaded to the gunwales with leather goods, onyx and Turkish delight, and the customs were quite fair and reasonable when we finally returned to UK after an absence of seven weeks.

February – March 1971

30 Signal Regiment

Winter Training

The turn of the year is a busy time in the Regiment, and especially for Headquarters Squadron, and the AMF(L) Force Radio Troop, who are now in the West of Norway, carrying out their winter training. The interval between returning from Turkey, in late October, and their departure, in mid-January, allows sufficient time for the preparations and administrative arrangements to be completed. Fortunately, Headquarters Squadron has an experienced team, especially in the QM 'Tech' Department, who resolve all the complications of drawing-up and issues of the winter clothing and equipment. Captain Dai Rees, RQMS John Cummins and SQMS Frank Gooding all have their moments of satisfaction and frustration before the process is completed, and some relief until three months later, when the items all have to be returned again. In the servicing bay, Sergeant Vic East, Corporals Watson, Sealeaf and Signalmen Barkess and Winter have worked for many long hours preparing the radio vehicles and Volvos for arctic conditions, and burning the midnight oil in the Pay Office, Major Ted Poole, Sergeant Johnson and the pay staff have put in much practice at converting pounds sterling to kroner.

This year's training includes much more skiing than in previous years and, due to the difficulties in accommodation, at the Norwegian School of Signals, the training is taking place at Ulven, near Bergen.

September – October 1971

30 Signal Regiment

The Right Honourable Geoffrey Johnson Smith MP, Undersecretary of State (Army) visits Army Strategic Command

1. Arrival of the Under Secretary of State accompanied by the Army Commander Lieutenant General Sir Mervyn Butler, KCB, CBE, MC.

2. Lance Corporal Bill Ridley of the UK Battalion AMF(L) Signal Troop plays it cool

Monday the 19th July was one of those brilliant summer days the Regiment reserves for their most important visitors.

At 11.40 hours The Under Secretary of State arrived by helicopter, accompanied by the Army Commander General Sir Mervyn Butler, KCB, CBE, DSO, MC. They were met by the Commanding Officer and given a briefing in the Regimental Mounting Centre. One of the most interesting displays was produced by the AMF(L) UK Battalion Signal Troop.

November - December 1971

30 Signal Regiment

During the latter part of August and in September the AMF(L) elements of 3 Squadron disappeared to the furthest extremities of BAOR and Greece. They were joined in Greece by the UK Battalion AMF(L) Signal Troop. As we were about to move into new accommodation at this time it was necessary to dispose of the stock of the Squadron Club - this irksome task was undertaken with surprising enthusiasm by all involved.

December - January 1972

30 Signal Regiment

AMF(L) Force Radio Troop in Greece

We are fortunate in obtaining this report from Captain Pat Dickinson, who has been severely pressed with recce in Norway and a visit to Italy since he returned from Greece earlier in the month.

The Troop left Blandford on 23rd August and headed for an 'overnight ' stop at Shorncliffe. The following morning, at 02.00 hours, the journey was resumed to Dover, where the Troop embarked for the Channel-crossing to Zeebrugge, and Birgelin as the destination for the second day. After enjoying the hospitality of 13th Regiment, the Troop were well fortified for the final leg of the journey to Mannheim, where all enjoyed a couple of days relaxation over the August Bank Holiday, and some accomplished sight-seeing tours in Southern Germany. Later, the opportunity was taken to polish up VHF rebroadcast procedure on a two-day exercise and during the brief stay with our US allies a shield was presented to Major Rice, US Army, the retiring AMF Headquarter Company Commander.

By 8th September, the Troop was reassembled and flown to Thessaloniki and four day later all were redeployed to start Exercise

'Hellenic Express'. There followed 12 days of hard, tiring, but generally interesting work. The Greek people were found to be extremely friendly towards the members of the Troop and frequently turned out in force to give greetings as we drove through the villages. The countryside was mainly mountainous and quite ruggedly beautiful, with breath-taking views from the high vantage points of the superb rebroadcast locations. Major Tom Blashill had the fortune to visit us before the exercise concluded on 21st September. After two days' grace we were embarked once again having had an opportunity to witness an impressive parade at Serrai and get in some bathing in the Aegean Sea at Epanorui.

The voyage was calm, and the weather continued throughout. The Troop put up a splendid show to reach the semi-final in the tug of war competition, especially against stiff opposition by the Royal Scots. The competition was won eventually by the Royal Marines who beat the Army officers in the final. By 12th October the Troop was returned complete to the UK after yet another memorable exercise with HQ AMF.

January – February 1973

30 Signal Regiment

Exercise 'Fjord Test/Strong Express' Exercising with NATO

Mid-August this year saw Force Radio Troop of 30 Signal Regiment leaving Blandford to take part in one of the largest NATO exercises ever held, Exercise 'Strong Express'. In preparation for this, the Troop crossed the Channel Dover to Zeebrugge, and motored down to Bruchsal in Southern Germany to take part in Exercise ' Fjord Test', the preliminary CPX for the Allied Command Europe Mobile Force (AMF(L)). En route to the south, we staged at 16 Signal Regiment, Krefeld, and spent a happy evening meeting old friends. After a rather hectic journey, during which a certain Yeoman (no names) decided to take his packet of vehicles to see the sight of Dusseldorf, we settled in with the German Parachute Signal Battalion at Eichelberg Kaserne.

After a free weekend to prepare for the exercise (or visit the Olympic Games at Munich) we moved out on Exercise 'Fjord Test.' The next three weeks were spent in the field where we worked closely with the Americans and at the end of which everyone seemed satisfied that at least the HQ of the Force knew what they were doing. Congratulations must go to Lance-Corporal John Taylor and Lance-Corporal Rod Wood who ran our bar so efficiently they are considering retiring on the profit!

At 1200 hours on 11th September, we redeployed to Northern Norway by courtesy of the USAFE and three hours later our Starlifter landed in the rain and mist of Bardufoss airfield. From here we moved straight into the field and spent the next two weeks communicating and trying to survive on 'good old compo'. The admin side of the Troop run by Staff Sergeant Tony McDonald, however, swear blind that the steaks they enjoyed grew in abundance on the trees in their part of the wood, and Lance-Corporal Bob Chesterman must be thanked for providing such an excellent restaurant in Tac HQ during the lull in the fighting. The weather remained poor throughout with continuous rain and cool weather which together with 8 inches of mud, provided us with a setting very similar to the Eastern Front. However, spirits remained high and everyone enjoyed working as part of a multi-national force, especially Sergeant Terry Peacock who was so obviously thrilled at the sight of so many stores in such a small area.

NATO Challenge Cup winners

On the last day of the exercise, Force Radio Troop entered a team of 26, led by Second-Lieutenant Mike Telfer, in the NATO Challenge Cup Competition, in which all units competed. The competition involved an eight-mile march and shoot within a set time and after a great effort by the Troop we succeeded in winning the Support Units Cup which was presented to us by Major-General J Groven, GOC, AMF(L) Belgian Army.

March – April 1973

30th Regiment's "ACE" Mobile Force Signallers

Tough, mentally alert, they will provide vital communications in a demanding Arctic environment

Standing, left to right: W02 (YofS) Wood, Captain PJK Dickinson, Lance-Corporal Jeffery, Lance-Corporal Siddle, Corporal Patterson, Corporal Hudson, Signalman Davies, Lance-Corporal Williams, Lance-Corporal Milne, Corporal Hindle, Lance-Corporal Barrington, Sergeant Geddes, Lance-Corporal Ireland, Signalman Rumford, Signalman Ormond, Lance-Corporal Parry, W02 (YofS) Bland

Kneeling, left to right: Signalman Gilyeat, Lance-Corporal Briers, Signalman Mcilvenny, Signalman Cook, Signalman Tomlinson, Corporal Wilkinson, Signalman Astle, Signalman Barron, Signalman Leggett

Once again 3 Squadron 30 Signal Regiment is deploying to far off places. The ACE Mobile Force is due to undergo six weeks of Winter Warfare Training.

Faraway places

Annually our Force Radio Troop which is a NATO funded force are exercised on the flanks of Western Europe. This includes Turkey, Greece, Italy, Denmark, Zealand and Norway. It is in Norway that the most severe winter conditions are met and for which careful training and planning must be done.

Fitness essential

The first requirement for all these men is physical fitness. This involves rigorous marches in full kit, gymnasium training and langlauf ski training. The ski training gives many the impression that the troop is to indulge in a winter holiday, but rest assured this is not so. The conditions in Northern Norway or even in the south of the country high in the hills, are not conducive to many holiday thoughts to the man who is living in a tent and has to carry enormous amounts of personal kit.

Well equipped

The excellent winter equipment provided for AMF(L) includes equipment not seen elsewhere in the British Army. The Volvo BV 202 is one of the over snow vehicles used. The vehicle, despite its appearance is neither articulated nor track driven. Any driver with a normal licence is able to drive it. The drive is from a central knuckle and steering is affected from the trailer! Although the steering allows for easier reversing the affect in forward is quite different from a standard vehicle. The great advantage of the vehicle is its over snow capability with minimum pressure per square inch on the surface. It makes a very useful rebroadcast station with a remarkable cross-country performance. Personal equipment includes extreme cold underwear, contact gloves, Bergen rucksacks, snow shoes, a mass of first-class equipment valued at nearly £200 per man. All that he needs in fact for survival in the Arctic during winter conditions.

April – May 1973

30th Signal Regiments Force Radio Troop in Norway

End of a day out in the snow and it's home sweet home - a tent

Ski patrol being towed by Volvo

You will remember in the last issue of THE WIRE we described the training undergone by members of the Force Radio Troop of 30 Signal Regiment. This Troop have now moved to Norway and are continuing the winter training that their employment with the ACE Mobile Force, demands of them.

They are now living near to the Arctic Circle in temperature which can be as low as 40 °C below freezing. This leaves no room for mistakes no one can take any chances. Clothing must be perfect, and the correct type of clothes must be used at all times. There can be no exemptions from the basic rules of survival for under these conditions it really is survival. Perhaps it is this aspect of life in the Arctic that appeals to the soldier. Skill and training must be used to their limit. Every man must play his pan in the tent group, looking after each other at all times. This sort of challenge issued by nature to anyone who wishes to take up the gauntlet is a wonderful aim for today's professional Signaller.

September - October 1973

30 Signal Regiment

An Inexperienced View of 'Hardfall' Training by 'Not Too Late as I Thought It Was'

Exercise 'Hardfall' took place in Voss, Norway, and for the duration of the exercise Force Radio Troop were based in a Norwegian Army camp. The training officer was Lieutenant Mike Telfer, who with the services and assistance of 2 Norwegian officers, Lieutenant ('Coffee') Junker and Lieutenant ('Sleepy') Mueller, aimed to have the Troop proficient in the use of skis and snow-shoes and become aware of Arctic communication problems and personal survival in just 4 weeks.

Three days' training in a valley 5 minutes from base enabled everyone to ski and be capable of covering average terrain and we then spent 4 days on the well-known ski slope Hangur where, as the pressure was piled on us, we learnt the techniques of snow ploughs, herring bones and turns. Each day finished with a trek across the slopes with Lieutenant Junker who always managed to make even the way back difficult or stubbornly uphill! The remainder of our training was carried out under canvas in 2 camps in the Rong Valley. In these camps we lived in Arctic tents, a situation where it had to be, one turn, all turn! A typical day began at 07.30 when first the cook rose to heat some water followed in rotation by the remainder of the group who dressed, rolled up sleeping bags and sat down to give the next man a chance to move. Before the day's skiing began, after a heavy fall of snow the previous night, the first task was to dry out packs and make the camp presentable.

Skijoring, the name given to the art of being towed behind a snowcat on skis, was a very popular exercise. Each snowcat, issued with 2 x 25ft lengths of nylon rope, then equipped itself with 6 men who then joined ski sticks ready to be towed. A 'Buzz boy' helped in operating a buzzer every time a skier fell to warn the driver to stop. On the other hand, if the driver decided to stop suddenly on a down-hill slope one had the spectacle of all the skiers unable to stop in time piling up behind the snowcat with assorted looks of horror on their faces.

Training ceased at 16.45 to prepare for night ski patrols which began at 18.30. After a brief by the instructor, came an hour of 'follow your leader' uphill on skis and down dale with cries of "Herring bone, snow plough and side step" and such like being passed back.

By 22.30 after the evening meal and the disappearance of washing and shaving gear, we, the happy campers, settled down quietly thinking of the days to come, skiing, trail break-up, snow-shoe walk-up, navigation and map reading, driver training and communication drills in the Arctic.

At the end of the training period 60% of the Troop gained their 10-kilometre bronze Medal (Norwegian) for langlauf and Signalman Molloy gained his well-deserved silver medal.

January - February 1974

30 Signal Regiment

3 Squadron - Visit by The Queen of Denmark to Force Radio Troop

During Exercise 'Absalon Express', an AMF(L) exercise in Denmark, Force Radio Troop were honoured by a visit from Her Majesty Queen Margarethe of Denmark. She spoke to Major Ron Clayton, Lieutenant Mike Telfer, Staff Sergeant Dougie Edmond, Staff Sergeant (YofS) Colin Eastland, Staff Sergeant (FofS) Pete Davis, Sergeant Bill Adams, Signalman Jim Buckberry and Signalman Ron Coughtry. It's ironic, but the day of the visit was the only day during the whole exercise that it didn't rain; it snowed.

VISIT BY HRH THE QUEEN OF DENMARK

Left to right: Accompanying Her Majesty Queen Margarethe of Denmark, Staff-Sergeant Edmonds, Major-General Groven (Commander AMF(L)), Major Ron Clayton and Lieutenant Mike Telfer.

April - May 1974

30 Signal Regiment

Exercise Hardfall 74 - A Report From 3 Squadron

In January Force Radio Troop participated m Exercise 'Hardfall 74'. The annual winter warfare training period for the UK contingent to the Ace Mobile Force. The exercise took place near Voss in Western Norway, where weather conditions can vary from very cold and dry (- 20°C) to a wet and slushy (0°C).

Prior to the departure for Norway, the Troop ran a four-week dry shod training period at Blandford, consisting of lectures, demonstrations, films, physical training and a Volvo snowcat familiarisation course. The Troop were fully prepared to face the hazards of Winter warfare, by the time Christmas came round. (Sic!)

The Troop deployed on 10th January by RAF and civil ferry and finally arrived at Mjolfjell Camp near Voss. On the 16th January the training began in earnest when we deployed into the mountains for a 6-day period under canvas practising survival, the construction of snow holes, snow caves and igloos and mobility, consisting of ski and snow shoes training and Volvo snowcat driving.

We were all very happy to see Lieutenant-Colonel Jarrett, who during his visit spent two days up the mountain with us and was also seen on skis. Rumour now has it that he is re-writing the SOP for 'rising after a fall.' We must also mention Corporal Rick Slade and Signalman Jock Wallace for their apparent coolness whilst skiing towards a Ravine.

Although the training was intense and physically demanding, it was very enjoyable and such subsidiary subjects as ski training and skijoring (towing up to 12 skiers behind the snowcat) kept moral high throughout. All the training instruction was accomplished by Captain David Gardiner, Lieutenants Vaughan Smedley and Mike Telfer and Corporal Dave Kemp with the assistance of two Norwegian Officers, a Lieutenant Arne Junker and Second-Lieutenant Kjell Selnes. Arne Junker, an old friend from previous

'Hardfall's', had arranged a release from his new staff appointment specially to be with us. We were delighted to see him again.

Norwegian Sense of Humour

The following connoisseur item was noted at approximately 1130 hrs on 27th January.

Norwegian Instructor, "Turn left! ... TURN LEFT!! ...TURN LEFT!!!"

Student: (Crashes in unbelievable tangle of skis etc).

Norwegian Instructor, (Sadly), "That-was not necessary"

May - June 1974

30 Signal Regiment

Life in the Swan Regiment has, as always, been busy this month, especially so with two major Exercises in progress 'Argus Express' to Norway, and 'Snowball' to Scotland.

'Argus Express' was held in the chill mountains of the Norwegian Arctic region with 3 Squadron adding communications to their previous antics galore on langlauf skis and snowshoes. Although it was very hard work everybody enjoyed this most successful exercise. The main talking point, in fact, seems to have been the food! 'Norwegian Porridge' is highly recommended by the ACC participants, and so is the high style of dining (eating) aboard the RFA 'Sir Geraint', the vessel which brought the Squadron back to England.

Our Cover Picture - Our cover picture this month features the Corps in a Norwegian setting. The photograph, which recently came into our possession, unfortunately omits the name of the soldier in the foreground and various enquiries made by us have not been successful in finding out who he is.

May - June 1975

30 Signal Regiment

Exercise 'Hardfall 1975"

On Monday, 17th February, Force Radio Troop arrived in Trondheim, Norway via Marchwood and the LSL Sir Lancelot for Exercise 'Hardfall 75'. During our four weeks stay we practised Arctic Survival, snow driving, communicating in adverse conditions, snow shoeing and skiing. We spent a great deal of our time training in the mountains, where we used our Snowcats for skijoring and moving our 5-man tent groups and their stores. Our skiing improved immensely during the exercise under instruction from Captain David Gardiner, Lieutenant Vaughan Smedley and our two Norwegian Army Liaison Officers.

We spent a night in ice-caves which we had to dig in one afternoon. Although the temperature outside was - 20°C., a relatively comfortable night was had by all. After one particular night in the mountains, we woke to find 'White Out' conditions all around which is confusing to say the least, however with expert Snowcat driving and navigating by Staff Sergeant (YofS) Colin Eastland, Sergeant 'Sandy' Geddes, and their team of drivers, the Troop came down out of the snowy mists to safety.

Our last week was spent at the Hjerkenn ranges, where we were visited by our Commanding Officer, Lieutenant-Colonel Michael Jarrett who accompanied us in a search for 'hairy cows' (Musk ox) in a nearby nature reserve close to Snohette, the third highest mountain in Norway. On our final training day at Hjerkenn, we carried out live firing and section tactics over a 2 km long course.

On Tuesday, 18th March, we loaded our vehicles and stores on the LSL Sir Lancelot and returned to Blandford for a week's leave and time to change our colours before our next exercise which takes place in Denmark.

May - June 1975

244 Signal Squadron (AS)

Exercise 'Hardfall'

This account has been received from Echo Troop. We deployed to Bergen, Norway on the RFA Sir Lancelot, and thence by road to the transit camp at Bømoen.

The morning after our arrival we drew skis and associated gear under Sergeant Dave Longhurst. Then Corporal Jim Hutchinson, Lance Corporal Dave Beattie, Signalman David Bragger and the technical Sergeant Brian Stow left the main party to set up their detachment with 72 Helicopter Squadron, RAF, this was to provide a voice SSB air safety link with the helicopters when they flew.

After three days preparation the main party left with four Land Rovers and two Volvos. We headed for Brandsec Camp where, Arctic cents pitched, 9 x 9 tents dug in and stoves going we were fed an excellent casserole by Flight-Lieutenant Dave Stanley from HQ 38 Group. We then proceeded with tuition in the gentle art of skiing under Flight-Lieutenant 'Ned' Sparks.

In the afternoon we were towed higher into the hills by the Volvos, during which process Corporal Dick Kilpatrick broke a ski and Signalman 'Geordie' Knox suffered an uncountable number of falls.

For eight days the training continued, climaxing with a 36-hour spell in snow-holes and a visit by the SASO, from HQ 38 Group, Air Commodore Latham. We then returned to Bømoen, joining Lance-Corporal Billy Malone who had returned early after a fall; during the journey Signalman John Morgans somehow managed to turn over one of the Volvos.

November - December 1975

30 Signal Regiment

3 AMF(L) Sqn - Adventures in Turkey

3 Sqn has been off on its travels again, this time to Turkey to practise operating on NATO's southern flank. The Sqn deployed by sea, taking seven sun-filled balmy days to arrive at Saros Bay in Turkey, W02 John Sydney was so taken by the life at sea that he is now universally known as the Yeoman of Sailors. SSgt FofS Gavin Spearpoint gained notoriety by wiping out all the scrabble opposition aboard, and our heavyweight troop tug of war team of Cpl's Brian Roxburgh, David Thompson, Bob Hill and Sig Simon Rose were both swift and sure in destroying every other team in sight.

However, all good things must come to an end and we exchanged the sedate restful sea voyage for the made helter-skelter 'Chicken run' that is Turkey's principal highway. As one urbane German staff officer put it: 'There is no problem, the road is just like a German autobahn but driving the other way'. Traffic accidents were numerous and serious, we can only thank providence and some very nervous passenger/observers riding in the hot seat of right-hand drive vehicles that we escaped without serious incident. Sig Jock Marshall, the veteran Tp Commander's driver took some pleasure at showing the new Tp Commander, Capt John Ambrose the AMF(L) ropes.

Communications went well throughout the exercise, with the troop managing to produce a couple of unscheduled 'one off' links to satisfy an anxious information starved staff. International relations were, as ever, very good, though Maj Peter Brunton, is still wondering about the background to Sig 'Tex' Saul's swop of one 'hats floppy ridiculous' for a brand-new American combat jacket complete with liner. Most of the troop are hoping the Americans don't manage to find any army surplus stores when they visit Salisbury Plain in November, it could mark the end of a happy trading relationship. Cpl Mick Kenny lost some comms time on the RATT net eventually reappearing to report he had been struck by lightning.

Since there had been no rain at all anywhere else on the exercise, let alone storms, this announcement was greeted with a certain scepticism by the powers that be. However, reliable technicians were despatched to the scene and reported that the detachment had indeed been struck. We have asked the padre to check through that crew's Regimental entries. We were visited on the exercise by Col JH Hild Comd 1 Signal Group and by the CO, Lt Col M. S. Jarrett. Both visits went well, and we hope they were satisfied with what they saw (CO's note-they were) we entertained them in the field and it was reliably reported that our General was jealous of our senior officers' accommodation. Certainly, our cook, LCpl John Thorpe ACC excelled himself in producing some excellent meals at some fairly odd times.

Next month we voyage fearlessly to Imber village on Salisbury Training Area (West), new territory for AMF(L). Then early in the new year, we don our Arctic kit and return to the more familiar NATO northern flank. Anyone for winter sports let us know quickly!

February 1976

30 Signal Regiment

3 Squadron Report

3 AMF(L) Sqn has again had a busy few months. Following their return from Turkey, we had time for a quick turn round at Blandford before heading for the wastes of Salisbury Plain. It made a change for the British contingents to act as hosts to an AMF(L) Exercise and we like to feel that what we lacked scenery and weather we made up for in hospitality to our allies.

The Exercise was much visited it was estimated we saw '72 stars worth' of generals, so that boots were cleaned in relays and LCpl Denny managed to shave by his gleaming toecaps. W02 'Sailor' Sydney was finally sunk by his OC Capt John Ambrose when they went for a nocturnal drive down a local mud bath. His nerve snapped when the Rover reached a 50-degree list and he abandoned ship. We had a bad fright when a large tree fell on SSgt

(FofS) Bob Chapman whilst he was in his tent. Luckily, he was not permanently damaged, though the tent and technicians' TV were write-offs, and it was not long before cracks about 'splinter groups' began circulating. He's not coming with us again, he said.

May 1976

30 Signal Regiment

3 AMF(L) Squadron News - Dartmoor in January

Other Squadrons' years may have started with a bang, ours began with a whimper of self-pity. Dartmoor in January didn't appeal too much, even to our hardiest warriors. Still, we went, the weather was fine, no one got lost (Sig Bob Shuker tended to go his own. way, but he assures us he was never lost) and, in the end, we quite enjoyed it. Sgt Pete Sellars, manning an exposed check point by moonlight was convinced his last hour had come when he heard a cow cough from the darkness behind him, the OC, Maj Peter Brunton, had been telling him about escaped cougars loose on the moors, but he quite enjoyed it, too. Anyway, it was a fine run up to the real thing - Norway in the winter!

And Then Norway

We left in early February, had a good sea voyage across and arrived in time to pitch our tents in the snow and settle in. The old hands, like Cpls John Watt and Bob Hill showed the new boys some of the wrinkles and we got organised. Long uphill snow shoe marches followed. Cpl 'Barrington' Hobbs reckoned he was better off on his own size 12 feet and probably was, but even his shoes weren't long enough for the ski down the other side. The rest of us were fine but Sig Robert Baker's body brake stops had to be seen to be really appreciated. After a few days we went up into the hills for more skiing and skijoring training. The skijoring (like water skiing on snow behind Volvos) was popular, particularly on the open stretches when the speed built up. Sgt 'Geordie' Longstaff swears he died at 50mph, and Sgt 'Sandy' Geddes who was driving the 'cat' thinks he's not that far out.

Members of AMF(L) Sqn skijoring in Norway. Speeds of 50 mph are said to have been reached

We were visited by the CO Lt Col Michael Jarrett who declined to ski on the grounds that he was out of practice. It was good to see him and we're only sorry he's posted soon and so won't be visiting the AMF(L) Sqn for a while. We couldn't persuade our other visitor to ski either, though by the time the group commander, Col J H Hild, MBE, visited us we were hard at work on exercise farther north. The exercise was successful and was combined with some useful trials work on the Clansman PRC320 manpack set. We renewed old acquaintances with our NATO allies and formed some new friendships. Perhaps the most impressive demonstration of NATO solidarity was when one of the allied Battalion Commanders, asked if he had any communication problems put his arm around the rear link det commander Cpl Pete Tyres' shoulders and replied, 'No problems, with my friend Peter here how could we have problems?' Tyres' request for a cross Army posting on democratic grounds has been turned down.

TRY US OUT

Incidentally, if you reckon we're shooting a line, just try settling down for the night in the bottom shelf of your deep-freeze -2Oc gets a bit parky in a tent. Then put in your preference of posting, but get it right, we're going independent soon.

244 Sig Sqn (AS) RAF Benson

Exercises Hardfall and Atlas Express

Early in February, 14 members of the Squadron left Benson on a three-day journey aboard the LSL Sir Lancelot, bound for Norway, there they were to stay until the end of March taking part in exercises Hardfall '76/Atlas Express.

The picturesque fjords greeted us on arrival and provided the camera enthusiasts with some good shots. After unloading the equipment by mexe-float we set off to the youth hostel at Mjolfjell where we spent the next 18 days. The first days were spent checking equipment, fitting our skis and learning the basic principles of skiing from Flt Lts 'Irish' McCartney and 'Neddy' Sparkes from RAF Odiham. Sgt 'Paddy' Law still insists that his skis had a will of their own, hence he was nearly always on his back. As time went by, we progressed to other things like, skiing with a Bergen rucksack and hauling five-man sledges uphill - not so easy if you've never skied before. Also, we went skijoring behind a Volvo Snow Cat; this, too, can have its nasty moments as Sqn Ldr Dave Griffiths knows only too well. When he fell most of the team skied right over him before LCpl Frank Collins was able to press the emergency stop button. One ski expert emerged overnight; this was LCpl 'Ginge' Craghill. His shouts of 'Shift', 'Move', ‘Look out' and 'Aaagh' were frequently heard on the slopes. Next year he hopes to be able to learn how to turn and even stop.

THE GOLDEN YEARS 1976 TO 1990

1976 to 1979 - Mal Channing - 249 Signal Squadron

I joined the Army at the age of 15 on 25th March 1962 and was posted to the All-Arms Junior Leader Regiment in Tonfanau, Wales where I completed 3 years' service ending up as a Junior Corporal. On reaching the age of 18 I was posted to 24 Signal Regiment, Catterick, Yorkshire to complete my trade training as a Communication Centre Operator.

My first posting after completing my Yeoman of Signals course in 1976 was as a SSgt (YofS) with 249 Signal Squadron (AMF(L)) which was based in Old Sarum, near Salisbury Wiltshire. This Squadron was part of the Allied Commander Europe Mobile Force (Land) and required deployment on Operations and Exercises throughout Europe, including Denmark, Sardinia, Germany, and Norway to mention a few.

Whilst in Old Sarum one of the main deployments was our annual visit to Norway, on Exercise Hardfall, for Arctic Survival Training. This meant a lot of physical training and issuing of Arctic survival equipment, which was done by our SQMS SSgt Vic Shillingford who ensured all members of the Squadron were fully issued with the correct equipment. The unit was also given tracked Volvo Snow Cat vehicles, which had to be painted white and driver training completed.

The deployment began in January and required a sea journey using LSL's from Marchwood, the sea crossings was to say the least an adventure and we were glad to see dry land. On arrival in Norway, we met up with our Norwegian Liaison Officer and travelled to our base, home for the next few months. The deployment was called Exercise Hardfall and during my first year I was selected to attend a Ski Instructors Course being held in Nordsetter, Norway.

I was accompanied by another member of the Squadron, Sgt Bernie Temmen. We both had an excellent course with a lot of hard work and miles of skiing which was going to be well used during the following years. Having two ski instructors the Squadron relied on us to train all members with the survival techniques required to fight and survive in Arctic conditions. The training took place in various locations and at times proved a challenge.

Resting after the first snow trek

I knew I should have worn snow shoes

The training undertaken was at times quite arduous having to teach skiing and survival overnighting in tents, snow holes in ultra-cold conditions. As an instructor I went out with the Norwegian Liaison Officer on recces to check areas for overnight stops, this meant the use of helicopters and long-distance skiing over rough terrain, during these recces we had on occasion to clear tracks and paths that were blocked by frozen water falls, this gave me a chance to learn how to fix and detonate explosives

which was something different. The only disappointment was that I expected a loud bang on blowing the waterfalls but only heard a dull thud, the hard work then began when we had to remove all the blown ice.

Fixing explosives to clear frozen water falls blocking track

It was not all skiing, one of the instructor's duties was to check the thickness of the ice covering the Fjords that had to take the weight of a vehicle, this was done by using a handheld winding drill whilst having a rope around your waist being held by someone else. This was in case I took an early dip and could be rescued. The most noticeable thing was the sound of the ice, it groaned like an old lady. Once the training had been completed at the end of the day the fun began by borrowing

Clearing the track of ice after detonation

a local farmers tractor and using it to pull people around on their ski's doing spins and tight turns. It certainly was enjoyable.
One of the important parts of the training was surviving in Snow Holes. This involved digging into the side of snow drifts to enable 4 or 6 soldiers to shelter safely. The hole had to be big enough to lay down and sleep, one member had to remain awake to ensure the

Setting up basecamp for first overnight camp

Awaiting Gazelle helicopter ride back to basecamp after recce candle that burnt all night remained lit, this indicated that the snow hole had enough air to maintain life. It was on one of these occasions that I led my group of twelve soldiers to an area selected for our overnight stay. After spending many hours digging and ensuring the snow holes were big and safe enough, we would normally have camped out but on this occasion the Liaison Officer and myself decided that it was too cold to start cooking but we would return to our overnight accommodation for a hot "all in stew". After having a hot meal and in the dark cold snowy night we made our way back to our overnight snow holes, I led in my snow cat with Cpl Dusty Miller driving with all the rucksacks and equipment and the second snow cat followed with the twelve Squadron members. As we slowly drove over the rough terrain, now being covered in fresh snow, we began to climb a slope when we noticed that the snow had a blue glaze to it, I checked the ground ahead and continued into the night, only to drive up another slope

Communicating with Base Camp

when the snow beneath us gave way and sent my snow cat tumbling 600 feet down the mountain side finally coming to a stop against a rock the size of a small house. The snow cat being on its side and Dusty and I trapped inside, it became an exercise of rescue and survival. Medevac Gazelle helicopters with medical teams landed and managed to get us both out, Dusty broke his arm and split his spleen and I severely injured my lower back. After being secured in the helicopters stretcher we were flown to Voss hospital where we were treated. On arrival at the hospital the helicopter Pilot asked me to sign his logbook as it was his first aero med evacuation he had undertaken at night in bad weather. The snow hole adventure for all had to be cancelled much to the relief of some of the soldiers. We were both eventually medevac'd back to the UK. The following year was safer for all and during the summer of 1978 I took a group over to Norway to assist in the annual summer clean-up of all areas used by the military, it was surprising how much compo, ammunition even the odd weapon and equipment had been mislaid in the snow during the winter training. It was during the clean-up that I had the privilege of visiting one of the Liaison Officers summer house which was on the side of a Fjord. Many an hour was spent fishing both from a row boat and the shore, a BBQ and beer and chats of all the war stories we could think of. Overall, the three years spent in the unit are memorable and missed.

My military service spanned 26 years and took me to postings in BAOR, Singapore, Belize, and UK. During which time I progressed through the ranks and reached Warrant Officer 2 (Yeoman of Signals) ending my career in the high-profile environment of Central London where I was involved with Ceremonial Duties and Liaison Officer to the FANY.

1978 to 1981 - Kevin Gifford - 249 Signal Squadron

My original exposure to the military was through the Army Cadet Force at the age of 13. I loved it and got to Cadet Cpl and then joined the Army in September 1977 as a Junior Soldier aged 16. I went to the Junior Soldier Wing of 11 Signal Regiment which was based at Ouston and joined White Swan Troop. From there I went to 8 Signal Regiment in Catterick for trade training as a Combat Radioman. My first posting to a working unit was 249 Signal Squadron (AMF(L).

I served with 249 Signal Squadron for 3 years from 1978 to mid 1981 and was part of Support Troop. I joined the unit at Old Sarum near Salisbury before the move to Ward barracks, Bulford Camp in March 1979. At this time, I was single and held the lofty rank of Signalman!

At this time, the Sqn OC was Maj Danny Fisher and The SSM was WO2 Steve Marshall. I had the privilege of serving with some great guys, some of whom I have stayed in touch with. A few names that come to mind are Mick Fitzpatrick, Tony Slaney, Steve Fielding, Steve Harris, Gary Lang, Bram Bratton, Sgt 'Skully' Walker, Lt Chris Cox and Steve Bushby.

During my time my deployments with the Sqn were to Germany, Belgium, Denmark, Turkey and Italy and I did my Arctic training in Norway on Ex Hardfall 1980. I loved every minute of Norway, especially driving the Volvo Snow Cat and felt part of something very special.

I remember a particular incident in Italy in May 1981. My Detachment was Rebro and I was crewed with Captain Nigel Hope who was the Sqn 2ic. In the middle of the Ex we were out overnight doing recce and O groups and I had been driving for around 8 to 10 hours. It was sunrise and the sun was shining brightly, like a brilliant Italian summers day.

We were proceeding along a long road with trees either side. At this time, I was so tired that I was playing 'noddy dog' at the wheel of the Land rover, which was a lightweight air portable version. Nigel told me to move over and get into the passenger side and he would now drive. It didn't take long for me to fall asleep, the next thing I remember is waking to a loud bang! When I looked up all I could see was smoke and a great tree embedded into the bonnet, the arctic heater system was almost on my lap and my right leg was trapped and very painful. I looked across to Nigel, he was unconscious and slumped forward with blood coming from his mouth. I managed to quickly extricate myself from the vehicle, with severe pain radiating from my right tib and fib up through my knee and into my femur.

What do I do! I was alone with an injured officer, in a country that I could not speak the language with people starting to arrive onto the scene and were now in my face. I looked at the vehicle, there was fuel pissing out all over the underside of the engine bay and smoke and steam coming from the front. My immediate concern was for Captain Hope stuck in the driver seat, so I pulled a jammed door open and lifted him a safe distance and placed him on his side, he was making mumbling noises but was incoherent. I proceeded to the back of the rover and retrieved the BID system boxes and our weapons, an SLR and SMG, and got myself back to where Nigel was. I sat by his side and waited as I could now hear sirens in the distance.

The ambulance arrived and loaded Nigel onto a stretcher and onto the vehicle, I sat in a spare seat in the back, two big bulging pockets with BID boxes and two weapons across my knees (I had refused treatment at this time as I had two weapons and BID's to secure), the medics were fantastic. On arrival at hospital I was wheeled by wheel chair behind Nigel's stretcher into the Emergency Department and was placed to one side of the room as again I had refused treatment until I could dispose of the BID's and weapons. I kept trying to communicate the need for them to get a policeman or NATO soldier to me asap. After an hour or so one of the biggest human beings I have ever seen walked in, he had a US Air Force Military Policeman uniform on. I explained what had happened and what I had in my jacket and gave it and the weapons to him. I don't remember much else after that, apart from waking up on a ward some hours later with my right leg in plaster. There was an empty bed next to mine which Captain Nigel Hope occupied later that evening. We were casevaced back to the UK some weeks later and spent a further few weeks in Wroughton Military Hospital.

I spent a lot of time in hospital wondering how this accident had occurred. I remember struggling due to the sun dazzling and blinking through the trees at the side of the road that seemed to go on for miles. I suspect that this monotony, along with our general tiredness contributed to the accident. This incident had a profound impact on my life as at the time I felt vulnerable and useless in this situation.

I left the Corps in June 1981 and went on to be a Fire-Fighter, then Ambulance Service Emergency Care Practitioner, qualified as both a Paramedic and Nurse. I also joined the RAMC(V) as a Combat Medical Technician retaining my original army number. I was later commissioned and was reissued an officers six figure number. My wife and I are now retired and live in Co Donegal, Ireland but remain in touch with fiends of that time. My time in the Corps was an excellent foundations for a career in the Emergency Services. I have very fond memories of my time and loved the travelling that serving with AMF(L) brought.

1980 to 1984 - Tony Slaney - 249 Signal Squadron

I Joined the Army in May 1978 as a junior soldier and completed my basic training and then my trade training in December 1979. I was posted to 249 Signal Squadron AMF(L) on 14th January 1980, straight from trade training at 8 Signal Regiment as a Combat Radio Operator. I served with 249 from 1980-1984 and completed 5 Norways in Support Troop as a crewman on Ech dets and then as the Crew Commander.

Arriving at Bulford, I was met by members of the rear party, issued with my Arctic Kit, given a bundle of poly whites, some mail and a set of false teeth and departed with the newly arrived quarter master, Captain Peck, to Brize Norton. There I boarded my first ever flight anywhere and eventually arrived in Norway. On landing in Norway, Captain Peck pushed to the front to disembark first and upon putting his feet on Norwegian soil, slipped over and broke his arm. I walked very carefully from there on.

What a Lovely Day for a stroll!

We eventually arrived at Bømoen camp, I was shown to my accommodation, which was empty as my Troop were already conducting their Arctic Training. I was placed under the tender care of Cpl Frank McAleer and Marty Hyett. Frank was, to my mind, a very funny but scary mad jock and initially terrified me I must admit.

We had some scoff and then later Frank took me to the bar for some drinks, this is when things got a tad tense. Some of the guys from the MT under Cpl Roger "Spider" Walters started to take the piss out of me as the new guy. Eventually Frank had heard enough, and he and Spider squared up to each other. Again, as the newly arrived guy straight from the factory, these guys seemed enormous and intimidating.

After a few days, my troop arrived back in camp and I got to meet them all, these were then, and still are some of the nicest, funniest and talented men I had ever met. I am proud to say I am friends with most of them to this day and with a small group we still go out onto the hills and mountains hiking and camping.

I was placed on the Ech det with Cpl Steve Brant, a very dapper and intelligent NCO and he took me over everything comms wise and admin wise to make sure I was up to speed. In those first weeks in the camp at Bømoen the famous Squadron Photo was taken. As my rifle and webbing was very well cammed with white tape, I was

Norway montage

placed as the right marker by WO2 (SSM) Steve Marshall, much to the annoyance of Cpl Phil Clifford who chuntered non-stop about the 'Nig' taking the best spot. Two anomalies which most people miss is that the QM, resplendent in a sling for his arm was the only man not on skis. I was also not wearing bindings as I had no idea how to put them on and was simply stood on my skis. It was during this time, that to date, the funniest thing I have ever seen was to happen. The holy grail at that time, was to find an unbreakable flask, as the Army versions were really delicate glass tube jobs. Mick "Fitz" Fitzpatrick and Geordie Taylor had gone shopping into Voss, I believe, and when they came back, we were all in the shared dormitory. The doors burst open and Fitz shouted out 'I've found it, an unbreakable flask'. Naturally there was pin drop silence, this was massive news after all. They described at length how they came across the shop, how good the shop owner was, his product range etc, Fitz describing and Geordie nodding along. They then got to the point of the flask (holy grail) and its test procedure to prove its durability 'the shop owner was kicking it all around the shop, dropping it from height and nothing happened. He bounced it off every surface and wall, nothing happened' We must have looked like monkeys seeing their reflection in a mirror for the first time, as

How deep is this snow??

not a word was spoken from the audience. This was when Fitz, took the flask out from his bag, he held it up triumphantly and then to prove his statements, held it by the neck and tapped it gently against the edge of the six foot GS table we had in the room. As soon as flask touched table we heard the familiar tinkle of shattering glass inside a thermos. There was a moments silence with Fitz and Geordie staring in disbelief at the plastic container of shattered glass before we all burst into hysterical laughter. The timing was comic genius. Mick later, much later, after we had stopped laughing said 'it was worth the money we spent just for the laugh'. I still cry with laughter to this day thinking about that event.

Squadron Photo

Shortly after the photo, we took the long drive North, this was my first time driving on snow and ice with a fully laden vehicle and trailer. I can confirm adrenaline is brown and it does smell.

Eventually we headed out for the Comms exercise and our Det was attached to the US Engineers. It was during this period that we developed a comms issue and the Technicians were sent to resolve the issue. As they arrived, one asked me 'Do you have your cold start handle?' Of course said I. 'Good, get your kit on and take it to the Gazelle crew who are repairing their helicopter, they need a cold start' I looked at my Det Commander who just nodded and I said okay, got my gear on, grabbed the starting handle and made my way to the helicopter. On arrival, the crew were inside the cockpit area, doing something or other. They had not noticed me, so I knocked on the cockpit. One of the doors opened and an irritable 'what!' came forth. Beaming a smile I held up the cold start handle and said 'I've come to give you a cold start'. I never saw the punch launched, but certainly felt it. I could hear the roars of laughter coming from our 9x9 as I approached it, twats.

On our return to Bulford from Norway, Gary "Chalkie" Lang, Paul "Ginge" Battle and I went into Salisbury for a few cheeky beers and a haircut. After several beers we went to the barbers, Chalkie first who said 'Skinhead please'. Ginge was next and said the same, I was last and as they had got it done, I got the same. As my haircut was almost completed Chalkie and Ginge said 'Lets get the lines cut in' As I was already in the chair, I said 'Go for it' as I was full of bravado (beer). As soon as the barber took the cape off, they both looked at each other and said 'Nope!' and nearly pissed themselves laughing. Twats!

On the Monday we were doubled up to the Kiwi for the very first clean up. As we were wearing civvie clothes for this I put on a wooly hat to hide my hair or lack of it. It was all going swimmingly until the SSM Steve Marshall was walking towards me and Steve Fielding ripped my hat off. To say the SSM was not impressed would be an under-statement, my word he could shout loud.

SSgt Sid Vivian was our Troop SSgt at the time, I loved winding him up. We had an infestation of cats at one point and they would crap and pee in our cam nets and hessian. One day I found a dead cat in the garage. It could not have had a pleasant death judging by the way it lay there all contorted. I took the dead cat and put it in Sids desk drawer. I waited for Sid to enter his office, imagining him going to his desk, sitting down……. All of a sudden there was an unholy shriek and then 'Slaney you little twat get your arse in here'. The extras were worth it.

Two Years later, as a newly married man and recently promoted LCpl and Det Commander, we were due to deploy on an Air Transportable Ex to Denmark. We had done the same Ex a year previously, but went through all the usual briefings and orders sessions as you would. The parade time for departure to Lyneham was set for 0430hrs and we were briefed 'Do not go out and get drunk'.

I had sent my wife to her parents for the duration and after several beers in the Saxon Warrior with my crewman Geordie Brown, we got a carry out and went back to my quarter for some food. After several more beers and food, I packed my crewman off to his room, cleaned up the kitchen, put my uniform on and set my alarm clock. I woke up to bright sunshine beaming through the curtain gaps and thought 'strange'. I looked at my alarm clock which read 0830hrs. Once more I proved adrenalin is brown and smelly. I raced over to the duty NCO bunk in SHQ and the Rear Duties NCO started to laugh, we got the duty vehicle and started off for the Air Head at South Cerney. About 10 miles short the duty vehicle broke down. Both of us were clueless how to get it going and so I flagged down the first passing car that came along. It was a middle aged lady in a VW Beetle, I explained that I needed to get to South Cerney and she immediately agreed to take me as she would pass by. Thanking her as I jumped out with all my kit, I never got her name sadly, I made my way into the Air Head. I gave the movements team a sob story about family bereavement and vehicle breakdown and they organised transport to Brize Norton. Immediately on arrival I went to the movements team there, repeated my sob story and got 'Don't worry there is an aircraft almost ready to depart'. They took me out and passed me over to the Chalk Commander. It was the newly arrived Para's who had taken over from 1 PWO as the UK battalion. The Chalk Commander put me on his manifest and shortly after we took off. On arrival in Denmark and remembering the briefings, I saw a convoy for 33 Sqn RAF about to leave. I knew they passed by our Squadron Box on the MSR to their location. I threw my kit in the back of a Bedford and climbed aboard. Looking out, I saw our Squadron Flag and as we passed threw my kit out and jumped. Walking into the Squadron area the first person I saw was SSgt Max Williams, my Troop Staffie. He was writing something on a clip board 'Morning Staff' says I, he looked up and nearly choked. 'WTF are you doing here, I was told you were in Bulford. Come with me' He took me to the SSM WO2 Ian Campbell who had no option but to place me on orders. The Sqn Commander had not arrived and the 2I/C Capt (JR) Ewing was in command. I was duly marched into his tent on orders by the SSM and the YofS, WO2 Mick Altham, was in attendance. I told the complete truth about what had happened, to silence apart from one or two giggles from the afore mentioned WO's. The 2i/c then asked me if I accepted his award or wished for trail by Courts Martial. I thought this is where I find out what is white and flies through the window (my Lance Jack tape) and said 'I accept your award sir' He responded '10 extra duties' The YofS said 'Ten, after getting here before his own packet has arrived. 5 maximum?' Then the SSM chimed in with 'Outstanding initiative sir, he should only get 3' I couldn't believe they were haggling down my punishment and thought 'that's proper man management right there' That was a lesson I never ever forgot. JR eventually said 'Fuck it, go and unbundle all the weapons, that's your punishment' As I left the tent gob smacked, I started to head over to the weapons as a packet of Rovers arrived. This was the packet I should have been on and had beaten to the location. All my mates, Joe Campbell, Mark Baxter, Geoff Vear were all betting who would get my tape. They could not believe I was there. They were also gutted I did not get bust.

On the major FTX's we had the NATO Challenge Cup, this was a race followed by (usually) an assault course and always a shoot. 249 was such a fit Sqn, thanks to Maj Danny Fisher, we always won not just the minor unit competition, but usually the Major Unit one as well. The names were drawn at random by the AMF(L) staff from the nominal role, but it never mattered who was chosen, we would still win. ID chits in lieu were sometimes used.

1982 To 1986 - Paddy Lynch - 249 Signal Squdron

I joined the Squadron in late 1982 as a Cpl from 2 Squadron, 21 Signal Regiment. I was 27 years old at the time and had been in the Corps for 9 years, having joined in July 1973 and trained as a Radio Op.

When I arrived in the Squadron, some of the personalities already there were Jock McAleer, Bob Cook and Shammy Leather.

My first time to Norway was on Ex Hardfall 1983 where we were based in the Stalheim Hotel. The hotel was modern with fantasic views over the valley, large recreational areas and a cellar where we kept the skis etc and which was also the main entrance and exit of the building. Luckily, I had a room to myself.

Stalheim Hotel

I did my ski training and artic warfare training at the Stalhiem and surrounding area. I learned to ski on nato planks at Stalhiem. Locals must have found it amusing to wtch us make our first tentative moves on skis, and there where some spectacular snotes as we slowly learned to manage the nato planks attached to out feet.

As a novice skier, it was hard going. Staying upright was difficult, then they added belt kit, weapon and bergen to make it more interesting. Finally they strapped you to a pulk to try and finish you off. The ski training was fun, especially the ski-jourring behind the volvos. The funniest casualty was fellow novice Cpl Terry Petherbridge, managing to get stabbed in the behind with a pair of ski sticks whilst doing the ski-jourring.

Pulk pulling was no fun whatsoever. I hated it and found it very hard going. Even after 3 Norways all that pulling pulks did was annoy me and produce a sense of humour failure after about 10mins.

Digging snow holes was fun. Hard work if you where in the entrance pushing out blocks of snow from the guy tunnelling out the snow hole itself, but once completed I found I it warm and comfortable. It could be a bit disconcerting when waking up to find that the roof had settled a bit overnight though.

Evenings where spent watching videos, playing board games or cards over a few beers. When we moved to Ulvik we could get out into the village in the evenings but there was no place to go at the Stalhiem.

One evening I was taken to one side by the Sqn 2ic, and told he had a job opportunity for me. 'How would you like to go on an OP behind 1 Para tomorrow night ready for an exercise start the day after. Sounded like fun, so Nigel Back, an ED whose name I have forgotten but who was a top guy and myself, where loaded up with massive Bergens, into a BV 202 and sent off in dead of night for other side of Voss.

A moonless night and Bergens weighing about 90 to 100lbs (or at least felt like that as there was 3 of us carrying 5 tent sheets, 4 days rations, cam net,enough 320 batteries to last 4 days, naptha for 4 days, plus personal kit) meant a slow night ski to a position on a cliff edge overlooking the valley that 1 Para was defending. The lack of moonlight made the terrain featureless and it was only when Nigel Back stepped left to take over breaking trail that we found out we where on the edge of a 30ft embankment, as he disappeared down the slop in a tangle of skis, poles and weapon.

When we found a good site, I was left to start putting up a tentsheet shelter, and guard the bergens, whilst the other two who where more profficient skiers, back tracked and then laid a false circular trail to hide where our position was. This paid off on the second night as a para patrol went off following that false trail rather than stummbling onto our shelter.

We set up under the shadow of a few trees, with a ledge to look out over the valley, and with the cam net deployed, we where pretty well hidden. Speaking to Jim Perry's team later, they dug in under a tree using tent sheets and the deep snow to shelter in.

Come daylight we could see every move the enemy made and spent the next three days calling in notional artillery fire on Echeolon sites, HQ's, Mortar sections and hides where the Scimitars and Volves where hiding up. On the second night a patrol got to within 30ft of our tent sheets but somehow missed us.

Every good job has to end and on fourth day, as the enemy retreated out of the valley, we where picked up by helicopter and taken back to Voss. There we met up with Sgt Jim Perry and his OP team, who had apparently been listening in to the Paras land lines for 3 days! All in all, it was a very successful Sqn exercise against 1 Para. To be fair it was their first Norway too, but it was nice to put one over on them.

I did deployments to both Turkey and Denmark while in the Squadron and can remember during one deployment to Turkey, teaching the American Para Bn how to play rugby and murder ball, as well as enjoying a few beers with some of them later. A trip to Istanbul was the highlight of that trip with several members learning that the bargain perfume they bought from street venders, did not really smell that much like the Channel you got from the duty free shop at an airport. I heard that it was described as cats pee by more than one wife!

My first deployment to Turkey was to the Erzerum area in Norther turkey. We arrived by herculese and had a few days in a tented camp on the base. We were most surprised that one of the Turkish conscripts, wearing old WW2 type battle dress uniforms, had a London accent. He explained that he grew up in London, but had come to Turkey to visit famly and ended up getting conscripted into his national servcies as he had dual citizenship. He was not a happy man! Another thing I remember of that camp was that we all had very clean boots, as the conscripts had a little sideline going cleaning everyones boots for 10 lira a go.

I left the Squadron in 1986 and moved to 200 Signal Squadron in Detmold. I left the Corp in 1987, on a Friday, handing in my kit at 11 Signal Regiment in Helles barracks in Catterick where I had started my carrier. I joined Leicestershire Police on the following Monday. Many years later, I went to my stepsons passing out parade at Helles barracks when he joined the Parachute Regiment, and found that little had changed from my final visit.

1985 to 1987 - David (Charlie) Rodgers - 249 Signal Squadron

My second tour was with 249 Signal Squadron AMF(L), based in Old Sarum, began in 1985 as the WO2 YofS. At that time Glen McArdle was the SSM and Maj Innocent was the OC. They always say "don't go back" and maybe I should have listened as the whole outlook of the Sqn had changed. The emphasis was now on fitness and skiing ability. Maj Innocent was in that mould and he was hard but fair. We had a good bunch of lads and a lot of hard working Senior Ranks and Officers. When we went to Norway this time we were housed in a big Hotel on the top of a hill, the training area was about 1 and a half miles down the hill and from the first day we had to ski down to it, there were vehicles driving up the road as we were skiing down it, this is where we had lots of falling over (or Boxes of Snot) as we called them. I carried out my AWT this time and, as you can see, had the press following me around.

During this exercise I found I had a turnour (non malignant) in the back of my eye and after the exercise was finished, I was told by the doctor not to go back on the next visit to Norway. I stayed with 249 for a good few months, organising the "Ten Tors Safety Net" and taking two young Sgt's through their prep for the YofS Selection Course. It was decided that me not being able to go to Norway was not in the interests of the Squadron so I left in 1987 and went to 8 Signal Regiment. All in all a great Squadron and a pleasure to say I served with them.

Arctic endurance

IT is minus 29 degrees and the temperature is falling fast. A Brandon man is about to spend his third night out in the snow.

Sgt. Maj. David Rogers, 35, whose mother, Mrs Edith Rodgers, lives at Willow Close, Sawmills, Brandon, is on a two-month Arctic winter exercise in Norway's fjord country.

David — above — is serving with 249 Signal Squadron, which forms part of the Allied Mobile Force (Land). In time of tension this deterrent force deploys from its barracks in Wiltshire to Norway, Greece or Turkey to secure the flanks of NATO.

Doing my Arctic Warfare Training with the press on our heels

International course for AMF(L) staff hosted by the Squadron

A few of the names that I remember: Glen McArdle, John Fielding, Jim Perry, Pete Wykes, Les Hoehne, Dave Beatie, Steve Armitage. I apologise for the names that I can't remember

Dinner night in the Sgt's Mess with wives: L-R, Pete Wykes, Steve Armitage, Charlie Rogers, and Dave Beatie.

1986 to 1989 - Jim Wentworth Brown - 249 Signal Squadron

I joined 249 Signal Squadron AMF(L) in 1986 as a Lance Corporal from 30 Signal Regiment. The picture below is of me on one of the landing vessels with my Line laying winterised Landrover carrying Arctic Camouflage netting in the foreground. This would later become a duty vehicle used for resupply and for Ferrying Senior Officers to meetings at Divisional HQ for exercise deployments and training. The authorities of Ulvik, Norway would only allow certain types of naval Landing Craft to

Waiting to unload in the Hardanger Fjord

dock in Haŕdanger fjord. 249 Signal Squadron vehicles offloaded and started off by road for The Brakanes Hotel which was to be for the sole occupancy of the squadron. On arrival, the hotel car park became the vehicle park and we booked into the Hotel, just as normal guests would, and were each allocated a room key. We were responsible for our rooms during the stay and gave it a general clean as you would do your room in barracks. You also had the use of most of the Hotels facilities which were leased to the Military. However, the Hotel reception was manned by duty military staff and became the de-facto Guardroom for the duration of our stay. In previous years the vehicles were normally offloaded at one of the public ferry jetties around Bruraviki, which is a ferry quay in the municipality of Ulvik in Vestland county, and then followed a convoy road route to Ulvik in groups of 12-15 vehicles.

One of the first things in training was that all those staff allocated or likely to drive a vehicle had to complete and pass a Winter driving course which was held at a dedicated centre run by the Norwegian Authorities this consisted of giant punchbags slung from overhead gantries and also had a skid pan style course, a driving examiner travelled around this course and when told to do so under control you had to steer safely around these punchbags easier said than done for some as you not only had to deal with snow and ice but also a large slippery skidpan.

'Road of the Trolls'

I was fortunate that this training was completed first, as one day, trying to return to Ulvik from Bergen via a road commonly known as 'Snake Pass' (its correct name is Trollstigen or translated, the 'Road of the Trolls'. This road held a deadly secret near the top as it had a pillbox carved into the mountainside. Apparently, this caught many a German out during WW2. During the 1980's, this road had no barrier to prevent vehicles tumbling off the edge during blizzards, so was quite dangerous. After dropping some officers off for a briefing, I found myself on this road, accompanied by new boy to Norway (it was compulsory to have a 2nd driver in vehicles in case of emergencies).

The weather had turned to blizzard conditions and as I rounded a bend, going down the road, I felt the Landrover going into a skid. I was fortunate to remember my training and the words 'turn into the direction of the skid' came immediately to mind. I was lucky as the co-driver, for some reason, opened his door of the Landrover and I could only see fresh air! He could see my left front wheel was within a couple of inches from going over the edge of the road. I was so lucky that I recovered from the skid only to then encounter a tanker coming up the hill! Thankfully, all turned out well and I received a round of applause from some Norwegians below who then offered to take the Landrover onto a frozen lake to race against them. Obviously I declined the offer as I'm not totally sure my bosses would have been too keen on me doing this. However, I did accept a ride in a VW beetle car doing 50mph around the frozen surface of the lake, watching and hearing the ice crack underneath the weight of over a dozen vehicles racing.

It was then onto cross country skiing. Learning the basics until they were mastered and then onto the use of pulks. Basically, if you imagine an Indian style canoe carrying everything a 5 man team would need for survival, tent sheets to form a tent, candles, fuel and food you will have an idea of the size of the pulk. All in, the weight of the pulk could amount to 300lbs or more. One guy would be in a harness to the front like a cart horse and would guide this canoe like object whilst 2 others, who had control of ropes leading off the rear would act has brakes if it should speed up rather than have the front guy run over. However, it wasn't always plain sailing. Squaddie humour was always cropping up and they just love to play around! You could be forgiven for wiping your eyes seeing a white-clad soldier trying to break the downhill landspeed record with a massive weighted load trying to run him over as his mates let go of their brake lines!

On the approach to some training areas, we could encounter some of the local kindergartens taking their charges of 4 to 5 year old's out on ski's which looked no bigger the a 12" ruler in length. Many a time someone would be overheard saying "well if that little bugger can do it then I can". But the truth was that in a few cases some people were not destined to ski or could simply not muster those skills. One of the lads from Mike admin troop who i had been asked to coach for about a week told everyone and anyone who would listen he wanted to ski, but was often found enacting the movements of an ostrich, when trying to ski he would be found with his head embedded in the snow, and yet when you helped him up he was roaring with laughter. No matter how hard he tried, he just could not get the hang of it.

During this biathlon I destroyed my right knee cruciate ligaments. I had just got to the top of a slope and then sped down the other side when I hit a small hump at the base, this caused my ski's to cross meaning I could not regain control and have my ski's side by side as normal. Race staff and those on light duties were tasked as Marshalls at various danger points around the course. In the case of an incident they were to form a wall and fended off anyone coming down the hill. One guy brought a Landrover and used that to replace the human wall of staff protecting me. This was to protect me from skiers coming down the same slope. This same vehicle was used to ferry me to the Norwegian Hospital in Bergen the hospital staff heavily strapped and splinted my leg and I was put into a Norwegian Ambulance, alongside another soldier from a different regiment who was also being returned to the UK for further treatment. The Journey in the ambulance was a bit funny for us as we found ourselves for the first 10 minutes of the journey to the airport singing the theme tune for Ghostbusters. The Norwegian medics had to stop and check we were ok until we explained why we were laughing and yes, if you haven't guessed it, it was because we were travelling in a 'Ghostbusters' ambulance. We ended up on a Hercules back to the UK.

Prior to starting the Unit 20k Biathlon, looking far happier than I would be at the end!

All troops received training in Cross country skiing, building shelters of brushwood or snow holes. Each unit would be given a training area along with a Norwegian liaison officer who had been allocated to your unit and was tasked with checking daily for safety before troops were taken into the training areas. Part of my role at one point was to train newbies to Arctic conditions. In my case this was to teach and demonstrate how to build different types of brushwood shelter and then insulate. I might also, depending on the team I was with, have to teach and demostrate the process for building a snowhole, which was a type of igloo under snow banks. We would dig into a snow bank to create part of it and then build a snow wall, while at the same time dig a tunnel from both ends which ended up as your access to a domed area within the bank. A pole poking out of a hole at the top was to indicate occupancy and location of the hole. Inside you laid your neoprene mats onto which went your sleeping bag.

The heat for the snowhole would be a single whale fat candle which would last all night. However, you would also use a single naptha fueled stove and this would cook your food and provide heat until you went to sleep. You would also strip down to your undies and inside your bivvy bag would dry out any damp clothing. This period, while someone was cooking for all, would be about personal admin; drying clothing, powdering anywhere needing a tender touch and ensuring each other had done so. The 'Tent Commander', who had a duty to do all of this on top of checking for frostbite and hyperthermia and looking for any kind of injury which might compromise a soldiers ability to fight and survive under arctic conitions.

I was there in 1986 when it was reported that an avalanche had happened on slopes near Narvik and the Norwegians had lost 12 or 13 guys. We heard on the news that they were on avalanche patrols exploding dangerous slopes prior to troop exercises. However, this group entered an area where previous detonations had altered the snow in that area, and they got caught in the avalanche. The papers tell a different story. Oslo, Norway (AP) reported 'The death toll in an avalanche that buried members of a Norwegian ski patrol during a NATO war game rose to 13 today'. The Norwegian NRK radio reported 'Hopes of finding three missing soldiers faded. A wall of snow buried 31 Norwegian ski troopers on Wednesday at Vassdalen near Narvik in northern Norway. Fifteen soldiers were injured'.

It was also reported; Lt. Gen. Ulf Berg, the Supreme Commander North Norway, announced today that military leaders of eight North Atlantic Treaty Organization countries called off their joint winter manoeuvre Anchor Express, involving 20,000 troops.

"We cannot possibly shoulder the responsibility for holding personnel in areas with such extreme risks of more avalanches, and where lives have already been lost" Berg announced. More than 200 military and civilian members of rescue teams, as well as dogs and helicopters, were searching today for the missing ski troopers. Sven Arne Simonsen, a survivor, said by radio from his hospital bed in Narvik that he was buried up to his neck in snow for 15 minutes. He said he managed to get out and helped dig out six more men before the first rescue team arrived an hour later. "It was terrible.

... my pals are dead" said Simonsen, who suffered an arm injury. Maj Hans Kloevstad of the Allied Information Centre announced that foreign soldiers in Norway for the three-week-long war games would not be sent home but would be regrouped to take part in improvised exercises.

When this occurred, I do remember looking at the slopes with others after hearing several distant rumbles and making out the fine mists which rose from the slopes. The Norwegian officer with us explaining what was taking place and why. To the Norwegians it was all normal. I remember a few us spoke aloud and blindly stated 'well let's hope they don't go walking into that before checking'

I instantly thought of the families and loved ones of those lost Norwegians and could not believe when we were told that due to the conditions, they may not try to recover them until much later. A few of us even asked if we might volunteer but all we heard in asking was that all training in the region had been stopped as a mark of respect.

1988 -1990 - Rob James - 249 Signal Squadron

The first time I came across 249 Sig Sqn was during my time at the School of Signals, Blandford, in the mid-1980`s, when some guys appeared in our cook-house wearing cravats and the AMF(L) badge on their jumpers which made them unique, compared to our own dress code. One of my mates at the School, Terry "Wally" Walton had previously served with the unit often quoting, "when I was at 249".

Moving on a few years to June 1988, I was just coming to the end of my 12-month posting in Northern Ireland, with Int and Security Group as a RTG, when I was anticipating my next posting. Having spent the previous 5 years in the UK, I was hoping to avoid BAOR, as I was looking at plans beyond the Army and a move back into "civvy street". Fortunately, in came my posting order and 249 Sig Sqn was going to be my next destination!

This was going to be a bit of a culture shock as I hadn`t worn a uniform for 12 months in NI and I knew the unit was a bit "army green" for fitness but I was still looking forward to it. This was spiced up with the unit having a reputation for travel and the immediate prospect of going on exercise to Turkey in September 1988.

I arrived at Ward Barracks, Bulford in July 1988 and joined Main Troop with Lt Mike Grimson, Sgt Simon Strapp and Sgt Steve Hughes the troop hierarchy. Morale appeared to be very good with the usual characters you find in a troop, with the star being Del Whyman, a good Ol' cockney lad who would back chat everybody, no matter what the rank! No doubt everyone serving at that time will remember Del. There was a lot of humour in both Main and Support Troops; an example of this would be "Chuck Beret". Waiting for parade, a guy's beret would be nicked off their head and sent whizzing over the garages like a Frisbee, with the comment "look...Chuck Beret!"

249 Signal Squadron HQ in Bulford

Around this time Main Troop were preparing to go off on summer camp up to Ambleside in the Lake District. We stayed in some type of youth hostel and days were spent practicing canoeing and abseiling, with pub crawls in the evening and getting to know the female population.

Turkey – 1988

We travelled for this exercise by plane from Brize Norton and this deployment was based in the area to the west of Istanbul, up near the border with Bulgaria (which was still a communist country back then) and it just seemed like a huge dust bowl.

The Turkish drivers were "nutters" and every few miles, you would pass a lorry on its side, usually with its cargo of melons scattered all over the place. Car drivers would overtake our convoys at breakneck speed and think nothing of what was heading in their direction!

Once in location the immediate advice from the lads who`d deployed before to Turkey, was to acquire or exchange kit with the "spams" in particular a camp cot. These were a sought-after item, as they were more robust than the crappy camp beds, we had and were vital for future deployments in particular Norway. Usually, a spare beret or some compo rations did the trick.

Scene across the Squadron location in Turkey 1988

My land rover was one of the Key Dets accompanied by "Happy" Phillips and we had been assigned some top brass from HQ Land South East (NATO/Turkey) in the name of a British Officer, Col HJ Lowles CBE. I had been used to taking young officers out on radio exercises at the School of Sigs as part of our job in Radex Troop but this was a different scale in terms of top brass!

We spent a lot of time driving to different locations with the Colonel during the exercise phase and he quite liked our "all in stews" and general banter. On one occasion, we stopped off at café in some small town and he was going to buy us a meal (we took it in turns to stay with the rover). The place was a bit of a hovel and we scoffed some dubious meatball dish. The locals were watching repeats of their Olympian weightlifter on a black and white TV on the wall, winning their only gold medal in that years` Olympic Games. The meal came to about 3 lira which hardly made a dent in the Colonel`s daily 25 lira Turkish Meal allowance! I still have the letter and photo the Colonel sent to me as a way of showing his thanks for looking after him during his time with myself and “Happy” Phillips.

Myself, Col Lowles and 'Happy' Phillips at end of ex

We had a day`s R & R in Istanbul towards the end of the deployment and much of this was spent haggling with the market traders in The Grand Bazaar and a visit to a "Maccy Ds". I haggled a new burgundy leather jacket in the Bazaar which I knew was going to soon look out of place back in the UK! It was not long after we returned to the UK by plane, back to Brize Norton.

On our return to Bulford, the next few weeks were spent getting back into Squadron routine with regular gym sessions, usually conducted by Gaz Waters (also previously at the School of Sigs) troop admin, range days and the obligatory Friday afternoon Bergan run. These were typically overseen by our SSM Gordon Shelley and YofS Terry Crosby.

I remember we had a guy in Main Troop, Al Potter. As a young 'Siggy' he was looking to boost his pay packet. The way he thought best to do this was to volunteer as a "guinea pig" for trials at nearby Porton Down for 3 weeks. I can`t remember how much extra a day you got paid for this but Al did seem oblivious to the funny stuff he was probably going to be injected with when we had a chat about it!

It wasn`t long before we would be preparing for the annual Winters` deployment to Norway. This was preceded by Ex Dryshod held around November time where we would undergo training, usually around Okehampton, to familiarize ourselves with what to expect in Norway.

Some of the guys in the squadron were "old sweats" having notched up a number of "Norway's" already under their belt. Cotswold camping was the place to go to upgrade our kit for gloves, gaiters, anything Gore-Tex as a lot of regular army issue kit wasn't up to scratch. You could easily spend up to £100 just to ensure a more comfortable existence. This was also a time when we`d be all walking round camp in "boots Frankenstein", the square toed ski boots and white "noggy socks" to break them in.

Norway – Ex Hardfall 1989

The Brakanes Hotel was our base for the next 5 weeks, having flown on a "Herc" from Brize Norton to Bergen and then the coaches up around the Hardanger Fjord until we arrived at Ulvik.

Brakanes Hotel, Ulvik 1989

Once we had settled in, we were soon into a period of ski training, taken up into the mountains by a group of Haglund BV 206s; usually driven by guys who had been to Norway in previous years. This was an introduction to skiing on the "NATO" planks which for us novices, you were doing well to stand upright on. Quite often in some of the public places, you would be overtaken by some little kid who made it look simple and was quite embarrassing!

Having gone through Arctic Survival Training, erecting tent sheets, pulling sledges, cooking on the Peak stoves and gaining some confidence on the NATO planks, one particular incident does spring to mind. We had deployed up to the Smoreggi peak area a fair drive from Ulvik, to further practice our ski and tent-sheet building drills.

Loading our skis onto the BV before heading up into the mountains

Once the BV`s had departed, we were soon left digging our tent-sheet camps on the mountain plateau.

Preparing our camp using tent sheets carried in the pulks

At some point the weather deteriorated rapidly and it wasn't before long we found ourselves in a complete white-out blizzard. This went on for hours and started to become serious when some of the tent sheets started to collapse under the weight of the snow. In one or two cases the guys had to abandon their camps and squeeze into other ones.

In our tent, we joked about writing our last Valentine's Day messages as it was Feb 14th and things were starting to get really hairy now. Comms were eventually established back at base and the BVs were sent out to rescue us, with flares being used by YofS Terry Crosby and Carl Bruce leading the BVs in. A break in the weather allowed us to de-camp but a lot of kit was buried in the snow and got left behind that day.

Some of the Sqn guys in Norway 1989

Following the AMF(L) Infantry on their exercise as an Umpire

Our deployment came to an end with the customary "skit show" in the Brakanes, although I haven`t a clue what`s going on below in this pic!

Taff George, Nige Wilson, Paul Culleton and a dog bowl watched by SSM Gordon Shelley.

Once we returned to Bulford there was the usual troop admin routine and post Norway clean-up of vehicles and putting in claims "for lost kit" which a lot of us did to boost payday.

Our next deployment would be to Denmark in June 1989 and prior to this, it was decided to have all the Rebro Dets based in Support Troop. By this time, I had declined to do my A1 RTG course and took on a Radio Op role, switching to Support Troop and a Rebro Det Commander. The Troop was led by Lt Kim Evans, Staff Sgt Shaun Wilson, Sgt Ray Ramsey (I knew Ray from the School of Sigs) and Sgt "Buck" Rogers.

Denmark 1989 - Ex Avenue Express

The deployment was quite a short one which lasted around 2 weeks in June 1989 but one that I was looking forward to. As previously with Norway, we flew out from Brize Norton over to Zealand, Denmark and it wasn`t long before we had collected our Landrovers and formed the customary "squadron box" where all the vehicles were arranged in a uniformed manner, with an echelon check-point at the front of the box.

249 Signal Squadron Box with the Key Dets lined up

There was the usual "comms" exercise, troop admin days and on this occasion, the NATO Challenge Cup. This was something the squadron excelled at and involved a 10km march and shoot event, against other units and in particular the "spams". Although we had trained hard for this event, I missed out on the random final selection, as this was a ploy to prevent any units entering all their "racing snakes". Needless to say, 249 Sig Sqn were winners yet again in Denmark 1989.

SSgt Sean Wilson overseeing range practice before the NATO Challenge Cup

On one occasion I had to drive Sgt Taff George to a location in a left-hand drive Landrover. Whilst attempting to find the gear lever I ended up stroking his leg, which wasn`t the smartest of moves. He retorted" Are you trying to get fresh with me Cpl James?"

R&R was spent with a visit to Copenhagen which included a visit to the Carlsberg brewery and quaffing bottles of elephant beer in a designated sampling room full of pictures of previous chairmen going back 100 years. The evening was spent in a nightclub in the city and some of us caught the last train back to Ringstad at 3am only to nearly miss our stop as we were all crashed out! Once back to the Squadron Box, it was a quick kip underneath the rover before getting ready for the days` parade!

As those who were present at the time, this was when "Mad" Jock Wylie decided to throw up and relieve himself on a high-ranking German Officer in his tent, after a heavy night on the piss which I`m sure caused some ramifications with our seniors. When his name was called out on parade, his hand appeared under the tent confirming his presence. The journey back home was uneventful and this time by sea on the RFA Sir Percivale, back to Portsmouth.

Fitness was never far away at 249 Sig Sqn and we had entered a team in the Morrison Cup (Inter Unit Team Athletic Championships) in Middlesbrough, stopping off overnight at 2 Div in York. I got a 2nd place in the 800m Minor Units race wearing the amber and black colours of our unit but got absolutely pasted when I entered the same 800m race, having qualified for the Army championships at Tidworth a few weeks later. This was the era of Kris Akabusi and these guys were in a totally different league!

The Kiwi Trophy was also held around this time of year which was based on an individual run with a Bergen and shoot at the end of it (as it was in 1989). Being held in Bulford it was up and down around the Kiwi, always hills somewhere along the way around Bulford ridge and pretty knackering. It was won by either Harry Kemp or Gaz Waters that year and I came 4th behind them.

Kim Evans handed over an AMF(L) pendant to the Carabinieri team captain.

I was also in the squadron football team, led by Lt Kim Evans, Support Troop and one of the highlights was playing against the Italian Carabinieri on our exercise in Italy in September 1989. I think we lost this game and the Boss broke the Italian goalies' arm...accidental of course!

One of the stranger things we did later in the year, was prison guard duty at an old army camp on the edge of Salisbury plain. The Government at the time was looking at ways of dealing with overcrowding and had designated some army camps to help with this. These were Cat C prisoners and quite often derogatory banter was exchanged from the watch towers with the lags when staging on.

October 1989 was now looming and 249 Sig Sqn had entered into another competition it had a great reputation at winning; the inter unit Lanyard Trophy. That year it was to be held on Dartmoor, with the start point being Okehampton camp. We headed off from Bulford in our land rovers and from recollection we had entered two teams of 4.

Okehampton camp is located on the northern edge of Dartmoor and is as bleak as you can imagine, made worse by the sparse transit accommodation block we found ourselves in. In our team there was myself, Mark "Harry" Harrop, Ian Ormerod and Harry Kemp and our start point was 2am in the morning. After a bit of kip, off we went into the pitch darkness, with the customary wind and rain to the first checkpoint. The map reading skills of the guys was brilliant and we were soon making great progress over the designated course. Although you felt sleep depraved at times you were soon brought back to life, climbing over the occasional electric fence which given the rain, gave you a bit of a boost!

Lanyard Trophy plaque from 1989`s competition

By mid-morning the weather had deteriorated so badly due to a storm blowing across Southern England, it was decided to pull the competition early due to a storm blowing and the designated leading team were the winners. That happened to be our own section and we were all presented with a nice gong for our efforts. That was knackering and made worse by the fact we had to drive the 120 miles back to Bulford. It wasn`t long before we were preparing for our annual pilgrimage to Norway again and on this occasion, I was designated a BV Hägglunds 206 driver. The drivers had to attend a snow and ice driving course somewhere near Bulford. This was great fun as it included skid-pan training, where some sort of bogey wheel contraption was attached to a land rover and simulated driving on ice. In addition, we got to drive the BV 206 around the hills around Bulford and Salisbury plain.

Norway 1990 – Ex Hardfall

Our deployment to Norway on 2nd January 1990 was earlier than the previous year, as this was going to be spent in the south as well as the far north and going to last a couple of months. We again flew from Brize Norton to Bergen with the same routine of being located at the Brakanes Hotel in Ulvik. Once the squadron had settled in, we were soon briefed on what the next few weeks training involved. This included BV driver training up on Smoreggi, ski orienteering, a couple of ski races and AST/AWT deployments. Being one of the 12 designated BV drivers was a great experience, as our skills were put to the test driving up the steep tracks in the snow, knowing we had a carriage full of guys in the back wagon.

Hägglunds BV 206 navigating the snow tracks up on Smoreggi

The couple of ski races we did at 10km and 20km provided an opportunity for some of the guys to show off their skiing skills at

Prep before one of the ski races on the legendary NATO planks

pace, on the NATO planks. I was fairly average at these and would finish somewhere middle in the pack, including a few customary falls for good measure, usually belted by the SA80 rifle in the chops.

Norway 1990 included the extended "Northern" element of our training which was named Ex Array Encounter in the inner Arctic circle and based around Bardufoss airfield. This meant a 2-hour flight from Bergen to cover the 1,600 kms to go "up North".

The main stark difference on arrival, was how much colder it was compared to our time spent around Ulvik and how clearer the skies were. On this Exercise I was a Rebro Det Commander accompanied by Taff Gareth (T Shirt) Owen and Paul Gubba in a BV 206. We would set up in the remotest of locations with the 9x9 tent attached to the side of the BV, 3 VHF masts set up with the "gene" up and running providing power. The whole of the det would be covered up using our white camo nets.

Rebro Det set up in Northern Norway 1990

On one particular night we were caught in a "whiteout" and discovered in the morning that the snow that had fallen was now the same height as the 9x9 and so a lot of digging had to take place to rescue the tent. It was also vital to maintain access to get outside the tent, due to fire risks, as we had heard rumours of accidents happening with other NATO units. The BV was great driving to these locations but sometimes going downhill, the vehicle would lose traction on the roads and go into skid mode which made for spine chilling moments.

One of the final aspects of our trip up "North" was a display by all the various countries that made up the AMF(L) on Bardufoss airfield, including a helicopter flypast.

Myself with the Squadron flag on my BV206 at the final parade of AMF(L) units.

By this point the Squadron were based in a covered tented area, near the airfield, where there was a delay of around 4 days to fly back to the UK due to ice on the runway. The temperature had dropped to -40 degrees outside and so we were confined to our "maggot bags" to keep warm. If a song ever reminds me of waiting for that plane to arrive, it was Sinead O`Connor's 'Nothing compares to you' which constantly got played on some Arctic radio station!

Once we eventually returned to the UK, time was spent repainting the wagons back to green and black and the usual routine of camp life. It was at this point I decided it was time to leave the Army as there were other things I wanted to do back in civilian life. By the end of April 1990, I had left 249 Signal Squadron and my 7 years in the Army. The memories stay with you forever and I`m sure the stories and humour were similar to those who served before and after my era of the late 1980`s.

30 years on I attended the reformation of 249 Sig Sqn in 2019, although a lot had changed around the old Ward Barracks and Bulford itself. More recently, I attended the Snowden walk in July 2021 and met up with Kev Read, Paul Culleton, Frank McGuinness and Gaz (T Shirt) Owen from my era, where the humour and banter was still there, as it was amongst the other guys who attended that reunion. Big thanks for Steve Westlake for organizing that.

249 was a great squadron to have served in and provided some great memories to cherish.

The Wire Magazine 1976 to 1990

Over this period, 'Winter Warfare' gradually became a more specialist role, requiring special training and specialist equipment.

May 1976

30 Signal Regiment

Re-Formation of 249 Signal Squadron

A parade was held at Blandford on July 19 to mark the independence of the AMF(L) Signal Squadron, ceasing to be 3 Sqn and assuming the title of 249 Signal Squadron. The Salute was taken by Col Hild, Commander 1 Signal Group, and four previous 249 Squadron Commanders were present. A pennant was presented to the Squadron Commander, Maj Rodney Clare, by the last 249 Sqn Commander, Lt Col Hamish McKinlay.

And now for something completely different ...

3 Squadron AMF(L) notes

Although this year has been, by comparison with past years, a quiet one so far for AMF(L), the Squadron was fully involved with the preparation for Signal View 1976. To this end most of the Squadron spent at least a week at Worcester toiling in the sun erecting tents and constructing the arena. This year's reward was granted immediately after Signal View, when the Squadron became independent, taking up the name of 249 Sig Sqn AMF(L).

Our new resting place, for at least two years, will be Old Sarum. In preparation for this event SSgt (SQMS) Fred, Sgt Bradshaw and our soon-to-be-left-behind civilian storeman, Jim, have been busily packing and despatching stores to our new home. Sgt Benson, the Squadron's Chief Clerk, has feverishly been indenting for untold numbers of publications. In fact, it is now a guaranteed certainty that our 2IC, Capt John Ambrose, thinks of a new publication every night. It has something to do with the five-hour bath that he takes (who said that there was a water shortage)! Earlier in June the Squadron, as a prelude to the visit of the new Commander of

AMF(L), put on a display of equipment for the Commander of 5 Brigade, Brigadier P M Welsh, OBE, MC. Sgts Sellars and Longstaff laboured hard and were well rewarded by a most professional display. This was closely followed by a NATO inspection of all vehicles and Radio Equipment. To this end Sgt Geddes lined up the vehicles and trailers on the square in true Guard's fashion (SSM take note!) whilst SSgt (FofS) Flanagan and his team attempted to present the radio equipment both to the Tels team and the NATO Representatives. Both bodies were suitably impressed, and the F of S was even seen to be smiling later.

The Squadron has welcomed its new OC, Maj Rodney Clare, and his wife, Marianne, and said au revoir to Maj Peter Brunt. Other notable departures have been Sgt Adams on promotion to Staff-Sergeant after four years and many, many exercises in different countries, and W02 (SSM) Friend (though it is rumoured that he is returning) who has been posted to Alderney as Fisherman Extraordinaire.

We wish good luck and thanks to Cpl Hughes and Sig Lythall on posting and Sig Bennett on his return to the civilian environment. We also welcome SSgt Garrod and Sig Ramsey to the Squadron. The SSM finally returned, but when fishing was mentioned to him, he just replied with a wry grin.

249 Signal Squadron (AMF(L)) Old Sarum

Beginning Anew

The restructuring of Royal Signals units within the UK includes, among other things, the move into independence of the AMF(L) Sig Sqn. Authority has been given by MOD(ASD) for the forming of 249 Sig Sqn (AMF(L)). And that's how 'Force Radio Troop' came of age. On August 1, 1976, we left 30 Signal Regiment (Cpl Cass Cassidy vividly expressed the parting in his cartoon of a flying swan and caption of 'free at last') and accepted the mantle of a proud name - 249 Signal Squadron (AMF(L)).

Maj W R Clare, OC 249 Sig Sqn (AMF(L)), receives the 249 Sig Sqn pennant from the last OC, Lt Col Mackinlay. Lt Col Byng (left) heads 30 Sig Regt on the independence parade

The new 249 Signal Squadron resurrects a unit title which was lost when 18 Signal Regiment disbanded in 1971. The old Squadron had enjoyed a particularly high reputation as an efficient and happy unit and the AMF(L) Squadron are proud to be given the chance of maintaining and then improving on the old high standards.

Send-off

In July, 30 Signal Regiment gave the new 249 Signal Squadron a fine send off. Lt Col Arthur Byng headed a regimental parade to see us on our way and the Squadron Commander, Maj Rodney Clare, was proud to receive the Squadron Pennant from the last OC 249, Lt Col A G MacKinlay. Col J H Hild, MBE, Commander 1 Signal Group, took the salute and recalled his time in Singapore when 249 Sqn formed part of his regiment. Col Hild was joined on the saluting base by yet another past-Squadron Commander, Brig P H F Webb, MBE. It would seem that command of this particular Squadron leads to better things and Maj Clare's eyes do sometimes seem to focus a little above our heads!

With the formalities of the parade over the Squadron settled down to the serious business of saying farewell to 30 Signal Regiment. SSM Tom Friend and his senior ranks had a right royal send off from the Sergeants Mess and the All Ranks Squadron party, ably organised by Cpl Billy Henderson and his committee, was a great success. Sig 'Taff' Duffy, pre-empting the Squadron Commander, accepted a ' Swan' shield from Lt Col Byng, and we're still trying to prise it from him for the OC' s office wall.

The Move

The move itself, from Blandford to Old Sarum has gone smoothly with our new QM, Capt Jack Simpson, arriving in the nick of time to help the 2IC, Capt John Ambrose, to coordinate the movement details. Jack's combination of experience and sporting prowess is going to stand us in good stead for the future and we welcome him to the AMF(L). We're not too sure how his Gurkhali will fit into the already multi-lingual set up.

Everyone has worked hard during the past months, but Sgts Sandy Geddes and Alan Benson deserve special mention for their success in organising their departments for the move and gaining excellent results on staff inspections during the process.

The Future

So now life goes on. The Mediterranean beckon in September, Southern Norway next January/February, and after that, something is sure to turn up. We're sorry to leave 30 Signal Regiment, but not too sorry to relish our new independence and to look forward to adding new laurels to the name of 249 Sig Sqn (AMF(L)).

December 1976

249 Sig Sqn (AMF(L)) Old Sarum

Squadron Personalities

OC - Maj W R Clare
OC Designate - Maj D J Walden
2IC - Capt JD Ambrose
QM - Capt A J Simpson
OC Support Troop - Lt PK Gorford
0C Main Tp Comms Offr - Capt R D Symonds
SSM - W02 T J Friend
YofS l - W02 R J Butcher
YofS 2 - SSgt M R Channing
FofS - SSgt M A Flanagan
Chief Clerk - Sgt C J Davies

Exercise Augustus Exchange

On September 19th the first part of the Squadron set out by road to Sardinia for exercise Augustus Exchange. By September 27th the final elements of the Squadron had arrived in Sardinia. Augustus Exchange was a CPX for the AMF(L). As always with this type of exercise the remainder of the force participated with small elements mostly travelling by air. We, however, had a full deployment moving in three convoys across Europe passing through Calais, Douic, Chaumont, Orange, Savona, Genoa, Gagliari. The problems of overnight stops and ferry crossings were numerous but were overcome by good humour, common sense, school-book French and ice cream Italian. Highlights of the exercise include the whole of the main party travelling first class from Genoa to Gagliari, sampling excellent Italian cuisine and wine on the ferry. The Squadron was marooned for a time on the beach outside Gagliari because of a dock strike. The term the 'forgotten army' was heard at this time!

Cpls Charlie Rodgers and Bob Hill and Sig Mark Fairclough 'resting' at Genoa

April 1977

249 Sig Sqn (AMF(L)) Old Sarum

Exercise Hardfall 1977

East of Bergen

A report on the exploits of 249 of Sig Sqn (AMF(L)) training for war in the Arctic region of Norway during January/February 1977. From the peace and quiet of Old Sarum we departed, on four different dates, in four modes of transport, in four phases and eventually through luck, good fortune or plain good organisation by RCT movements, we arrived as one unit in Voss, some 55km east of Bergen. Dalane Hostel Voss was to be our home for the duration of our stay in Norway, from where, we were to carry out our annual Arctic acclimatisation programme, the theme of Exercise Hardfall as many before us are only too aware.

Hectic programme with Norwegian liaison

The training programme for this year was master minded in the luxury of heated rooms, carpeted floors, soft chairs and coffee by the Squadron 2IC and Training Officer, Capt John Ambrose. Training waws to consist of snow-shoe walks, bivouacking, snow caving, skiing, ranges, skijoring and a Volvo driver course; a hectic programme that had to be fitted into the 14 days we had available. We were ably assisted in our tasks by three Norwegian liaison officers, who became very much part of the Squadron. Their sense of humour was as twisted as ours by the time we parted company. Capt ('Warx the skis') Hagen, Lt (Double push) Fed, and 2 Lt (don't forget to service the tractor) Gutraume, helped make the training most enjoyable, though at times, it was extremely hard work.

A la Eskimo

Training commenced with a ' breaking in' night spent in a five-man Arctic tent in the grounds of the hostel, followed by a 5km snow-shoe march. A further night in Arctic tents was then spent 'half way' up the mountain. The climax to the nights out was the snow cave. A chance to live a la Eskimo was not to be missed. The part we could have done without was digging the damn thing! Unfortunately, snow caves do not come ready made so the back-aching task of digging them out began-five hours later-a five-man snow hole. The final night out brought us to our mountain hut, a remotely situated, ski training hut some 3,000ft up, where, when the wind blows. inside the hut is the only sensible place to be.

Circus Britannica

Then the entertainment started. Now it seems we are to be known as the Royal Signals White Plank Cross-country Display Team, or to put it in a nutshell, Circus Britannica. It does not help matters when one commences ski lessons at lesson No. 6 instead of lesson No. 1, but this was how it was to be. A short sharp rise in the ground contours lay in our way to the basic ski training area. Amidst cries of 'Our leader has fallen', the OC, Maj David Walden, followed by his equally painful ally SSgt (the one with the short fat hairy legs) Rick Garrod,' made their way forwards, backwards, sideways, one ski over the other to learn what it was all about. Those NATO 'planks' received an abundance of abuse during the next few days. To some the idea came naturally, to some it was a struggle, to others it was pure aggravation. We were beginning to wonder if we were doing the right thing when we observed members of the Squadron talking to their skis, begging them to co-operate, while everyone's favourite Lineman, Sig Quasey Aitken spoke of insufferable consequences if his skis did not do as they were told. Twenty-three broken skis, numerous sprains, knocks and bruises ably dealt with by the way of our resident doctor, Sgt 'Doc' Wroe, assisted in every way by Sig 'Nurse Chalky' White. The ski training ended up with a 10km ski race. This was a two-event affair, the advance skier's plaque was won by Cpl Dave Turner, the novices by Sig Shaun Wilson-well done.

Some found it easy!

Advanced Skiers, led by a Norwegian LO and Lt Paul Gorford

Distinguished visitors earn Arctic goggles

Visitors during the exercise were plentiful, the highlight though being that of the SO in C, Maj Gen Tighe, and Commander 1 Sig Group, Col Benbow. They spent two days with the Squadron, who impressed upon them that Exercise Hardfall is not one big holiday but that plenty of good, hard, useful training does take place. Their second day with us saw Sgt 'Sandy' Geddes, our resident Volvo instructor, insisting that our two distinguished visitors earn their Volvo driver Arctic goggles. So, after a quick brief on driving techniques, two Volvos with Sandy Geddes and LCpl Kev Frogget as co-drivers, disappeared over the snow-clad hills enroute to the mountain hut where Lt Paul (Grass-hopper) Gorford was in action with the advanced skiers, the Volvo driver's course were busy changing tracks and, finally, where our mountain cook, Sig 'Geordie' Ramsey, with his excellent morning porridge, proved he could do better than any laxative on the market.

An important thank you

An army marches on its stomach, so they say. A mention must be made, therefore, of our 'chef' as he demands we 'Jimmies' call him. Sgt Phil Roe provided us with food of quality and quantity. The problems were with his own cooks, broken windows and falling out of bunk beds!

Force 11 and Helicopter lift

February 19 came too quickly for most of us. A short trip to Ulvik, our port of departure, and there, awaiting our pleasure, was the LSL Sir Geraint. Events were not at an end though, for on the second day at sea, having experienced a force 11 storm, LCpl Ross Miller, vomiting blood, had to be helicopter lifted from the ship, off the coast of Lincolnshire. He was transferred to a hospital in Norwich. LCpl Miller had earlier been involved in an accident when a Volvo overturned on the mountainside; Miller bruised his shoulder while his co-driver, SSgt (YofS) Mal Channing, suffered injuries to his back that resulted in his being Casevac to England (still not Hardfall trained). Happily, both are now well on the road to recovery.

Relief

Our Squadron 'sailor', SSgt (short fat hairy legs) Rick Garrod, tried to ease a rather unpleasant journey back with some nautical lessons, but most of us were feeling a little uneasy in the stomach to digest(!) the information. It was with some relief when we reached port, green grass, no snow, warm weather and home!

(Photo courtesy of Public Relations. UKLF Mobile Team (York), HQ North East District) SO in C, Maj Gen P A M Tighe, MBE, with LCpl Chris Rogan, Sig Jim McMahon and Sig Fred Dudden

Cpl Dave Turner, winner of the 10km ski race

May 1978

249 Sig Sqn (AMF(L)) Old Sarum

All Go

Again, another busy year and for the Squadron, with exercises in Sardinia, Denmark and the inevitable Salisbury Plain.

Add to this local Troop and Squadron exercises, demonstrations, summer camps, battle camps and leave where possible, one can see what a busy unit we are. All in all, however, the Squadron seems to thrive on this hectic life made all the more interesting in having to work with so many different nationalities and in exciting places.

Norway Bound

Dryshod training, the build-up exercise to Norway normally held in late December was cancelled at the last minute and after an early Christmas leave, the OC Maj David Walden, and the majority of the Squadron sampled the delights of Chester and surrounding districts on fire-fighting duties. A brief period of leave followed, and the Squadron deployed to Norway in three separate phases; the Advance Party leaving on January 15, the remainder on the 19th in two separate parties. The base camp for Hardfall training was

Flatlandsmo Camping Site, which is situated 4km south-east of Voss and consisted of a main house and 12 four-man chalets. The secondary camp – Espland - was to be the Survival Training Camp and consisted of 10 four-man chalets supplemented with Norwegian tentage.

Production and Direction

The training programme for the next three weeks – devised, written, produced and directed by 2IC C apt Rob Symons consisted of three separate seven-day phases. Apart from a small admin party and rebroadcast crews who trained separately, the Squadron split into three groups, each group doing the round of the three phases.

Marksman of the Year

W02 (YofS) Ron (How's ya lumps) Butcher was OC Espland, the training (?) staff being Sgt Bernie Temmen and one of the three Norwegian Liaison Officers attached to the Squadron, L t (Compo) Thoreson. The object of this phase was to teach personnel how to move and survive with the minimum equipment, all carried by the individual, in mountainous terrain for a period of four days and three nights. The first night was spent in five-man tents and the next two in Brushwood shelters built by each individual and which proved to be very comfortable. Marksman of the year must go to Sig Raymond (Titch) Fallowfield who killed a rabbit from 14 yards with a well-aimed (?) mallet.

Over the period of the four days the distance covered was something like 38km on the map. However, bearing in mind the mountainous terrain and the fact that all movement was on skis, the actual distance was much greater and all those completing the course had every right to feel pleased. Apart from the usual blisters and injuries caused by uncontrollable skis the only two accidents to speak of were Sig (The Hulk) Gaskell who dislocated vertebrae in his neck and SSgt (YofS) Steve MacQueen who, after many visits to hospital, was told he'd broken his back. Happily, both are now well on the road to recovery. YofS still claims he holds the record for the most falls in one day (not quite three figures).

Phase 2

This took the form of a four-day Communications Exercise preceded by a 2-day 'Plan and Prep' stage. A COI had to be produced by each group and presented to the overseer, Sgt Pete (Wait Out) Sellars, for scrutinisation and inevitable alteration before the exercise.

Sgt (Klondike) Pete Coll thought he had defied all the rules of communications when two of his outstations were heard working to each other without using a Rebro. Oh Joy! Until it was realised he had deployed both detachments to the same location - Techs Ugh! However, many useful lessons on both VHF and HF comms in the Arctic were learnt on this phase.

Basic Skiing

Give an English soldier skis, show him how to put them on and you have, 'on tap', the funniest show on earth. Leave him alone for a day or two and after many bruises, encounters with fellow skiers, holes, trees, and hedges he'll be back asking how to stop and turn. SSgt (YofS) Mal (Planks) Channing with LO, Capt Lynam, had the unenviable task of turning these raw novices into crack British Alpine Corps troops, within seven days. At the end of this period most people, although perhaps not 'Franz Klammer', certainly knew the meaning of Snow Plough, Double Gait, etc, even if the skis didn't. It's rumoured that W0 2 (SSM) Dave Wilcox came near to physically attacking his skis after a particularly arduous day.

The training programme finally finished on February 13 with the 10km ski race following on the 14th and 16th. All participants, apart from eight, managed to get within the time required for their particular medal. The fastest student to complete the course was LCpl 'Taff' Duffy with a time of 36 mins. Due to pressure of work the REME contingent had to forgo much of the training and hence could not participate in the 10krn race. However, it was rumoured that Sgt Jim (Jim Lad) Stokes and his merry crew held their own 25metre toboggan dash. Even then Cpl Allen managed to turn it over and injure himself but put the blame on something which sounded like 'Crankcase Breather trouble'. Capt (QM) Jack Simson, who flew out to join us on February 6, managed to take time off to enjoy a few hours skiing. However, his practises were done in such secrecy and the personnel involved threatened with such dire consequences on the utterance of even one word, that, even today no one really knows what happened the day the QM took to skis. Whether the Squadron has set a precedent or not I don' t know but our senior ACC rep, Sgt Phil (The Cook) Roe, has been allocated his own appointment title, namely 'Pan cake'. As always, good things must come to an end, and on February 18 the Advance Party departed for Exercise Arctic Express.

The Sharp End

Readers may like to know that from here on the notes from Exercise Arctic Express have been taken over by a second author. We now have an account of life at the sharp end of AMF(L) exercises. Whilst taking nothing away from the 'Victory through Logistics' boys it has to be left to the front-line boys to tell of what war is all about. It was a three-day LSL cruise from Ulvik (our Hardfall port of call) to Sorreisa (our Arctic Express port of call). What a wonderful opportunity now presented itself to get those ship's washing machines working and to dry ourselves out. Having then disposed of the dirt and damp of Voss the OC (Maj David Walden) and Main Troop Staff-Sergeant Ricky Garrod (still with the short, fat hairy legs - why do ' they' always get a mention) decided the one thing that they would bring with them was the dreaded 'lurgy', a form of bronchitis that had plagued the Squadron since its arrival in Norway. The exercise period saw frequent 'happy trips' by our two patients as they were observed pouring medicine and pills by courtesy of MASH, down their parched throats. We welcomed our latest recruit to the RADCON team, Sgt John 'Jock' Johnston, amongst many other things, the Squadron helicopter expert. His moment of fame came one hectic evening when he decided to route a telephone call through the German-manned exercise switchboard. 'Please speak English, Sir' was the retort to his connection request. His answer is not to be found in the Oxford English dictionary.

So now some 250 miles inside the Arctic Circle, this was to be our life for the next two weeks. Surprisingly, it was not so cold as down South, although the snow falls were far heavier. 'Ah! but we also had snow', commented our Chief Clerk, Sgt Geoff (Welfare problems fixed) Hughes, back in Old Sarum, kid's stuff, Geoff, to we Arctic-trained boys.

Not Without Incident

Arctic Express was for the Squadron a very successful communications exercise. Slight damage was reported though by one of our RRB station commanders, Cpl Mick Moseley, who, being lumbered with the task of preparing a dismounted RRB station to one of the many hilltops that surrounded us reported that the helicopter pilot had dropped the load from some 20 feet! Over to you Sgt Tony (I'll get it replaced) Scrase, who tells us by the way that he has done his last shift in RADCON. Wait and see Tony! But at least it was dropped in the right place unlike LCpl Chris Pottage and his dismounted Rebro crew who, after four days on a cold mountain, were picked up by helicopter and deposited 100km away from where they should have been. Once they had recovered from the shock though they didn't complain as they were in our redeployment area 24 hours ahead of the rest of us. Did someone mention bribery? It was not only 20ft drops by helicopter that made our bowels cringe. Nature also had its say. Of immense interest were the Norwegian produced build-it-yourself cardboard loos. All very good if you are of average weight. LCpl (Slug-all 18 stone of

Exercise Arctic Express-Stand to ...

him) Henry proved they were not made for the 'big boys' as his loo unceremoniously collapsed under him one morning - messy business!

By March 6 the thoughts of the green grass of home loomed in our minds, so it was not with too many misgivings that we drifted from the shores of Norway-for one more year- back to dear old Blighty. Ah well, after our winter skiing I suppose that we shall have to make do with Dartmoor and Hythe until we set off for the Mediterranean in September.

May 1978

A Tp, 244 Signal Squadron (AS)

Capt Jack Boyle's troop deployed to Norway in May; he had been assured that the snow would have disappeared by then. What a sense of humour the Norwegians have. The OC Maj Leslie Steane and Capt Jim Cadwallader spent the first 36 hours motoring around trying to locate sites with less than 5ft of snow on them, we will not mention how many times they had to dig themselves out of snow drifts. Not so lucky was Cpl Smudge Smith and Sig Boyle who went searching for kit previously hidden but gradually being revealed as the snow cleared, they found out what the Norwegians mean by 'rotten' snow. On the last part of the exercise, we left our vehicles behind and started marching. As always with this Squadron, the route was planned with a river crossing involved. The second in command (who is quite tall) waded through and found it waist deep. Sig Dave (Paddy) McGaughey (who is not so tall) took a slightly different line and found it neck deep. We all finished it however and were pleased to get back to the relative comfort of the Base Camp.

September 1978

249 Sig Sqn (AMF(L)) Old Sarum

Norway - Again

The Squadron, after spending three months on Exercise Hardfall, were tasked with this year's clean-up in Norway. This involved a party of 15, led by SSgt (YofS) Mal Channing, visiting all locations used by the British troops during their winter training. Although the trip involved a lot of hard work the hot weather made it enjoyable.

Good Driving

As some of the locations were in remote areas the two drivers, LCpl Roger 'Spider' Walters and Sig Raymond 'Titch' Fallowfield, had to use all their skill and judgement as they negotiated the tight bends and bad roads. It was said that the Norwegian LO, 2Lt Ivar Flatabe, started to gibber in an unknown language until he was reminded that he was a Viking.

Back Home Again

After a few days off it was time to return to flatter pastures, although not for long. Within five days we were to join the rest of the Squadron at Dibgate. We were surprised to find that we had covered over 2,500 miles in 20 days.

Exercise 'Double Whiskey'

On 19 June the Squadron, less their Clk Techs and Techs who, as normal, say they have too much work to do (it's funny how it accumulates when there is an exercise on), departed for Dibgate, the soldier's Butlins' holiday camp where everything is laid on free; morning runs, ranges, 24-hour Infantry exercises under 1 R Anglian and 1 RGJ, not to mention the summer weather (RAIN) and the cold showers. It was heard to be said that W02 (SSM) Dave Wilcox didn't need a Tannoy system when he did reveille, as his voice could be heard miles away.

Training

The Squadron split into three platoons under command of 2Lt Chris Cox, Sgt Phil 'Pancake' Roe, ACC, and SSgt (YofS) Mal Channing. Each platoon covered the same programme although 1 and 2 platoons got wetter than their sunburnt 3 platoon who only did the second week of training.

Weapon Classification

All members of the Squadron took this opportunity to attempt to pass their APWT. After a morning of zeroing weapons and explaining that the rounds come out of the pointed end, most people crossed over to the electric target range run by the 2IC, Capt Rob Symonds, and ably assisted by SSgt (YofS) Steve (all these switches look the same to me) MacQueen. Over three quarters of the Squadron classified. During the following days the three platoons took to the Individual Battle Simulation Range where for some it was the 'real thing', nobody had trouble finding the correct cover, it was hitting the target that was the problem. One member, who should remain nameless, decided his weapon would work better with the gas plug upside down, needless to say it didn't.

Local Squadron Exercise

1 and 2 platoons spent 24 hours on an Urban Guerrilla type exercise, this involved Red and Blue forces moving between locations trying to avoid ambushes set up by Sgt Bernie 'Survival expert' Temmen and sifting through information given by the two secret agents W02 (SSM) Dave 'Dago' Wilcox and Sgt Ted 'Phillpo' Jinman. Cpl Wally Calow trusted these two as much as he did the weather holding out.

Exercise 'Kentish Air'

This was the 24-hour Infantry exercise run by members of 1 R Anglian and 1 RGJ. This proved to be hard work involving section attacks (thank goodness the enemy can't see us), a tact1cal defence phase and night patrols. The biggest problem was the trench digging during the defence phase, this proved that blisters not only formed on your hands but on many other unlikely places. After five hours of digging, and just when most of us were starting to eat, the patrols started, first recce and standing patrols followed by fighting patrols, the latter being enjoyed by all except LCpl Paul Fisher who was wounded in the eye by a flying shell case (anything to get out of the march and shoot). 1 and 2 platoons had the pleasure of marching the five miles back to camp after the exercise while 3 platoon had transport (moan! moan!).

March and Shoot

This consisted of a shortened march of three miles in 35 minutes in full battle order, followed by a falling plate competition. The teams were drawn from all the AMF(L) units involved at Dibgate and proved to be very competitive. Before starting the march, all teams had their kit checked for deficient items, then off we went, 1 platoon first, 2 platoon fifth and 3 platoon ninth, the route involved a steep downhill section, a track march alongside the canal and the last section through Hythe and onto the ranges, all teams were over time but 3 platoon had the second fastest time of the competition. The falling plate competition was then fired (it is still believed by many that the plates were, in fact, glued to the butts - but this is strongly denied). The shooting practice we had proved valuable as Sig John Sibley hit four plates out of five shots and helped to bring 3 platoon to a final position of fourth overall.

Home Again

The weather remained unchanged for the trip home - rain – but now smiles were appearing on 'battle worn' faces. The Squadron split in to three parties travelling by vehicles, car and coach. Needless to say, a few war stories were told to the younger members of the family.

Northern Ireland Detachment

Since May this year the Squadron has had a detachment serving with 51 Fd Sqn (Const) RE, namely Cpl Taff Thomas, Sigs Len Fairclough and Bob Shortis. 'The Three' went to Ripon, Yorkshire, on 3 May 1978, to join 51 Sqn and after a week of being 'looked at' and 'prodded ' to see if they were 'real' they went to Lydd for their NI Training.

The training went well, and the detachment managed to make a name for themselves (omitted for fear of incrimination), although doing quite well on different ranges it was decided that they would not actually be involved with the RE Search Teams (or Construction Teams come to that).

The reason for this had a lot to do, we think, with Cpl Taff Thomas getting himself 'blown up', once 'What's this dustbin doing here?), twice (Oh No! Here we go again), Sig Len Fairclough (Medic. Medic? - Reply - Sorry No House Calls) 'blown up', getting contagious, and Sig Bob Shortis' (I thought it would be all right Taff) magnetic attraction to abandoned cars. After arriving in Castledillon in Armagh it was their job to teach the RE members of the Ops Room to communicate and use the equipment therein, which proved quite a novel experience for both groups, a case of the 'child' teaching the 'parent'.

The Three - Sig Bob Shortis, Cpl Taff Thomas, Sig Len Fairclough

May 1979

244 Signal Squadron (AS)

Personalities

OC - Maj ALWG Steane
2IC - Capt MN Grieves
A Troop - 2Lt C Burtenshaw
B Troop - Lt LK Byrne
M Troop - W02 (FofS) MP Coley
RQMS - W02 (RQMS) P Hardwick
YofS - SSgt (YofS) AD Janaway
Chief Clerk -SSgt (ORSQMS) M Kennedy

On the Move

The New Year has seen the 'Red Hand Gang' off on its travels again. Within a week of each other, the two radio troops deployed to opposite ends of Europe. A Troop commanded by 2Lt Colin

LCpl Nick Bahado prepares to spend a night out in the snow

Burtenshaw, departed for the snowy wastes of Northern Norway to join up with the remainder of AMF(L) on its annual pilgrimage to the Arctic Circle. Initially concentrating on winter training, the newer members of the troop, including LCpl Nick Bahado and Sigs Steve Clark and John Reiffer provided a remarkable display of free-fall skiing. Having mastered the Black Arts. under the instruction of Cpl Smudge Smith, the troop moved 'up country' for the serious aspect of its work. The OC joined them during the last week of January just to see how it's done, Sgt Mac McClelland taking great delight in making sure that he spent time out in the snow. Returning from their snowy wastes A Troop found themselves re-deployed to Germany within the week. Reports are slowly filtering through of their doings, but I expect we will have to wait until their return for a blow-by-blow account.

Some of the members of the FASC having completed their package tour of Norwegian woods

249 Sig Sqn (AMF(L)) Bulford

Photo Report Ex Hardfall 1979

After an extended tour of the Ice and Snow, living in tree and canvas houses, Sgt Bob Hassall's group pause for lunch. The DS for this phase of training were in front of the Volvo (left to right), Sgt Bernie (Grizzly Bear) Temmen, Norwegian LO Lt Morton Loden and WO 2 (FofS) Mick Flanagan

A two-man brushwood lean-to (tree house) occupied by 'squatter' Cpl Jeff Smythe, quietly doing his thing in the snow

Demonstrating the Norwegian five-man pulk (Grunt and Groan Machine!). Empty at the moment 'cos they're still learning. Cpl Dick Hughes leading his band of crack British Arctic Trained men across the frozen wastelands of Norway. Namely, Sigs Andy Marson, 'Piggy' Burkill, LCpl Martin Hoy, Cpl Paul Hickinbottom, Sigs Ron Curtis and Ian 'Flo' Philo

Even 'experts' fall occasionally, especially in a pulk harness

The Natives Are Friendly - Sgt Ted Jinman, W02 (SSM) Dave Wilcox, and Sgt Phil 'Pancake' Roe ACC with friends

Gazelles of 2 Flt AAC performing yet another of their lifts for the Squadron. In the foreground 2Lt Chris Cox discusses IA Drills with Sgt John West before emplaning. In the background, wearing helmet, SSgt Bob Morris (ex Royal Signals) of 2 Flt AAC discusses the flight plan with his observer. We wish to express our thanks to the men and machines of 2 Flt AAC who flew in excess of 100 sorties for the Squadron during the exercise.

September 1979

249 Sig Sqn (AMF(L)) Bulford

Wrong Again

Someone in the Squadron said that the period between coming back from Norway in February and going to Greece in September was going to be a 'quiet' time for us. He was wrong.

The Squadron had arrived back from Norway and had completed its move from Old Sarum to Ward Barracks, Bulford. We were all glad to be rid of the snow for another year, when due to importation of snow by QM Maj Jack Simpson Royal Signals into north England we were in it again. The eight unfortunates, Cpl Jock Greig, Cpl Bob Shortis, LCpl Dave Browne, LCpl Brian Monkman, Sigs Geordie Turner, Gary Pitts, Marty Hyett and Bob Weeks, plus the inevitable REME support, duly departed for the barren wastes of Catterick and surrounding area. We travelled to Catterick by train, and after settling into our accommodation for what was promised to be 'just a few days', we collected our Volvo (Snowcats) from Stockton-on-Tees amid acclaim from both national and local press. After a short journey lasting 'six hours' we arrived back at Catterick, two of the vehicles being towed in.

The next day spare parts were airlifted in and Op Barrow was under way.

Livestock Targets

The object of the operation was to deliver foodstuffs and also to rescue livestock on the dales. The party was split into detachments and sent to different areas of the dales where they worked in conjunction with the farmers. LCpl Brian Monkman and Sig Bob Weeks along with Cfn Jackson REME were sent to Cumbria where they carried out their tasks from the comparative luxury of a 'Hotel'. Cpl Jock Greig and Sig Gary Pitts were sent to Weardale and during their time there were accommodated by various farmers. During the operation they moved 30 tons of foodstuffs through drifts of up to 20 feet, to outlying areas and rescued numerous sheep which had become buried in drifts. They were also interested spectators to a pitched battle between rival TV crews and managed to supplement their vocabulary quite considerably. During this time the REME worked non-stop to maintain vehicles. The only serious mishap was when LCpl Dave Browne was injured in a collision with a horse box, which had become buried in the snow; happily, he is now fully recovered. Cpl Bob Shortis and Sig Marty Hyett took over his remaining tasks. They also carried out the recovery of another Snowcat which had become stranded high up on the dales.

After 11 days ('just a few days?'), strenuous effort the operation stood down, Cpl John Levins and Cfns Reed, Robinson and Bateman REME arriving just in time to be too late.

Ten Tors Support

On Wednesday 16 May a large proportion of the Squadron Deployed in support of the Annual Ten Tors Expedition. This expedition is mounted by the Armed Forces and youth groups between 14 and 19 years old compete over distances of 25 to 55 miles. We were required to provide communications on all the manned Tors for control and safety purposes. Though the Squadron is exclusively a radio unit we also engineered and ran a multiplex telegraph land line between Holming Beam and Okehampton Camp. This line was provided courtesy of SWS Troop Okehampton and has been dug in by them straight across Dartmoor. Three of the Tors are totally inaccessible by vehicle so these dets were dismounted and air lifted into location by Royal Marine Wessex. The comms achieved during the exercise were the best standard we have achieved for a long time and there was hardly an Officer or Senior rank in sight!

Exercise Agate Exchange

Early on Sunday 3 June the Squadron main party left Bulford for Marchwood, near Southampton. By evening all personnel and vehicles were safely on board RFA LSL Sir Lancelot. It should have been a quiet uneventful journey as the weather was perfect, however there were a few notable incidents. A fishing competition was arranged by the ship's crew using drop lines over the port side.

No fish were caught, but they caught Sigs Bimson and Cowie, they put their names down on the list!

To relieve the boredom on ship we had PT on the flight deck. Maj Fisher was obviously very keen, he attended all four sessions. LCpl Fisher (not the OC's son) ran German Lessons. As dawn broke on the 6th June we landed somewhere on the mainland of Europe, to begin the exercise.

Historically, communications in this area have always been difficult and there were some fears that the Exercise could become troublesome for the Squadron.

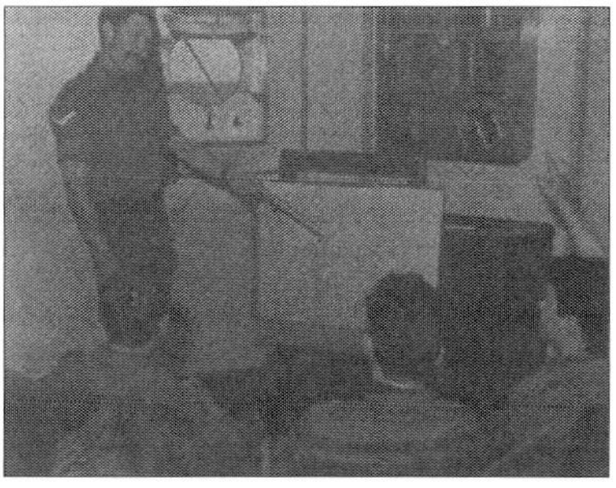

LCpl Fisher takes a German lesson on board LSL Sir Lancelot

Maj Fisher takes PT on the Flight deck of LSL Sir Lancelot

During the warm up phase Mobile Troop lived up to their name and by moving all over the area were able to build up a good local communications picture. This gave indications that some smaller hills were better than nearby larger ones as RRB sites, that some areas were virtually 'dead' as far as VHF communication were concerned. At the same time Main Troop were producing the goods by maintaining HF comms both locally and back to UK. As a result of the hard work put in early in the exercise what could have been a bad exercise turned into a very successful one. Even the Soldier who went to Copenhagen and back twice, because he overslept, managed to catch his plane out in time!

May 1980

249 Sig Sqn (AMF(L)) Bulford

Whilst The Wire was giving coverage to the glamourous ski boys (tremendous though they were}, the AMF Signal Squadron was quietly fulfilling one of its War Options in the Northern Flank, some 200 miles North of the Arctic Circle.

As our squadron spread shows all 249 Signal Squadron soldiers (less the QM with a broken arm) are ski and arctic trained.

The Professional Skiers

Royal Signals ready for war! 249 Signal Squadron AMF(L)

After refresher and basic ski courses using our own instructors, we were ready for our and rigorous training carrying everything on our own backs.

Which way did you say the laundry was? Sig Albert Schweitzer

I'm sure I left my troop herel Lt Jim Barry

Should I be double gaiting or diagonal polling now? Sig Cowie

The Squadron vehicle were left in base camp-if only we hadn't complained about servicing them at -20"C! But once we got going it was fun, after all we are 249 Men! Leadership and planning at the Detachment Commander Level were severely tested with all NCO's working hard for the Arctic JNCO's Leadership Cadre.

Is this really Marlboro' country? LCpls Douglas, Williamson, Shortis and McAleer

As a little relaxation after the end of Exercise Hardfall all the soldiers of the squadron took part in a 15km biathlon. The standard of shooting would have been quite high if only the target balloons had stood still in the wind.

This snow isn't shown on my map! SSM Steve Marshall, Sunray and Sgt Bernie Temmen

Smile lads, he's right behind us! Sigs Cowie, Hollet, LCpl Catchpole, Cpl Clark, Sig Deane, LCpl Norrie and Sunray

In early March the squadron deployed North to join the German and US elements of HQ AMF(L) for the FTX Exercise Anorak Express.

The FTX had troops from the Canadian, UK, Italian armies as well as Dutch, US and our own Marines fighting under command of the multi-national HQ AMF(L) and various Norwegian HQs. 249 Squadron is responsible for 'both end' communications sending detachments to all component parts of the AMF(L). Not only did this ensure 100% communications on all nets, but considerably reduced the language problems. However, the Italian Detachment did complain that their daily issue of wine froze!

Couldn't you just give me a parking ticket??

The centre of the universe!!

November 1980

249 Sig Sqn (AMF(L)) Bulford

An Infantry Role

LCpl's Gus Webster, Vic Hoy and Mark Nelson

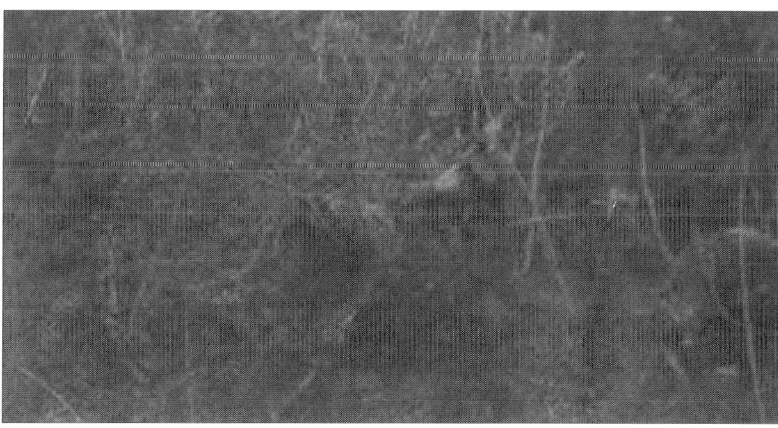

LCpl Gus Webster guarding the 'Basha'

The Professional Skiers of our last Wire notes have spent the summer training hard for our Southern Flank operations in Turkey,

Italy and Greece. On return from Norway our first major exercise was in an infantry role as 'C' Company 1/2 GR acting as enemy on 6 Fd Force exercise *Tiger Head*. The exercise, apart from being great fun, demonstrated the high standards R Signals soldiers can achieve as infantry men.

Ten Tors

Apart from running the Corp Officer Recruiting programme for ORLO. our next commitment was to provide the communications for Ex Ten Tors. Since this is run by Corporals and below, the Seniors of the Squadron "volunteered' to accompany Sunray and complete the course on foot.

Here and There

The early summer saw our shooting team trying to break (unsuccessfully) the Gurkhas grip on Corp shooting. Our congratulations go to HK Gurkha Signal Squadron and particularly to YofS Cochrane on winning the Queen' Medal. In July the complete Squadron drove down to Southern Germany for a CPX with the other AMF(L) nations. We were able to trial our new Clansman sets, which we were proud to demonstrate to other NATO nations. Clearly a great step forward for us. The Squadron stopped over in Dover on our return from Germany to have a quick week's military training just to sharpen up the boys.

Back Row: LCpl McIntyre, Sig Graven, Sig Williams, Cpl Walmsley, Sig Hoolahan, Sig Hayward. Front Row: LCpl Johnston, SSgt Vivian, Lt Ewing, Cpl Clifford, Sig Phillips.

Before departing on our Summer leave a team of volunteers took part in the 6 Fd Force *South Downs Way* 37-mile bash. Although we didn't win the event (congratulations to 6 Fd Force) most of our team finished in excellent times.

Commanders Cup

Whilst having many commitments over the period the Squadron found time to continue the all-important military training.

Not even puffed! Sig Phillips, Cpl Walmsley, Sig Craven, Sig Williams, LCpl McIntyre, Sig Hayward, OC, Cpl Clifford, SSgt Vivian

Was promotion worth it? SSgt Sid Vivian after the Obstacle Course

Respirator? - I have taken it off!

Sig Williams and Lt Scan Ewing

The success of our training and the professionalism of our soldiers was demonstrated in the Commander 1 Sig Gp **'Commanders Cup'** summarised below:

Endurance March	249 Sig Sqn	1st
Obstacle Course	249 Sig Sqn	1st
NBC	249 Sig Sqn	1st
Shooting	249 Sig Sqn	1st
First Aid	249 Sig Sqn	1st
Driving	249 Sig Sqn	LAST
Overall winners	249 Sig Sqn AMF(L)	

March 1981

249 Sig Sqn (AMF(L)) Bulford

The Squadron worked hard to keep up its Arctic Training despite having returned from Norway in April. Recruiting engagements included some 10.000 people on the Sqn Snowshoe Walk at the Aldershot display.

After the Coup

Arriving in Turkey only a week after the military coup the advance party of Lt Jim Barry and the PAP net found only sunshine and smiles but still seemed a little relieved when the rest of the sqn deployed to join them. This was the first Southern Flank Exercise for the AMF(L) for six years. It was also very important for the Corps. Despite the very dry and dusty conditions ('just like Salisbury Plain without the trees'-anon) the Clansman equipment worked well and impressed our allies. Like the Clansman the Sqn was put through its paces but was always made sure to remain inside the exercise perimeter after dark, especially because of the helpful armed Turkish guards!

Rewarding

Multi National Squadron, Cpl Rameshkaji Rai, Cpl Greig and Cpl Oswin RAS during deterrent Ops

'It's the same as any other country only harder'. Lineman Sig Conchie and Sig Richmond dig in

As the exercise ended the Sqn returned the best time in the NATO march and shoot competition but narrowly failed to win the competition outright due to mediocre shooting. Members of the sqn had to say goodbye to their various pets, lizards. tortoises and a host of insects and depart back to wintry Bulford after a very rewarding exercise.

'What do you mean move it'. Sgt Calow keeping his sense of humour

Visit of Dep SACEUR

Lt Gen Sir Jack Harman KCB, OBE, MC with the OC talking to LCpl Nelson, Cpl Oswin and Sig Vear

May 1981

249 Sig Sqn (AMF(L)) Bulford

SW District Marathon

Shortly after Christmas the squadron hosted the SW District Marathon. The event was organised by Lt Scott Ewing and SSgt (YofS) Wilson with over 120 competitors taking part. The squadron entered a team of eight who put on a very creditable performance. The best time being run by Cpl Fitzpatrick, 3 hrs 2 mins 45 secs.

The squadron Marathon Team: L to R. Cpl Chopping, Sig George, Maj Fisher, W02 (SSM) Marshall, Cpl Fitzpatrick, LCpl Dawson, LCpl Dean, Cpl Riding

Ex 'Hardfall 81'

At the beginning of February, the squadron deployed on Ex Hardfall 81 for its annual winter warfare training in Norway. The advance party, led by the QM Capt Ray Danells, was ably assisted by our three Liaison Officers, Capt Magen Fosse, Fenriks Morten Lodoen and Toro Moller, who made sure of our comfortable reception in Norway.

Ski Training

All soldiers in 249 have to be Arctic and ski-trained. In addition, this year we had A Troop 244 Sig Sqn and some members of 11 Sig Regt attached to us. This made for a record number of students on our ski cadre. However almost ideal weather conditions made for extremely high standards as can be seen below.

Survival Training

But it's amazing what a difference 10 days concentrated practice makes: at the completion of ski training, and after the 10-kilometre ski race, the squadron was Heli-lifted up into the mountains to practise survival shelters. During one night 128 members of the squadron lived in snow holes that they had freshly dug.

Tactical Training

Once all the Arctic skills had been acquired Main and Support Troops were pitted against each other in Ex Wolverine Ambush, the squadron tactical winter training exercise. The final outcome was much argued about, however, no one disagreed that a lot of valuable lessons had been learnt by all those involved.

Final Test

The climax of Hardfall 81 was the Inter-Troop Biathlon competition skied over a 15-kilometre course. The winners this year were again Mam Troop although some pretty creditable performances were put up elsewhere. Notably LCpl Bunt who succeeded in doing 22 kilometres and 'OC Des' who was silly enough to arrive out in Norway for takeover just before the race.

The 'Cossack' Turn - as illustrated by Maj Danny Fisher

Sig Kingston (11 Sig Regt) illustrating how not to keep your balance

The Troops deploy. Members of Support Troop high above Haugsvik in the Vossevangen mountains

On stag again! - Sgt Calow manning the radio during Ex Wolverine Ambush

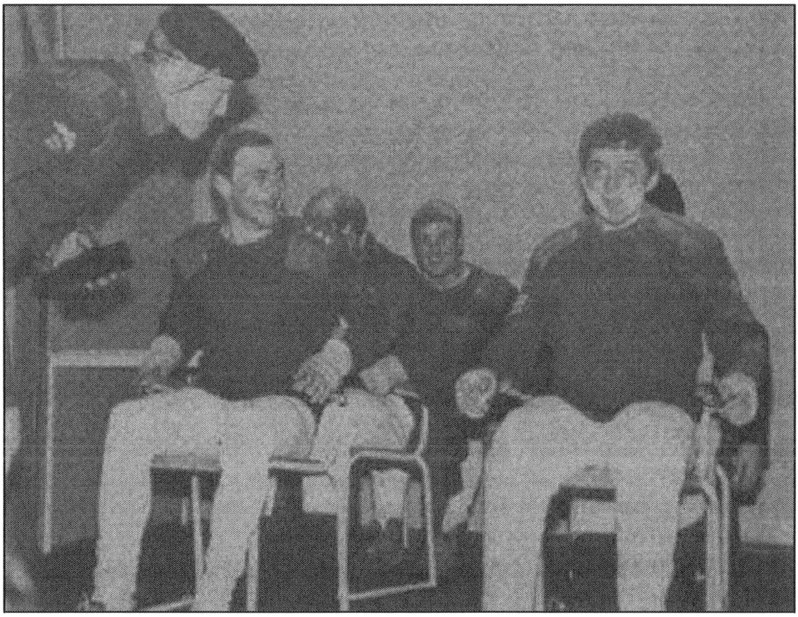

The Chelsea Pensioners: Sig Slaney alias 'Sergeant-Major Spud Marshall' and Pensioners Redman, Hoolahan and Barker in wheelchairs at the squadron concert

May 1981

249 Sig Sqn (AMF(L)) Bulford

OC	Maj MPS Shaw
2IC	Capt NKP Hope
QM	Capt RL Danells
Comms Offr	Lt JA Barry
OC Main Tp	2Lt AW McComb
OC Support Tp	Lt DS Ewing
SSM	W02 SG Marshall
YofS	W02 M Altham BEM
FofS	W02 KJ Bradley

In Northern Italy

The beginning of May arrived to find the squadron deploying to Northern Italy for an Ace Mobile Force (AMF) CPX. In true AMF fashion we despatched our vehicles by sea, having been given vague assurances that we would see them about a week later at Venice docks. For anyone who lives by the saying 'Never separate a soldier from his kit', the AMF can sometimes be a bit of a nightmare. Following a week of extensive military training in Bulford, we flew to the exercise area to find, that not only had the vehicles actually arrived as promised, but that the rain that we had left behind in the UK had somehow found its way to Italy as well. We felt quite at home. However, within 24 hours of our arrival the weather changed, and, in glorious sunshine, the squadron settled down to its daily routine of battle PT and 'pokey' drill followed after breakfast by the testing of all radio equipment prior to the onset of deterrent operations.

The Key detachments were duly despatched to their various national host units and favourable reports on their performance were received from all. Cpl Kevin McGready and Sig Phil Harris, both attached to the 509th US Airborne Battalion, not only took a full part in deterrent patrolling, but even joined in the early morning PT sessions lasting, we are told, longer than many of their American hosts.

With the onset of combat operations, the squadron, in true Jekyll and Hyde fashion, melted away beneath its camnets and set about the business of providing the staff with communications. Endex arrived to find trips to Venice on many minds and over half of the unit managed to visit the 'sinking city' before we were eventually whisked by VC10 back to Brize Norton and yes, the rain.

A field somewhere in Northern Italy. Deterrent Operations or 'showing the flag' AMF style. The Alps form the backdrop

LCpl Andy Dawson and a German airborne soldier during deterrent operations

The Bulford Kiwi

The week immediately following the units return from Italy witnessed much activity. BFTs and range work were the order of the day as preparation for the annual march and shoot competition got under way. Fitness training was augmented by the bi-annual Kiwi clean up, when all available members of the squadron, suitably armed with shovels and sandbags, spent Wed 20 May weeding and refilling the famous Bulford Kiwi.

Readers of previous issues of both the Wire and Soldier magazines will be aware that the Kiwi has now become a firm part of squadron life and that a bond of friendship has been cemented between 249 and the old comrades of the New Zealand Retired Services Association. This bond was recognised recently when the OC, Maj Mike Shaw, was invited to New Zealand House to meet the Chief of the New Zealand Army General Staff, Maj Gen BM Poananga CB CBE. The general presented the OC with a very fine plaque in recognition of the squadron's efforts in keeping alive a part of our Commonwealth heritage.

With apologies to our friends in New Zealand we now publish the following poem which was found lying around the squadron office. The author is, of course, anonymous but rumour has it that Cpl Gus (Wordsworth) Taylor of the LAD has been at work again.

Our Pet Kiwi

It sits on a hillside
gleaming and bright
but it takes too much hard graft
to keep Kiwi white
They left it behind them
when they all went back
Oh, how that I wish
we could paint it all black
We're all tired of taking
sacks and spades from the shelf

so, comeback you skivers
and clean it yourselves

Don't worry Kiwis, by the time autumn comes he'll be ready to do it all over again.

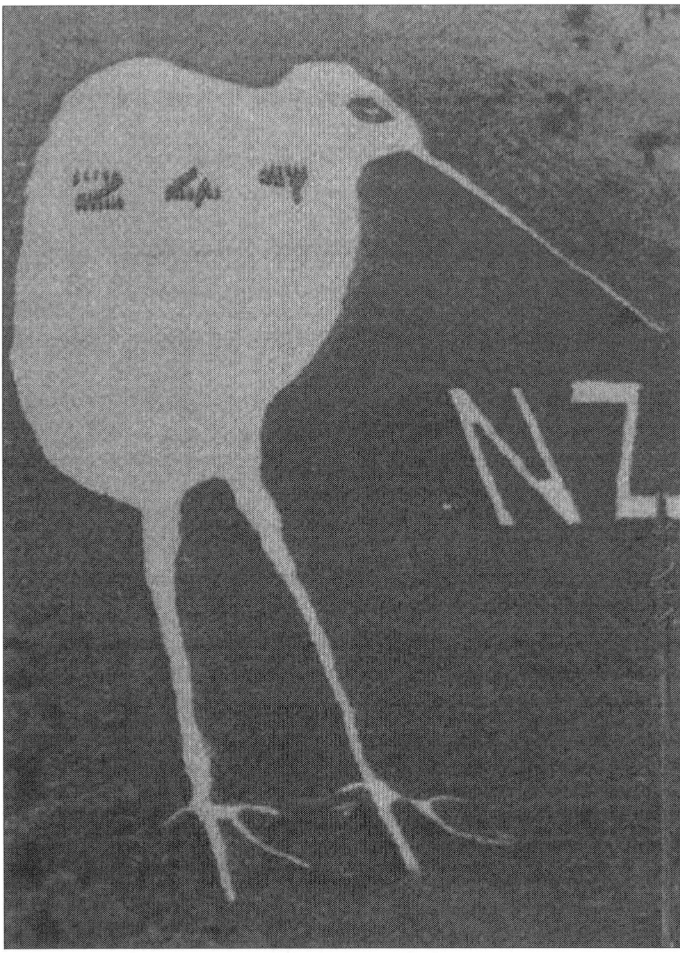

The finished product

March and Shoot Competition

Our photograph shows the Deputy Commander South West District, Brig JG Starling CBE MC ADC, presenting the winner's trophy to the Yeoman, W0 2 (FofS) Kev Bradley and LCpl Paul Norrie look on.

On Fri 22 May the annual Inter· Troop March and Shoot competition got under way and by mid-morning it became apparent that the whole affair would be a close-run thing. The 'old style' 10-mile bash placed the Support Troop 'D' team, under Cpl Mick Fitzpatrick, one of our best Marathon runners, in the favourite position with a time of 107 minutes. However, as is so often the case, the final positions were to be decided by the range phase of the competition and the Admin Troop team with W02 (YofS) Mick Altham in command eventually won the day with an overall average of 87 per cent hits on their targets.

May 1981

249 Sig Sqn (AMF(L)) Bulford

Commander's Cup Competition

The squadron, having returned from a wet and windy exercise in Northern Italy, has been as usual involved in many and various activities. One such being the Commander's Cup Competition which this year the squadron retained in a keenly fought battle. The team led by Lt Jim Barry practiced and competed vigorously and will no doubt pass on this expertise to next year's team.

Norway Clean Up

Also, during June elements of the squadron returned to Norway to pick up litter left from the winter exercise. Expecting to find a sunny and green land they were surprised to find areas still locked in mid-winter.

Offa's Dyke

As part of our fitness training and to add variety to life in Bulford, the unit recently walked the length of Offa's Dyke in Wales; half the squadron going from north to south (downhill?) and the other from south to north (uphill?). The total distance of 180 miles was covered in 8 very strenuous and tiring days.

The team hard at work picking up litter, Sgt Wand, LCpl Catchpole, Sig Leach and Sig Holt

GOC Visit

The quarter guard: SSgt Vivian, Cpl Johnston, Sigs Barker, Redman, Slaney, Campbell, Johnson, Kirk, Slaney, Hayward

On 24 Jul Maj Gen Acland, GOC SW DIST, briefly visited the squadron on one of his periodic visits. Whilst with the squadron he inspected a quarter guard and visited a display of the squadron's equipment.

Farewells

Sadly, we have to say farewell to the SSM W02 Marshall and his wife Myrtle. He moves onto bigger (possibly not better) things at 3 Armd Div HQ & Sig Regt as the RSM. By the time members of that regiment read this, he will already have arrived so we cannot warn you about his sporting instincts.

The art of public speaking. The SSM with an attentive audience at his dining out

November 1981

Our cover picture shows the successful 249 Sig Sqn. (AMF(L)) team which won both the NATO Challenge Cup and the Shooting Cup. The successful NATO Challenge Cup Team. L to R: Top Row: Sgt Cook, LCpls Talbot, George, YofS Altham, Lt Foxley. SSM Campbell, Sigs Payne, Slaney, LCpl Fraser, Cpl Yeomans Centre Row: Cpl Clifford, LCpl Vowden, Sigs Burnett, Goddard, O'Shaughnessy, Barker, Cpl Iverson, Sig Holt, LCpl Ball Front Row: Cpl Griffin, Sigs Leach, Tambs, Hartshorne, Sgt Barnard, Cpl Douglas, Sig Williams

Kiwi To the Fore

Discerning readers of the Peterborough column of the Daily Telegraph and viewers of the Southern Television News will have seen that the squadron recently received quite some coverage in connection with its association with the Bulford Kiwi. It all concerned the vis it of the New Zealand High Commissioner, who came down to see the Kiwi itself, and present the Squadron with a model in recognition of our hard work in restoring this well-loved national memento. Of course, the bird had to be spruced up in honour of our visitors and the appearance on orders of such words as 'Kiwi Clean' produced muttered oaths, moans and groans from the longer serving members of the Squadron. However, all put their backs into the arduous task of de-weeding, cleaning and scrubbing to such effect that within one and a half days our prized posse ion was again gleaming forth over the Plain.

'Trimming the Kiwi's locks'. Left to Right: Sig Tony Redman, Cpl John Murray, LCpl Phil Harris. Sig Sid Payne, LCpl Phil Hesketh, Cpl Dave Catchpole

On the day of the visit, we held an individual March and Shoot competition in order to find a suitable winner for the Kiwi Trophy. The Vorlaufer was none other than the OC, Maj Mike Shaw, who, accompanied by his dog Wellington. set the bogey time of 100 minutes for the ten miles. The competition was eventually won by

LCpl Tony Ball of Admin Tp, by a combination of hard running (!) and good shooting with an overall time of 99 minutes.

Presentations by High Commissioner

The New Zealand High Commissioner His Excellency The Honourable Leslie Gandar spent the morning with us, and after a full inspection of his national landmark, presented the prizes to the winners of the competition.

LCpl Tony Ball receives the Kiwi Trophy from the NZ High Commissioner. Admin Tp look on

To Denmark

Immediately after the Kiwi day, the squadron departed for Denmark and Exercise Amber Express. The airborne deployment passed relatively painlessly, and we settled into our patch of real estate at Ringsted ready for the onset of the exercise. Neither the rain nor the sidelong glances from the other nations' soldiery, deterred us from our routine of Battle PT commencing at the ungodly hour of five o'clock (Zulu). Running concurrently were checks of all our radio equipment and 'R & R' trips to Copenhagen; it isn't hard to guess which alternative was always over-subscribed. Because of an active EW threat, a large proportion of the combat operations was spent on radio silence, testing the alertness and endurance of all concerned. Cpls Mick Fitzpatrick, Jeff Smyth and (now Sergeant) Jimmy Jameson were given their heads, using their rebroadcast stations as tactical decoys; a good test of their wiliness and cunning in staying one jump in front, and sometimes behind. the 'live' enemy.

NATO Challenge Cup

LCpl Tony Ball, Cpl Dave Iverson and LCpl Butch Vowden grind out the last few miles of the March

The end of all large AMF(L) FTX's is always feted by the NATO Challenge Cup Competition, which is an international march and shoot competition. Memories of the Kiwi Competition coursed through the minds of those 'lucky' enough to be selected to participate. However, with the pride of the squadron, Corps, Army and country at stake, the gallant 26, banners waving, coasted home to a well-earned victory. Beating not only all the non-infantry units but also the infantry of the four nations competing, winning both the Challenge Cup and the Shooting Cup.

'The boys come home', featured Left to Right: Sigs Taff Williams, Keith Goddard, Ian Holt, Lt Ian Foxley, SSM Ian Campbell and Sig 'Brummy' Tambs

January 1982

244 Signal Squadron (AS)

Exercises

The Squadron is fortunate with its exercises, as they vary in location from Norway in the North to Turkey in the South. September found the whole of the Red Hand Gang in Denmark for Exercise Amber Express, a NATO Exercise which involved both AMF(L) and UKMF deploying to the same area at the same time which is quite a unique experience. Although the exercise was very demanding the majority managed to visit and enjoy Copenhagen even it if was the umpteenth visit for the stalwarts of the squadron. A keen interest by members of the squadron was shown in the Chinook helicopter which was exercising for the first time on Amber Express. The reason for the enthusiasm is the forming of a new troop within the squadron, aptly to be called Charlie Troop, which will deal with the VHF communications required by the Chinook. A few members were able to get a ride in the Chinook, afterwards Sig 'Gronk' Davis's comments were 'noisy and just like a here,' complacent aren't we!

249 Sig Sqn (AMF(L)) Bulford

Home Again

After the squadron's return from Denmark, it was all hands to the wheel in preparation for PRE. Everyone worked hard and must be congratulated on achieving the aim of passing.

Exercise Dryshod 81

Dryshod took place in the first two weeks in November in Sennybridge. It is the annual ' beat-up' exercise prior to deploying to Norway in January. It began with instruction in Arctic survival, map reading and mountain safety; these lessons were then confirmed in a series of one day marches and a night navigation patrol over the training area. In the case of Cpl John ' Sherpa' Murray though, it was decidedly doubtful whether he was using a map or not. We also used the many range facilities Sennybridge had to offer. Sig ' Shags' O'Shaughnessy particularly, enjoyed the SLR CQB; he leopard crawled the entire range through every patch of water he could find. Whilst on the SMG CQB Cpl Andy Dawson decided to go swimming whilst crossing a stream. On the section in defence shoot Sig Ian Holt (who was giving fire control orders) was lost for words for the first time ever, when a section of enemy appeared 25m from his trench. Dryshod culminated in a four-day, 60-mile forced march in the Brecon's, called Ex Wet Foot, which certainly lived up to its name. During the march the Deputy Commander SW District, Brig Walker visited the squadron for its ARU and joined one patrol for the day's march.

Norway, somewhere between Tromso and Cape North. If you like the view why not come and join us

March 1982

244 Signal Squadron (AS)

'The Red Hand Gang'

OC	Maj RCA Thwaites
21C	Capt SW Jones
OC ATp	Lt ND Couch
OC BTp	Lt G Smith
OC CTp	Lt SP Wallis
SSM	W02 (SSM) TK Muir
RQMS	W02 (RQMS) R Jeffery
YofS	W02 (YofS) DA Gruncell
FofS	W02 (FofS) RL Gibson
Chief Clerk	SSgt (ORSQMS) JS Symes

As our regular readers can see from the above list of personalities the squadron is going through a big change. To all the people who have left us we wish you all the best in your new units and thank you for all the hard work done whilst members of a very elite Gang. To all new members, welcome to the squadron and we hope that your stay will be an enjoyable one.

Initiative and Courage

Whilst participating in Ex Hardfall 82. in Norway, four members of the squadron, with their RAF officer, rescued a Norwegian fisherman and his son from a frozen lake after the ice had cracked beneath them. Whilst other fishermen stood by afraid to go and rescue their colleagues, the MAOTS (Mobile Air Operations Teams), drove their Snowcat vehicles out onto the ice getting as close as possible to the fisherman. Led by Flt Lt John Dungate RAF, Cpl Bob Smith, LCpl Fred Dudden, Sigs Jeremy Edwards and Brian Thom then went further forward and pulled the men out of the water.

249 Sig Sqn (AMF(L)) Bulford

Ex 'St Nicholas Stakes'

In early December the squadron provided commumcat1ons for a North East District Home Defence Exercise. We were tasked with providing the majority of the unit rear links on the District wide net. It certainly was a different experience from working with our NATO allies. Cpl Andy Dawson and LCpl Steven McNally certainly made themselves very comfortable with 3 Fl t AAC. LCpl Chalkie Lang found it was quite like the Arctic on his Rebro up on Sutton Bank.

Arctic Training in Bulford

The great freeze-up of December and January proved to be an asset to the Squadron. Whilst England stopped work, we carried on with snow training. Sgt Frank McAleer and Sgt George Cook took the Volvo drivers up onto Salisbury plain to practise their over snow techniques. The ski-instructors who had just returned from a course in Norway, Cpl Jimmy Johnston, Cpl Flo Philo and Cpl Fitz Fitzpatrick and others attempted to teach some basic ski techniques (with varying degrees of success).

The ARU

Brigadier RMB Walker, OBE, MC, visited the squadron in camp checking equipment, procedures and compulsory training. A blizzard that morning covered a multitude of sins.

Can I have a hat like that too? Brig Rory Walker visiting the QM 's stores during the ARU. SSM Ian Campbell and Sgt Terry Hughes look on. SQMS John Stanley sports the tropical version after his recent trip to Zimbabwe

Visits

In December, the permanent representative (Ambassador) to ATO, Sir John Graham BT, KCMG, visited. the squadron before taking up his new post. He saw a number of displays portraying the squadron on exercise and also watched some pre-Hardfall training

Sir John Graham talks to Cpl Bob Nixon while Sgt Barney Barnard and Sig Macfarlane look on

Maj Gen Reynolds, inspecting the quarter guard, talks to LCpl Hardwidge

In January the Commander AMF(L) Maj Gen Mike Reynolds visited the squadron. Fortunately, he could view our training for Norway at first hand as we were still under six inches of snow.

Maj Gen Reynolds talks to LCpl Dave Gosney (a novice) and Cpl Flo Philo (an expert) whilst the OC Maj Mike Shaw looks on

At present five soldiers from the squadron are spending four weeks in Italy learning Italian. Learning Italian, you might well exclaim indeed, but as they are the RLD to the Italian mountain battalion in the AMF(L) it all makes sense. Still, they are there to work as well, mainly keeping their skiing up to scratch in the Italian Alps. The five lucky soldiers are Cpl Kev McGready, LCpls John Lynch and Paul Cowie and Sigs Joe Campbell and Trib Slaney. News of their escapades will figure in the next Wire along with a report from our Norwegian correspondent.

May 1982

244 Signal Squadron (AS)

The Red Hand

As the squadron travels extensively throughout Europe to fulfil its roles with both AMF(L) and UKMF a question regularly asked is 'Why are you know as the Red Hand Gang and have a red hand on your vehicles and trailers? The answer is:

The first two Close Support Bomber Controls were formed as experimental units in 1941. They were formed by the War Office for reasons learned in the close Army/Air Force cooperation practised so successfully by the Germans in their 'Blitzkrieg' through Europe prior to Dunkirk. No 2 CSBC was commanded by Lt Col JM McNeill RA and was attached to HQ 13 Corps, 8th Army at the end of 1941. It soon became apparent that there was an urgent need for an immediately identifiable sign, as most traffic was high precedence. For lack of anything better Lt Col JM McNeill chose the 'Bloody Red Hand', his family Armorial sign. (The McNeill's being direct descendants of the Kings of Ulster). The red hand sign was immediately queried by the BGS. However, some persuasive talks resulted in the Red Hand being kept, provided that 'performance justified it'. The Red Hand was carried on the vehicles of No 2 CSBC throughout North Africa, Sicily and Italy.

The CSBC Signal Officer. Lt Bryn Davies returned to England at the end of the Tunisian campaign to form No1 Air Support Signal Unit (ASSU) in preparation for the Normandy invasion. The tradition of carrying the Red Hand spread to all ASSU's as they formed. The close cooperation between ground and air provided by these ASSU's proved so successful that they became top priority for the supply of men and equipment. The ASSU's consequently became the envy of every CSO.

After 1945 only one ASSU remained in existence and eventually it was reduced in size until by 1963 it was a squadron of 22 Signal Regiment. In 1963 there was a motion to remove the Red Hand.

However, an official reprieve was granted and now 244 Signal Squadron (Air Support) is virtually unique by still retaining a tactical sign. In 1964 the Air Support Signal Squadron was disbanded but reformed in 1969 at RAF Tangmere as 244 Signal Squadron (Air Support). From there, the squadron moved to RAF Benson and in 1976 it moved to its present location at RAF Brize Norton.

July 1982

249 Signal Squadron (AMF(L)) Bulford

Exercise 'Hardfall South'

On 15 January the Q advance party led by Capt QM Ray Danells left Bulford for the Voss area of Norway, to take over the accommodation which would be the squadrons home for the next six weeks while we carried out our annual Arctic Training. With the squadron split between three different locations, the furthest being 30 minutes away, the admin problem looked difficult but actually posed no problems for the Admin Staff.

Arctic Survival Course

With the new policy, of all troops going north of the Arctic Circle being properly prepared, the Arctic Survival Course was started this year. The squadron with many novices going to Norway, provided 47 students for the course run at Myrkdalen. Two Royal Marine Instructors, the experts, ably assisted by Squadron Instructors, nearly experts, put the novices through their paces for a period of ten days. Stories emerged from the course, far too many to tell here, suffice to say LCpl Keith (Legs) Talbot, has now found his ski. Sig Eddie O'Kelly and LCpl Bill (Humpty) Hesketh have been enrolled in the 'Banzai Brigade' and Capt Ian Foxley and Lt Kevin Fisher have found out that 'Naphtha' does burn.

Squadron Training

Immediately after the Survival Course had finished, squadron training started with a patrol exercise between Main Troop, with A Troop 244 Sig Sqn (AS) and Support Troop with Admin Troop, in the hills between Myrkdalen and Vossesstolen. The exercise started with both forces being inserted by helicopter. Support Troop using the helicopter to greater effect captured both Main Troop OP's led by Cpl Dave Catchpole and Cpl Bob Nixon in the first 24 hours whereas their OP led by Sgt Barney Barnard remained undetected for the full exercise. Pity they could not communicate, due to a faulty set at platoon base to pass on all info. The exercise finished with Support Troop and Admin Troop putting in a ski borne attack on Main and Alpha Troops base which, of course, Main Troop say the repulsed. The arguments continue!

With the troops reassembled, vehicles were prepared for the communications exercise. This brought home to the operators the difficulties of VHF communications in Norway. Many lessons were learned and put into good use on *Ex Alloy Express*.

A dismounted Rebro is prepared for Heli lift by (Left to Right) LCpl Smudge Smith and Sig Paul Madine, while Sgt Jamie Jameson looks on. Cpl (it's not a wig) Charles is hidden

Exercise 'Eagles Lair'

Platoon Radio Operator from 249 Sig Sqn's Special Ski Unit, at platoon base on Exercise Eagles Lair high in the mountains above Myrkdalen

The Deputy Commander SW District, Brigadier RMB Walker OBE, MC, planned Exercise *Eagles Lair* to test the military skills of the supporting arms, RCT, REME and RAOC with Signals providing the teeth to act as enemy to 1PWO. This force of about 300 strong, led by the OC Sqn Maj Mike Shaw (Never mind, even the best people get captured, Sir) acquitted itself very well. None more so than the Special Ski Unit of the Signals, led by Capt Scott (JR) Ewing who had at one time captured 2 Scimitars, 5 Volvos and the SQMS of D Coy 1PWO.

249 Sig Sqn's Special Ski Unit on patrol high in the mountains above Myrkdalen on Exercise Eagles Lair

Squadron Biathlon

Timing was now critical before going north for Exercise Alloy Express, could we fit in the Bi-Annual Biathlon, of course we could. Capt Ray Danells with the assistance of SSgt SQMS John Stanley and Sgt Terry Hughes selected and marked the course even though the QM injured himself in the process. The SQMS did not really mean to laugh! The course proved to be excellent as did some of the performances recorded. The winner of the individual was LCpl Paul George, with Main Troop winning the Team Trophy.

Exercise 'Alloy Express'

Exercise Alloy Express was an FTX north of the Arctic Circle, where all we learned down south was put into practice. The squadron once again came away with flying colours producing all that was asked of them. Our trip to Norway finished on a high note when the squadron retained the NATO Challenge Cup with a time in the speed march, two excellent pacesetters in Cpl Pete Griffin and Cpl Phil Clifford, that left the infantry and non-infantry teams, gasping in our wake. Well done lads!

July 1982

244 Signal Squadron (AS)

Norway

In January of this year Alfa Troop took 29 men to Norway for the annual Arctic training exercise, Ex Hardfall. The first five weeks were spent in Southern Norway learning to ski, survive and Patrol in the Arctic. Those who had been before completed refresher training. Whilst those who had not were taken under the wing of Royal Marine Mountain leaders for a 10-day Arctic Survival Course. This completed, everybody joined up for continuation training, including ski patrol exercises, biathlon, 10km ski race and Ex Eagles Lair, a five-day ski exercise for all British AMF troops in Norway. After completing Ex Hardfall, redeployment to north Norway in the form of a three day remarkably calm LSL voyage. for the AMF FTX Ex Alloy Express. All national elements of AMF joined together to practice the Arctic Warfare role. Here there was less skiing and more communicating to be done, it had to come some time. Altogether a long time, 8 weeks, for all and more for some, to spend in the 'Arctic Wastes' but a rewarding and enjoyable exercise.

249 Signal Squadron (AMF(L)) Bulford

About The Squadron

For those of you still in the dark, 249 Sig Sqn is the Force Radio Squadron to the AMF(L), a multi-national quick reaction force for deployment to either of NATO's Southern or Northern flanks. If you thrive on physical fitness, like cross-country skiing, enjoy seeing countries ranging from North Norway to East Turkey, working in differing mountainous terrain and weather conditions to BAOR and want your trade to have a touch of variety, why not think about 249 as your next posting.

Kiwi Cutter Returns

In April we were pleased to host David McCullen, one of the original Kiwi-cutters. The Bulford Kiwi was originally carved by one of the New Zealand Services whilst stationed on Salisbury Plain in 1918. It was dug into the western slope of Beacon Hill which lies to the north of Bulford Camp. Mr McCullen was hosted to lunch by the Squadron Officers on ANZAC Day and Lt Col Danny Fisher, ex OC 249, with his wife Stephanie attended. An enjoyable day was had by all and we hope the visit will be beneficial to the up keep of the Kiwi in the future.

Ex 'Ten Tors'

The squadron once again provided comms for Ex Ten Tors between 12-17 May. The weather was on the side of the walkers, which accounted for the low fall out of competitors. Main Troop provided the majority of the Radio detachments, whilst Support Troop provided the telephone operators for the TOR parties. Comms were going well when LCpl Tony Pope walked into the control cell, complaining that his TOR didn't have a telephone, rumour has it he was on the wrong hill. Cpl Pete (TSB) Vowden kept Radcon happy with sausage sandwiches. The REME Sgt, Mick Ward ensured that no one woke him up by putting an Alsatian dog on guard outside his tent. Capt Scott Ewing and sidekick Lt Alan 'Tufty' McComb, budding Travolta's in their own right, provided the entertainment.

Cpl Jimmy Johnston with Mr McCullen. Cpl Johnston who leaves soon on an exchange visit to NZ shortly holds the Kiwi Trophy awarded to the winner of the Annual biathlon event

Ex 'Clear Voice 82'

With Mr McCullen departed, the squadron officers raced for three Amesbury hotels to meet officers from six NATO countries, who were arriving for a week's instruction on AMF radio and voice procedure. The social side of events seemed to escalate from Day 1. Comd 1 Sig Gp held a welcoming party the first night, followed by a skittles evening at a 'local' pub. Sgt Pete Mallinson our MT rep, wasn't impressed with the course officer, when he was informed that 'local' meant 18 miles away. The week progressed with demonstrations and lectures and culminated in a 24-hour exercise.

After the debrief, twenty or so extremely tired NATO officers were rewarded with a happy hour. During this, the course officer was asked by several Italian and Canadian officers if they had booked London hotel reservations. Two days previously, he had asked them if they wanted rooms, but got a negative response. The NATO officers wanted somewhere cheap. Smiling quietly to himself the course officer Lt Kevin Fisher, booked them all into the Hilton.

Officers and seniors of the six participating nations pictured here with the Comd 1 Sig Gp and 249 officers and seniors

November 1982

249 Signal Squadron (AMF(L)) Bulford

Inter Troop March and Shoot

Before block leave in August the squadron ran its annual Inter Troop March and Shoot. Fine performances were produced by all team and Support Troop were awarded victory. Sgt McAleer led his section to overall first place.

Sgt Frank McAleer leads the winning section. Sigs O'Shaughnessy and Hamer and Cpl Dawson to the fore

Ex ' Bold Guard/Bold Anticipation'

On return from leave we entered a very busy exercise season. Ex Bold Anticipation was the I Inf Bde run-up exercise for Bold Guard and took place on Salisbury Plain between 1 - 5 September. The squadron found itself out of its normal role, producing the umpire communications for the exercise, down to Company level. Many detachments found themselves in different guises, Cpl 'Chamois' Leather and LCpl Tom Dooley (both normally Rebro commanders) found themselves acting as umpires to the Recce regiment. Unfortunately, their umpires thought they were driving Scimitars and they spent the entire exercise chasing tanks across the plain. Then on 16 Sep the squadron deployed to Schleswig Holstein on Ex Bold Guard until 24 Sep. LCpl Tony Slaney earned himself the~ nickname of Scammel, as he spent the majority of the exercise being towed out of ditches. Sgt Willy Riding gamed some practical experience speaking German to the local farmers. The exercise was very fast flowing, and no sooner had we finished than we were on the boat back to UK.

Squadron Battle Camp

The day after Bold Anticipation finished, the squadron went to Okehampton on the annual Battle Camp. The majority of the time was spent on the ranges where much of the work was new to the younger soldiers. LCpl Alan Griffiths on 84mm while SSgt 'Stretch' Dalton supervises. LCpl Tom Dooley kept up his record on the field firing grenade range. Three throws and three blinds. During the week SSM Ian Campbell had devised numerous light hearted activities to relieve the boredom. The log race (enough said, the SSM is Ex 216). To climax the week the SSM had organised a mini exercise based on the Cambrian marches. It was a two-day march across the moor with various military skill stands. The best-looking section of all, at the NBC stand.

Cambrian Marches

While the majority of the squadron were enjoying themselves on Battle Camp. Capt Ian Foxley and Sgt Frank McAleer and a team from the squadron took part in the Cambrian Marches. A very creditable performance was given by all, being the only minor unit to finish the four-day event. Cpl 'Fitz' Fitzpatrick and Cpl 'Griff' Griffin deserve a special mention for gritty performance.

The Future

At present the squadron is in the middle of PRE preparation and expecting to go to Greece in November, although because of the political situation it is still 50/50 whether we go.

January 1983

249 Signal Squadron (AMF(L)) Bulford

Visit Of the Master of Signals

Maj Gen Bradley talks to Sgt Willy Riding and Cpl Andy Dawson at the arctic display

During his round of farewell visits Maj Gen PEM Bradley CB, CBE, DSO, visited the Squadron in October. He saw a display of arctic equipment and talked lo soldiers during the inter-troop rugby XV's which was won by Main Troop.

Summer Biathlon

In September the Squadron held its annual summer biathlon, an individual 10-mile march across Salisbury Plain finishing with a timed SLR shoot. The event was won by Sgt Frank McAleer, who was presented with the Kiwi Trop by Col EJ Torrence OBE, the New Zealand Military Attaché.

The Lt James Barry Memorial Trophy

The summer biathlon was the final event in the competition for the Lt James Barry Memorial Trophy. As readers of the Wire will know, Lt James Barry had served for four years in the Squadron before joining 2 Para on an attachment. He died in action whilst serving with that battalion in the Falklands. The memorial trophy was presented to the Squadron by his parents. The competition is based on three events, a 10km ski race, a winter biathlon, and the summer biathlon, together with a grading for individual performance during the year. On 30 September Lt Col D. A. Barry (Retd) presented the trophy to the first recipient, Cpl Peter Griffin.

Cpl Griffin enjoys a welcome 'cuppa'

Salisbury Plain

Ex Active Elbow was a radio exercise conducted on Salisbury Plain during October. It was designed as a run-up exercise to Ex Apex Express: an AMF(L) exercise in Greece.

During the first phase detachment commanders put into practice the theory of HF techniques and PPAs which they had been taught the previous week. The aim was to work back to Bulford over the longest possible distance. Some Det Comd's worked out their PPAs correctly and managed to work in excess of 160km: others like Cpl Andy Dawson spent two happy days on the beach at Minehead, but not on the radio!

The second phase was combat operations on the Plain. Whilst one troop provided communications the other played 'the staff. They then changed roles so that everyone got a chance to 'pressurise' the communicators. During this period Col Mike Marples, OBE, Commander 1 Signal Group visited the squadron and carried out the ARU.

On the last evening of combat ops. the OC Designate Support Troop. 2Lt Peter Holliday visited various detachments. Whilst being shown round a very busy RADCO by SSgt (YofS) Bob Waller, he spotted a square fan heater. Hearing radio type noises coming from somewhere he put his ear to the heater, stood back and proclaimed. 'Ah Yeoman! An HF speaker?' Welcome to the Squadron Mr Holliday. On completion of the exercise, we discovered that the Greek government had cancelled Ex Apex Express and that we would spend November in wet. cold, Bulford.

Stop Press: The Lanyard Trophy

On the 27 November the Squadron entered a team in the I Inf Bde Lanyard Trophy competition, a 40-mile march across Salisbury Plain carrying a 30lb load.

The Lanyard Trophy contingent from the Squadron

Everyone who took part produced commendable results, especially Cpl Peter Griffin who was the Overall winner in a time of 9hrs 28mins. The Squadron also won the overall team competition: the team being Cpls Griffin, Fitzpatrick, Iverson and LCpl Dean. A notable performance was given by Cpl Grant Yeomans who completed the last 20 miles with torn shoulder ligaments and carried his bergen on one arm. The support team of Sgt Barney Barnard and Sgt George Cook deserve a mention for the hard work they put in keeping morale high and ensuring there was a hot brew at each rest stop.

March 1983

249 Signal Squadron (AMF(L)) Bulford

Since last going to press the squadron has had a full and busy programme including the Christmas leave period where for once the squadron lines were deserted and peace and tranquillity reigned for ten days or so.

Back in November the squadron saw a change of CO with Maj MPS Shaw leaving for Shrivenham on promotion to Lt Col and Maj PT Innocent taking over the squadron.

Ex Close Encounter 22/23 Nov

Due to the requirement to practise the military skills learnt in the summer months the two communicating troops, main and support, with admin troop under command of SSM Ian Campbell took part in Exercise Close Encounter on SPTA.

Cpl (Tech) Wright and Sig 'Trib' Slaney under basher cover somewhere on Salisbury Plain during Ex Close Encounter

The communicating troops set up platoon bases on the plain and sent out recce and fighting patrols in an attempt to locate the well-hidden enemy provided by admin troop. Patrol techniques and night navigation were the aim, but the two troops spent the night of the 22 Nov trying to locate the enemy without too much success! By first light on the 23 Nov the enemy position had at least been located and dawn attacks were put in by the troops. The exercise was considered to be good training and as always, each side claimed to have out-manoeuvred the other.

Communications Training

Military skills having been practised it was now time to turn our attention to communication skills and to this end the OC held a communications exercise once again on SPTA. With so many recent new arrivals the exercise was designed to introduce new members of the squadron to the format of the AMF(L) exercise and to the communications provided by the squadron for the AMF. The exercise proved successful with good communications and interesting tactics resulting from over inventive minds moving 60 T64's into a single grid square at the drop of a hat!

Dryshod Training 1983

The evil minds of the 2IC Capt Scott Ewing and SSM Ian Campbell devised this year's Dryshod training which was held in January in Sennybridge with the aim of preparing both hearts and minds for the rigours of Hardfall in Norway.

Night Navigation and Ranges

The initial two days were devoted to ranges taking advantage of the CQB and Section in Defence facilities with a night navigation exercise on the first night. All sections completed the course within the time limit and returned soaked and windswept but more trusting in the use of the Silva compass and not their instinct for direction.

Ex Mild Winter

With the words 'Pen-y-Fan' ringing in the ears, the squadron including Alfa Troop 244 Sig Sqn left the relative comfort of the Sennybridge Camp mid-week to carry out a foot tour of the Brecon Beacons. Ten-man patrols, with packs loaded, maps and compasses at the ready, sallied forth from the SP to various check points. The weather on the first day was kind and by 9pm all patrols were in the 1st base camp at the foot of Pen-y-Fan tasting the delights of the 24-hour ration pack and living in self constructed bashers.

Day two heralded the first snows of Winter 83 falling on the base camp but after a reassuring word from the weatherman: 'snow showers and sunny periods'; the gallant patrols set off for day two by scaling Pen-y-Fan. The weather forecast was unfortunately not entirely accurate and the patrols appearing at the second night's base camp looked as if they had passed through the ice age enroute. Snow and bad visibility had considerably slowed the pace. Once again bashers were constructed and all prepared for a good night's sleep. The snow had ceased, and all looked set fair for a good night. The Welsh weather still had some cards to deal however and by 1am some of the well-established bashers were no more as howling winds and driving rain had plucked the accommodation from the ground. The safety vehicles (FFRs) were rapidly filled with evicted residents and when the 2IC appeared at 6am seeking refuge from the gale, he was hard pushed to find space.

As first light dawned on the bivouac sight it was apparent by the soaked but cheerfully resilient campers that they had experienced probably one of the worst nights weather for a long time. The last leg of the exercise was an 5km walk back to the transport and then to the comforts of Sennybridge. Many stories of daring and intrigue were discussed over a pint in the Red Lion that night! We are now in the throes of preparing for and deploying to Ex Hardfall in Southern Norway and our next report will no doubt contain tales of daring skiing expertise.

May 1983

249 Signal Squadron (AMF(L)) Bulford

Arctic Training

With over 50 new members to the Squadron who had never undergone arctic training-many having just come from basic training, this year's exercise in Norway (Hardfall South) was to prove hard work on the part of administrators and instructor, whilst students were to have some unique experiences. Mid-January saw all the instructors completing their own courses and awaiting the arrival of the QM, Capt R L Danells and the remainder of the advance party. Prior to taking over the accommodation, however, the instructors decided to warm up by putting the admin wallahs through a basic arctic survival course.

The Stalheim Hotel was our home for the duration of Hardfall. Set amongst picturesque snow-covered mountains, with each room having private bathroom, this excellent hotel normally offers 4-star treatment to the tourist trade. Unfortunately to prevent damage many minor irritating, but necessary restrictions were placed on the soldiers to ensure the best possible PR with the management. Thus the 4-star hotel rapidly became known to the soldiers as the 4-star Colditz.

This year the Squadron bas managed to get sufficient of our own personnel trained as instructors and therefore both novice and refresher courses were under Squadron auspices; the former by Lt 'Tufty' McComb; the latter by Sgt ' Barney' Barnard with the 21C Capt Scott 'JR' Ewing acting as chief instructor. The courses ran very smoothly, though one would not get that impression when reviewing the morning sick parade. Notable casualties returned to the UK were W02(YofS) Mick Altham, Sgt Jimmy Jameson, LCpl Bob Mills and LCpl 'Mad Eddie' O'Kelly. Happy to say that all are now rapidly recovering.

Ex 'Pronto's Skirmish'

Immediately after the courses were finished the Squadron was reorganised for Ex Pronto's Skirmish. This was a Squadron military training exercise to re-enforce the points learned on the basic survival course and to practice JNCO's and Tp Comd's in leadership and minor tactics. The Squadron personnel, with Alpha Tp 244 Sig Sqn (AS), were equally divided into three forces with the aim being for each force to find and eliminate the other two. The exercise started with each force moving into base locations previously recce'd by the force commanders. Sig 'Andy' Picton found the move extremely difficult as trees seemed to have the habit of springing up between his skis. Midnight came, and the battle was joined, Lt McComb being of a generous nature, decided to assist the other 2 forces by sending all his locations in clear, (not again). 2Lt Peter Holliday's Black Force produced the most effective OP under the command of Cpl 'Steve' Martin, but Blue Force under Lt Neil Couch produced the most effective patrolling. The results of all the final attacks will never truly be known, but many valuable and exhausting lessons were learnt.

Ex Eagles Return

After 24hrs respite, the Squadron deployed on to the contingent FTX, providing command/control/umpire communications plus a very effective ski-borne company in the infantry role. Throughout the exercise the Squadron distinguished itself in all its different tasks and justifiably earned the praise received from the British and Norwegian Commanders.

Ex Norwegian Wander

After the rigours of the FTX and the exhausting business of the 10km ski Race; ably won by LCpl Frazer; the OC Squadron decided fun skiing was the order of the day, with camera's and personal hi-fi's to the fore. Alas, the weather gods had not been consulted. A rise in temperature produced 'White Out' and very poor snow conditions which made both vehicle and foot movement not only difficult but extremely dangerous in the mountains. After fighting the conditions for 48hrs the OC called in the 3-day trekking party and the 2IC started to move the comms vehicles down into the valleys. The move down saw the Volvo over snow vehicles of LCpl Bill 'Humpty' Hesketh and Cpl 'Hairpiece' Charles preferring the horizontal to the vertical position, causing much alarm to Sig Steve Armstrong and LCpl Ray Pritchard who were in the back.

The poor now conditions caused the cancellation of the Biathlon and so a live firing day was held on the local firing ranges to teach novice the Nordic military skills.

Redeployment

Hardfall 83 closed for the majority of the Squadron on the ides of March though the QM, Capt Danells, SSgt (SQMS) Terry Hughes and cook Sgt Richardson took an extra few days to hand back the hotel. With everyone now back in Bulford, it's all hands to the pumps as we clean and hand in stores in preparation for a well-earned Easter Block Leave, followed by an AMF(L) deployment to Turkey.

Basic survival course practises the art of shooting on skis. Cpl Pete Griffin looks on

(L to R) Sig John Hamer, Keith Goddard and Colin Burnett 'Smiling again' at the end of the 10km Ski race

'Nearly Gone' Sig Steve Armstrong looking pensive

'Gone' Cpl Steve McNally reviews his handiwork while LCpl 'Legs' Talbot and Cpl Sam Simcox smile knowingly

Cpl Jimmy Johnston an Instructor demonstrating the Hardfall

Volvo over snow vehicles being put through their paces on the basic Volvo driver's course

July 1983

244 Signal Squadron (AS)

Alpha Troop - Basic Arctic Survival Course in Norway

The course started with an introduction to NATO Planks (Army Cross Country Skis). After a few days learning to balance on this precision-made equipment we put on our Bergens and were told to 'ski up that mountain!', easier said than done! On reaching our destination we set about putting our evening lectures into practise and making little homes for ourselves. We dug furiously for several hours and our icy residences finally took shape. They did look inviting! The night passed slowly and to our relief the snow walls were still around us, not on us! Filling in the hole is a lot easier and we were soon speeding back down to the Hotel. The culmination of three nights out was a Puma helicopter lift back to base.

The Refresher Course

After Hardfall '82 we all thought this was going to be easy! It was, apart from the skiing! Lt 'Frans Klammer' Couch just couldn't master the snow plough at first but improved as time progressed. We believe he was doing some secret practise under flood lights. LCpl Pig Stannage bottled out in the first week before we started the course due to some strained muscle we think!! Subsequently he was put in his rightful place, behind the desk at reception! LCpl Kew had something against skis, he kept breaking them, luckily that is all he broke. The course lasted for 10 days and was designed to refresh all that we were taught last year. This included survival in the elements and living in snow holes and snow trenches. Cpl 'Big Nose' Robinson just watched and ate his Rollo's. Despite an early Spring, there was no shortage of snow.

September 1983

249 Signal Squadron (AMF(L)) Bulford

Ex Adventure Express

Report by Sig Russell

When in June the Squadron deployed to Turkey with the rest of the AMF(L) we looked forward to a pleasant change from a somewhat wet British climate. We arrived at the USAF Base at Incirlik on the first leg of our journey in blistering heat and immediately went in search of our advance party who, we were assured, had been having it tough. They were eventually found roughing it beside the base swimming pool, one of a number of amenities kindly made available to us during our short stay. For those members of the Squadron who had never been to Turkey before, the exotic insect life came as something of a shock. Sgt Milford soon discovered that the best way to make friends with a Scorpion is not to sit on it. The Scorpion was duly arrested, charged with assaulting the dignity of a SNCO, found guilty and sentenced to death.

More work was provided for the medical staff the next night by Sig 'Betty' Lynch, who while sleeping on top of his Landrover dreamed he was a helicopter and decided to go for a flight. (You won't get your pilot's licence that way John). All good things must come to an end and eventually we flew north to the exercise area around Sarakamis. Heavy rain bad turned many of the tracks into virtual bogs, but despite this the Squadron carried on as normal. Deterrent Ops were carried out in torrential rain, but the sun reappeared with Combat Ops and remained until we finally left. The weather was a bit deceiving however, as Capt Ewin in his Rebro Reece role was to find out. While guiding two Rebros into location he experienced a slight sinking sensation which required a tracked wrecker to remedy. (Maybe someone should have recce'd the route for you Sir).

After Endex, members of the Squadron took part in the Change of Command ceremony to welcome COMAMF(L) designate Gen Christy of the Canadian Armed Forces. During the parade Sig

COMAMF(L) Maj Gen M. F. Reynold s inspecting the Sqn parade contingent accompanied by Lt Alan McComb

Wilkinson decided to take a keen interest in something he saw at his feet, so keen in fact, he lay down to get a closer look. (Probably just a bit tired, poor lad). A couple of days later the Squadron returned to Bulford, slightly browner than we left and already planning for the Danish exercise in September. See you then.

'Not quite what I had in mind'. Capt Ewing (centre) carefully sites some Rebros.
L to R: Cpl Vowden, Sig Goddard and O'Driscoll

Cpl 'Brummy' Seaton keeping Sig Armstrong's morale up during stand-to with a cuppa

Lt 'Tufty' McComb and 2Lt 'Doc' Holliday 'roughing it' in Turkey

Sig Paisey and Williams enjoying a few home comforts in Turkey

November 1983

249 Signal Squadron (AMF(L)) Bulford

Preparation For Denmark

The Squadron returned from block leave on 22 August minus the late arrival who had the usual lame excuse. Those present received the good news of the following promotions: Cpl Gordon McKenzie and Sgt Dale Fuller, who now joins Main Tp. The first task in hand was the preparation of the Vehicles for Denmark. Ex Adventure Express in Turkey had taken its toll and a lot of hard graft was needed from the troops in order to get the vehicles back on the road.

Kiwi Clean Up

Once again, this responsibility had to be met and the task went to Main Tp. The clean-up was completed in a day and various new vocations in life were discovered: Cpl Geordie Storey posing as a Canadian 'look-a-like' on the Strimmer and LCpl Eddie O'Kelly discovered that it was possible to get a ¾ Ton GS into top while driving down a 1:1 chalk slope.

Summer Biathlon

Following a week of early morning runs, designed to loosen everybody up after the summer break, some good times were expected from the event this year. However, the event result was finally decided on shooting ability and not on running time. Sig Barker took first place after recording a maximum score of 20 at the range. LCpl Redman and Cpl McNally taking 2nd and 3rd places, Lt Col Leonard representing the Comd HQ I Sig Gp presented the Kiwi Trophy.

Echelon

Echelon CP set up independently and was able to provide better support for both Headquarter elements. This produced an extra task for the line section at Alternate. They completed this after getting a lift from a grounded Gazelle helicopter which they had to literally 'bump start'. Sig Oscar Clutterbuck suffered the pre-posting blues and failed to impress the SSM, W02 Glenn McArdle, with his erratic driving skills. The high point of the exercise was when all stood to, only to find that the enemy advance had by-passed them and that their location was now a few miles in front of the blue forces FLOT. The problem was solved when echelon reappeared near Alternate's new location with big smiles and no questions asked (white mine tape possibly?).

Main

Meanwhile up at the sharp end the enemy had succeeded in finding Main Headquarters, if only in patrol strength. Radio Village however was ready for them with trenches dug, despite LCpl Wilkinson's insistence on using the pick on his foot and not on the ground. The attack was broken off (rumour has it that they tasted some of LCpl O'Kelly's curry) and life returned to normal. The following day it was proved beyond reasonable doubt that after two weeks on compo rations, burdened down with a 'loo' roll and a pistol, a Squadron OC is quicker than a 'Senior' Yeoman over 50 metres.

Alt

Alternate had a quiet exercise, only having command for a brief period. The initial night move, completed in a storm proved interesting, especially when the no light rule was actually enforced. Stand-to produced a new meaning to the term "interlocking arcs of fire" when Sgt Jimmy Jameson pointed out to OC Main Tp that his arc of fire included four members of the US HQ Coy. The highlight of the exercise was when the Radcon crew, assisted by the 2IC, went to the aid of Sig Shawn Brookes, who had reported being attacked by a large rat. (For Sale, one very small field mouse, 5 DKr ONO).

PR

The Squadron participated in a four-sided football tournament which took place at the Danish Signal School. The 12-man squad assembled having travelled the length and breadth of Denmark via various forms of transport. The other three teams were provided by the German Wire Company, the Danish Sgts School and a team from the Signals School itself. The squadron beat the Signal School 5-1 in the first round and met the German Wire Company, who had an easy 5-0 victory over the Sgts School, in the final. The match itself was quite hard, with a lot of niggling tackles taking place. However, in the words of the Captain, Sgt George Cook, 'we kept our cool' and the squadron went on to win 3-2. Sig Steve Barker scored four goals in total and LCpl Tony Redman had two good warm up games prior to joining the Corps squad.

NATO Challenge Cup

With two previous successive victories, the first exactly two years ago on the 25 September 81, the Squadron was looking for its third win. The opposition was known to be harder this year, other minor units being keen to acquire the cup. Also, although competing in the Major Units cup, the team from the 1st Parachute Battalion were obvious contenders for being outright winners. The run went well, determined leadership being shown by the 2IC Capt Scott Ewing, whose career was in the balance. The squadron team was one of the fastest up to and through the assault course and after experienced pace making from YofS Mick Altham the team finished with a running time of 75 minutes. Despite being unable to zero their weapons, the team shot well and achieved the highest SLR score, beating all teams entered by 1 Para! The only Team to beat us at the range was the AMF(L) Workshop who fired SMGs from 75 metres. Overall, the Squadron retained the challenge cup having a joint second fastest running time with a team from 1 Para but winning the minor units outright.

Sig Stephen Barker receiving the Kiwi Trophy from Lt Col Leonard 1 Signal Group

Sig Paddy Harkness stealing rations from Sgt Jimmy Jameson during the NATO Challenge Cup assault course

January 1984

249 Signal Squadron (AMF(L)) Bulford

NATO Challenge Cup - Denmark

A full account of the Squadron's performance was reflected in November's issue of The Wire, we are now able to publish our group photograph.

The winning team shown with Maj Gen A. G. Christie CD- Commander Allied Mobile Force (Land)

The Lanyard Trophy 27-28 October 83

Report by Cpl 'Taff' Griffiths and Sig JJ 'Scouse' Johnston It was a brisk Autumn morning when well over 200 men (loyal and true) from 30 Sig Regt, I Inf Bde Sig Sqn, 5 Airborne Bde Sig Sqn, 244 Sig Sqn (AS) and 249 Sig Sqn (AMF (L)) arrived at the start of the 1983 Lanyard Trophy Competition.

The origin of the competition dates from the time when 1 Inf Bde were the old 216 (Para) Sig Sqn in Aldershot and devised a 40 mile 'undulating' route over the South Downs with a pack/bergen in excess of 30 lbs and carrying an SLR. Since the move to Tidworth the event has taken place on SPTA.

This year the '249' team were spearheaded by 2LT 'Doc' Holliday and Sgt George Cook. We arrived with the intention of retaining the cup which we won last year, but aware that in particular 5 Airborne Bde Sig Sqn may have information on our tactics from WOI (RSM) Ian Campbell who was SSM of the Squadron last year.

The outstanding performer from this year's team was LCpl Tom Fraser who was the overall winner in a time of 10 hours 9 minutes. He was followed in by Cpl Smudge Smith and Sig 'Mad Eddie' Okelly who were joint fourth; LCpl Dixie Dean and Sig Dougie Eaglesham finished in joint fifth and completing the team and finishing in sixth place LCpl 'Shags' O'Shaughnessy. Sig Dougie Eaglesham was the first soldier under 20 years of age to finish the course. There were many other creditable performances in the team: too numerous to mention here but it was generally agreed that the build-up of carbohydrate level the night before does the trick! Finally, we would like to thank Sgt Barney Barnard and his team of eight men who provided us with much needed moral support, first aid cover and liquid sustenance.

The winning team complete with trophies (and sore feet)

May 1984

244 Signal Squadron (AS)

Exercise Hardfall - Avalanche Express

After a hectic start to April the squadron is settling down to normal pace of life: It all started with the return from Norway of Alpha Troop on completion of their annual winter holiday in the snow. The troop departed to Norway in mid-January, all, or rather most having completed basic training in Wales. Sgt Terry German, Cpl Dave Oughtred and Sig Andy Fearn being the exceptions, having only joined the troop a few days before departure. As usual, accommodation for Hardfall was shared with 249 Sig Sqn who kept a watchful eye on events in the Stalheim Hotel and basic training started.

Although most completed the full two weeks, a few stepped, or rather fell forward for early release and much to the rest of the squadron's amusement SSgt Chippy Chambers, LCpl Pete Hayes and LCpl Dixie Dean had an early flight back escorted by the Wroughton Medicav beauties. We are pleased to announce that their various injuries are now well on the way to being mended.

The rest of Hardfall was spent converting those remaining into fully trained Arctic Warriors, with just a little time taken out to win the 249 Sig Sqn team and individual winter biathlon, 2Lt David Halstead being the overall winner.

During the R&R, some of the troop managed to go downhill skiing, which fortunately did not result in injury. Having seen Sig Dave 'I headbutt trees' Gray and LCpl Cliff Franz Barker hurtling down the Hangar, this was more by luck than judgement.

At the beginning of March, the troop deployed North to the Bardufoss area of Norway to provide the AMF(L) with their air support communications on Ex Avalanche Express. Throughout the exercise, 2Lt David Halstead and Sgt Terry German were operated on a number of times to remove their sleeping bags from their backs.

It would be fair to say that both the exercises went well and as one young Signalman was heard to say 'There was no comms problem even though we were working to foreigners'. A few other minor amusing incidents that spring to mind are Cpl Duncan Ware passing comment on some hapless young driver who had hit a tree, as he happily sailed into a ditch and the 'accidental borrowing' of Maj Gen AG Christie's (Comd AMF(L)) chocolate cake that raised the odd comment or two.

Despite Alfa Troops belief that the rest of the world rotates around them, RAF Brize Norton have got other ideas and the first week in April was spent being Tacevalled. A harrowing experience for even the most placid of people and an event that sorely strained inter Service relations.

28 March saw Cpl Dave Almond being presented with a GOC's commendation by Lt Gen Sir Geoffrey Howlett in Headquarters South East District. Cpl Almond earned the commendation whilst on Ex Gryphons Gold in November 1983. He was flagged down by a lorry driver who had found a man having a heart attack in a parked car. The lorry driver was unsure what to do so Cpl Almond took control of the situation taking the man to the nearest hospital in his car. This prompt action undoubtedly saved the man's life.

Sgt Terry 'where is my trophy' German coming home in fine style at the end of the biathlon

Cpl Duncan 'Who says I'm a poser' Ware showing off a neat line in Arctic Camouflage to the Italians

July 1984

249 Signal Squadron (AMF(L)) Bulford

A Look Back

1984 got off to a brisk start with the Squadron preparing for yet another Ex Hardfall South in Norway. Even during this period of frenzied activity, we took time off to visit the Tidworth Oval to watch the Squadron team win the 'York's and Lancs' Minor units Football Cup beating the holders 3-1 in a keenly contested match.

Hardfall 84

January 10 saw the OC Squadron depart for Norway with his team of instructors to prepare for the Squadron's Arctic Warfare Course. With the instructors, admin staff and vehicles all dispatched it was then the turn of the Squadrons WO's to lead the main parties out to Norway. The only problem being the ill-fated 'Chalk 21' commanded by the SSM, who had to sample the fine sleeping facilities on hand in RAF Lyneham's waiting room. After some 19 hours travelling the weary band of trainee arctic warriors reached their destination, the Stalheim Hotel (No Joke).

The following morning training started with the fitting of the dreaded Norge plank, which tends to have a Jekyll and Hyde effect on the wearer. The next few days were taken up with basic ski training, with very few injuries, thanks to the banning of the dreaded 'Banzai'. Sunday not being a day of rest we saw the Squadron happy on the slopes while the OC and his AWI's led a small group to dig demonstration snowholes. The highlight of the day being Lt 'Doc' Holliday giving the OC and SSM a 'Demo' on his new Peak stove, with encouragement from the onlookers and a lot of assistance from his fellow AWI's he finally managed a cup-a-soup some two hours later.

Since the Falklands War, we have all come to know the meaning of the terms 'Tabbing' and 'Yomping', we would now like to add a new method of travelling across country to the list, and this we call 'Bimbling'. All you require to practise this new mode of travel is 150 men on skis, wearing bergens and a few thousand square miles of snow. Some members of the Squadron found they could pursue other tasks while 'Bimbling' as a means of breaking the boring swish of skis. One such person was the QM, Capt Nick Nicoll who decided to start a write-off programme, unfortunately most of the equipment he was trying to write-off was being worn by the SQMS Terry 'Just Married' Hughes.

The Arctic Warfare Course

It was Saturday when the Squadron together with A troop 244 Signal Squadron set off in search of their Arctic Warfare Qualification. We left the warmth of the Hotel and moved up the Brekkedalen for our first night in the snow, this was spent in five men tents: luxury! Night two we moved into tent sheets, next morning we pulled poles and moved back to the hotel much to the disgust of the old hands and the smokers. The next couple of days were taken up with basic arctic warfare skills, then came the major event on the winter sporting calendar (second only to the Olympics) the 10km ski race. This gave our class skiers their chance to show us their skills. The race was won by Lt Graham Norris with a time of around 32 mins. The next day was a real blot on the social calendar as we were introduced to the pulk, which I can only describe as a man trap. After a first-class demonstration by the instructors, we students were lashed to the evil contraptions and were made to pull them up hill and down dale, for the morning.

Saturday and a well-earned R&R Day except for the QM and his band of Arctic Survival students who, under the watchful eyes of the OC and SSM, with just a 24-hour pack between four men and their sleeping bags (we must be getting soft) spent a night out. On Sunday it was the AWC who had the chance to build their shelters and managed to clear a couple of acres of woodland in the process.

Next day we were off again, as a company we skijored up the valley to our Coy RV. The PL's were quickly located and settled into digging a Coy defence location, in a near (in fact very near) blizzard. Next morning the Coy bugged out and withdrew to our next location and quickly started to dig-in. Position dug, we then started patrolling. Day three, once again we bugged out and withdrew. At the Coy RV the OC was waiting to inform LCpl Brian Mills that while he had been snug in his trench his wife had presented him with a fine baby boy. Good news received; we all started a two hour climb to our Snow holes. By six o'clock the mountain side looked like a giant rabbit warren. A good night's sleep was had by all, it was then time for a pleasant 10km ski down to the Hotel, with some people spending more time in the snow than on it.

After a couple of days clean up and R&R it was time for the Biathlon. The race was won by 2Lt David Halstead of A troop 244 Sig Sqn, with the SSM a close second and also picking up the Richmond Trophy for the old timers. With most of the stars of the previous race spending a lot of their time going around in circles asking each other the way. All that was left for the students to complete was the final exercise to test our new found skills.

Prontos Skirmish

The Squadron warm up exercise returned to the Brandset Valley, with the Squadron split into two forces pitted against each other. Both forces kept their tactical plans very close to the chest and spent as much time trying to outwit the umpires as they did each other. Orange forces tactic seemed to be to keep Blue forces awake for as long as possible. This task being given to the long-range patrol group of LCpls Jim Stubley, Tony Redman, Cpl Steve McNally, Sig Chris Loughlin who not only can ski well but are also bullet proof. The exercise ended with an early morning attack by Blue on Oranges base location, with the umpires awarding a draw. So, it's same time, same place, next year and we will try again.

Eagles Revenge

The last major event of our Hardfall programme before we prepared to go north was exercise Eagles Revenge when 249 Signal Squadron and LOG SP BN took on 1 Para, which was our chance to test our arctic and infantry skills. We, as a Squadron were tasked with providing the communications for both sides and the umpires and this involved two thirds of the squadron. The other third of the squadron was renamed D Coy of the Orange Force with the nickname of Leaches Lepers! As their gallant Coy Commander was Capt Steven Leach better known as 'Dez'. D Coy moved from the Stalheim to a tented camp at Bømoen where we were given our ration of suicide missions. One such mission was to be Hele lifted in the early hours of the morning onto a frozen lake in the mountains. Then four hours to a Coy RV on skis and then finally an assault on a I Para location wearing snow shoes. The assault taking the enemy by complete surprise, was ruled a victory for us much to the 1 Para Pl Commander's disgust.

January 1985

249 Signal Squadron (AMF(L)) Bulford

Exercise Bold Gannet 1984

The view of a newly commissioned YO.

Friday 9 September 1984 saw over 60 vehicles from the Squadron and assorted other units formed up ready to move to Colchester enroute to Denmark and Ex Bold Gannet. With Lt 'Doc' Holliday leading, the move started well and everybody duly arrived, refuelled, ate and bedded down in Colchester Barracks. However, next morning it was clear that things would not be plain sailing when it was learnt that the ship which was to take our vehicles was strike bound in Rotterdam courtesy of British dockers. Alternative transport was found in the form of an LSL, and the Squadron boarded the Dana Anglia, leaving our vehicles in Harwich docks, to be ferried across later.

Never Again

It was very plain that by travelling in such a ship, amply stocked with Danish blondes and beer, that we were going to enjoy ourselves. Indeed, Sig (I'm not really drunk) Higgins was discovered inspecting the radar from the top of the mast and after being coaxed down from his perch, decided that the top of the funnel was a safer vantage point. Hence the squadron arrived in Esjberg in good spirits, where the 'hurry up and wait' syndrome continued as we waited for our vehicles to arrive. On Monday the LSL arrived and we collected our vehicles accompanied by four very green faced members of the Squadron who swore never to travel in a floating garage again!

The Role

The Squadron's role in the exercise was to provide communications and control for the Umpire Organisation, so after arriving at our deployment locations, we set about establishing the area of communications and testing radio paths. Once communications were established and the exercise phase begun, there was relatively little to do for those based in Rinstead or Skalstrup. There was thus much time for R & R and contact with the 'indigenous population' who were found to be very friendly and obliging. Most of the Squadron discovered the pleasures of Copenhagen more than once.

A Different Story

For the operator drivers who had umpires it was a very different matter. They found themselves charging across the countryside after hectic battles so that their Umpires could agree on the score. Ex Bold Gannet gave the Squadron much insight into the conduct of a major battle from both the staff side, and actually on the ground, as well as the opportunity to see much of Denmark.

The Return

Yeoman (I know the way) Wykes aw rather more of it than he intended, and three subalterns all saw it sitting on the same bicycle (until it crashed!). After packing up we began redeploying to UK on Thursday 20 September. Moving via Skalstrup and Yarde to Esjberg we once again discovered that movers not only 'do it all over the world' but that they also do it very slowly. The return boat crossing promised to be as pleasant and relaxing as before. Much fun was had, and everybody enjoyed themselves; certain young officer being repeatedly woken from their bunks to ret urn to the bar. Whilst waiting to embark, Cpl Chris Nutt discovered that his. Trailer was no longer attached to his vehicle. Whilst he was away looking for it on the tow hooks of all the other vehicles. Lt Frazer (my name's Scottish) Grant, organised the man-handling of Cpl Chris Nutt's Landrover out of the packet and disappearance into a sea of green Landrovers, much to the amusement of the rest of the Squadron.

Enjoyable and Worthwhile

We completed the move back to Bulford with no major incidents, but a number of breakdowns. And as Sig Bob Littlewood put it after being towed into camp three hours after the main body ‘There is always one, Sir!’ And so began the clean-up after an enjoyable and worthwhile exercise.

January 1985

249 Signal Squadron (AMF(L)) Bulford

Exercise Hardfall 85

The Hardfall exercise in Norway from January to March is the culmination of the Squadron training year. It is the annual' winter training period for the UK contingent to the AMF (L), it gave approximately a third of the squadron the opportunity to go on to northern Norway to participate in Ex Cold Winter with the Marines and I PARA.

So, after deployment by either Hercules, VC10 or LSL to Stalheim, near Voss, the unit shelved their communicating skills and went in search of their ski legs. For the instructors and Hardfall veterans it was merely a case of waxing-up and brushing up on Telemark turns but for the novice, it was to be a sometimes painful but always an enjoyable period in which to discover as many ways as possible to fall - or 'snot' as it was affectionately known. The main aim of the ski instructors in these first 10 days, was to impart to the beginner, the skills of turning and stopping on skis. However, the beginner's aim was to reach, and once there, maintain terminal velocity for as long as possible. It was soon discovered that the time taken to reach this speed was greatly reduced with the addition of a rifle, bergen and pulk.

Arctic Warfare Training

With the squadron now declared 'safe to ski' Arctic training began in earnest with a four-day exercise. After a long 5Km skijor, (with Sig Morris doing most of the 'snotting' and so providing the rests), the dreaded pulks were unloaded from the Volvos. After a nearly perfect demonstration of pulk pulling by the continuation course, (and would you believe that apparently, they got it right every time in practice? and no, we didn't), we set off for the company base area with pulks in tow. Having broken the first rule of the Arctic not to sweat several times, the base area was reached, and the five man tents quickly erected. At once the benefits of carrying the tents around all day were realised, for with a Coleman lamp and several Peak stoves running, it was warm within minutes. Before turning in for the night, there was a noise and light demo, during which SSgt (YofS) Wykes proved just how far a voice can carry in the Arctic even from the prone position.

Luxury Left

The luxury of the Arctic tent and the burden of the pulk were left behind the following morning, and the squadron skied in the relative comfort of carrying just a bergen. That night was spent under the shelter of tent sheets, having initially discovered the numerous different ways of fastening them together to resemble everything but a tent. 12 hours later, these once pliable canvas sheets, were frozen solid, and took a Jot of coaxing to reduce them to a size small enough to fit inside a bergen, but eventually the squadron skied off for the 3rd day and 3rd form of shelter, snow holes.

The Advantage

Now the advantage of living in a snowhole, is that it does not have to be carried around. The disadvantage is that it takes four hours plus to dig. However, much to everyone's delight, they were fairly comfortable on what turned out to be the coldest night outside -25°C with a high wind blowing.

Survival Phase

This format of exercise was repeated the following week with the introduction of tactics, so in preparation, white cam tape was stuck on everything. The last 24 hours of the week was to be a survival phase in brushwood shelters. The provision of the brushwood came courtesy of our Norge LO. Armed with a chain-saw, Axel (grizzly Adam's stand-in) proceeded to defoliate the forest. After a few hours he had cut down everything resembling a tree or plank (Cpl 'Dithers' Petherbridge just falling outside this description, escaped narrowly). Unfortunately, the finer side of lumberjacking-such as where to actually saw through the tree to determine where it will fall, was not one of Axel's (half-shaft to his friends) strong points, and he managed to demolish a brushwood shelter and LCpl John Lynch's fourth brew; a pity as it was to be the one he had promised to share around.

Exercise Pronto's Skirmish

With knowledge such as the exact role of the lollipop stick in the Arctic ration pack now known the squadron split into two platoons for Ex Pronto's Skirmish. That was the chance for the two troop commanders Lt Mike Wise (in devil's disguise) and Lt Frazer (anything gimmicky with Berghaus written on, I'll buy) Grant, to display their ski-borne tactics. From day one, Lt Wise went 100% covert, only making one appearance from his Arctic sleeping bag (purchased from Sgt Jim Perry at very little profit to the latter) for such essentials as changing his 'Jack-box' batteries. Mr Grant, however, put out numerous aggressive patrols. A mention must go to the special ski patrol who were Heli-dropped behind enemy lines and succeeded within 24 hours to bump their own OP.

The OC, Maj (time for another hot Ribena I think) Cook, injected a little excitement into the exercise by telling each side where everyone else was. Unfortunately, the information was sent in BATCO which took the radio operators the remaining two days of the exercise to decode. However, acting on this intelligence (certainly not his own), Lt Grant pinpointed the enemy patrol base and prepared for a dawn attack. By mid-morning, the platoon had fought through a forest and came across the enemy position, won the firefight and won the day.

The Ski Races

For the majority of this time, SSgt (YofS) Wykes and Sgt Perry were always 'just off to cut the track' for the ski race. It was never discovered exactly what they were up to, but the ski races (on the well-cut tracks) were both a success. The 10Km competition was a straight forward race, with Sig Guy Ashton winning in a time of 41m 15s in front of 2nd placed Cpl Pete Plevin. The 'Richmond Trophy', a 20Km biathlon was, however, quite different. The organisers had a much more difficult job on their hands to cut a track in snow that was rapidly changing to slush. After a week's postponement, the event was run and enjoyed by all who took part. Sig Ashton after the success of the 10k, even imposed a handicap on himself by not carrying his ammunition with him. Mr Grant and SSgt Dave Beattie were so moved by this selfless gesture, that they both followed suit. The OC refused to allow. LCpl 'Gripper' Jackson to carry him around anymore, and skied into 4th place, behind LCpl Doug Eaglesham (good luck at 264 Sig Sqn). Cpl Schofield (244 Sig Sqn) came in 2nd and Cpl Plevin won with a very quick time of l hr 31 mins Cpl 'shades' Barton was unavailable for comment on the event from his Volvo seat, although it was rumoured that he complained of lack of time in which to practise.

Exercise Eagles Talon

The Arctic training had all been leading up to the Brigadiers exercise, Eagles Talon, which took place in the final week. 249 had to provide a ski company and the comms for the exercise which was geared towards testing I PARAs mobility. The ski company had a difficult job under the command of the 2IC, Capt Steve Leach (incidentally, the OC would like to take this opportunity to thank him for bringing out his St Valentines love cake from his wife) and the SSM. In an attempt to ensure the PARAs were the victors this time they advanced towards the squadron's defended positions, which included reserve demolitions on both bridges and tunnels, minefields and finally a well-prepared company position.

I PARA put in a dawn attack and took a full hour to fight through the position, complete with its ski-traps which caught more than a few by surprise. All that remained now was to fill in the trenches and return to the hotel for a wind-down and to start the war stories going. Cpl Peter Mclnally and LCpl Mark Ridley hung around the exercise area until everyone had left, muttering something about the possibility of finding a ridge tent laying by the roadside, as if anyone would leave one there just for the taking.

End Ex

For the fortunate minority, there was now a further fortnight of LOA to be earned at Bardufoss, providing the comms for Ex Cold Winter. However, for the remainder it was a case of packing the skis away for nine months and reminiscing over dehydrated mutton and rolled oats. In case the impression has been given that ii was all work and no play, there was time in the evenings for Trivial Pursuits and a darts competition to be run. Some SNCO's and young Subalterns also turned their hand to singing and held several private choir practices, their voices being heard well into the early hours.

A rare shot of Support Troop on their feet (thanks go to the REME for getting three Volvos on the road for this photo). Spot the hedgehog

Flying weather-good news for us, a five-minute flight can save a morning's skiing

Pulk pulling-everyone's favourite

Skijoring - man and machine in perfect harmony?

July 1985

244 Signal Squadron (AS)

Exercise Hardfall 85

At the end of January Alpha Troop made the now familiar trip to the Voss area of Norway for their Arctic Warfare Training. Training was mostly carried out under the watchful eye of 249 Sig Sqn (AMF(L)) whom we thank for looking after us in the Stalheim Hotel. Our MAOTs continued to train with 33 Sqn RAF at Bømoen. The OC Sqn, Maj DJ Mclean, visited and during his stay was seen flying past the Troop at amazing speeds on his trial skis.

On one social evening we said farewell to Col Mike Marples Comd I Sig Gp, which culminated in a rendering of the word famous Air Support Song by Sig 'Walter' Gray. Congratulations go to Cpl 'Mark' Schofield for coming second in 249 Sig Sqn (AMF(L)) biathlon event and to the whole of Alpha Troop for clocking the fastest average time. Also, to our MAOTs for their successes on behalf of 33 Sqn RAF. If 2Lt S Purser is reading this we want to ask him, where are the photographs?

Our next job was in Portugal.

Exercise Ardent Ground 85 Portugal

Ex Ardent Ground '85 was the annual live firing exercise for the Artillery and Offensive Support Aircraft of the AMF(L) and AMF(A). It took part on the Sante Margarida Training Area in central Portugal between 18 April and 9 May 1985. Alpha Troop had the enviable task of providing the Air Support Communications for the RAF and other air forces within NATO.

The deployment plan looked simple, this soon changed when half the Troop were placed on an LSL at Marchwood, the 'vessel' unfortunately developed engine trouble halfway across the Bay of Biscay, finally arriving in the exercise area two days late. Meanwhile the air move had gone well which meant that 10 members of the Troop were stranded in Santa Margarida Camp with no food, accommodation or, most important of all, no sleeping bags, (which may teach them not to be separated from their kit)! The intrepid 10 were not to be disheartened, especially after finding out the supermarket sold crates of beer for less than two pounds. The two night's waiting were spent with Lt David Halstead wrapped in towels, LCpl 'Spud' Eaton dressed in four combat suits and the rest of the Troop huddled around Cpl 'One Eye' Hearn's sleeping bag, hoping to take advantage of the two second rule.

The vehicles finally arrived, and the exercise progressed. Some good FAC experience was gained by the offensive support detachment, although inflating the blow-up tank targets is not everyone's idea of fun as LCpl Jock 'Blacky' Adams pointed out to everyone within 10 miles of the exercise area.

The highlight of the excursion was the Troop outing to Lisbon, during which much food and some drink was consumed by all concerned. The trip can be summed up by saying the OC and Sgt German caught a taxi, Sig 'Walter' Gray caught a train and LCpl 'Jock' Adams and big 'Bri' Heslop caught a cold!

At Endex the Troop was involved in a mini football tournament, finally winning by beating the Portuguese 8-2 after fine goalkeeping performances by Sig ' Oliver Tobias' Harris and 'Willy' Wilson. The recovery went smoothly, and the Troop moved on to 16 hrs leave before Ex Northern Trapper.

July 1985

249 Signal Squadron (AMF(L)) Bulford

Diary

The squadron has had a busy two months since our return from Norway at the end of March. After a well-deserved Easter leave and a hectic ten days preparation a full PRE inspection brought us down to earth! Sgt 'I can fix anything' McClune and the boys in the LAD nearly succeeded in doing the impossible. Nice try, next attempt in July. Early May saw the squadron playing host to 28 NATO officers and CO's of the AMF(L) for an annual bout of voice procedure and command post procedures instruction on Ex Clear Voice. Whilst the instruction proved straight forward, the Admin Officer 2Lt Nigel Godbolt spent most of the time tearing his hair out. Clear Voice ended on 7 May and the squadron moved to Okehampton for a weekend basking in the sun providing comms for Ex Ten Tors. Such was the popularity of the event that two German officers from 11 Fermeldebattalion and eight cadets from two of our sponsored CCFs joined us in ogling the young girls. Meanwhile in sunny Portugal one of our RATT detachments and its crew were providing a rear link to UK for Ex Ardent Ground 85. Having got the bug from Ten Tors, 2Lt Nigel Godbolt led a team of erstwhile runners around the Welsh 1,000. The team gave a very creditable performance considering they had only three days to train (in contrast to six weeks given to Maj Jonathan Cook when he was a subaltern!).

All is hectic again as the squadron prepare for Ex Albatross Exchange in Denmark in early June. The LAD is again working overtime and the 2IC keeps muttering 'Thank heavens I've resigned' every time an amendment is made to the Mov Order.

Exercise Clear Voice

Report by a frustrated Admin Officer

Under normal circumstances, the appointment of Admin Officer (course administrator?) incorporates a multitude of sins. Inject 28 NATO officers and NCO's, speaking five different languages and the formula for a few headaches emerges. Ex Clear Voice was run by 249 Sig Sqn from 30 April to 7 May; it is a biennial exercise to review voice procedure and standardise command post techniques for AMF(L) personnel.

Arrival at Bulford, be it either by private plane for one German Commandant or 'A Team' style minibus for the Belgian Special Forces, was accomplished in relative ease by Tuesday evening. A slight misunderstanding by an American Staff Sergeant, when told in his joining instructions to 'phone for collection from the station', did so from Victoria station. It was tactfully explained to him that although 'little ole' England was so much smaller than the US of A' he would still have to endeavour to get a little closer to Bulford before we could pick him up.

To increase the stress on the AO, the students were accommodated in four separate messes and a hotel. Using three minibuses, it was just possible to coordinate the collection and depositing of the course at the right place at the right time. So naturally, there were only two buses available leading to an increase in the Valium dosage and a potential patient for the shrink.

The opening address by the Comd I Sig Gp was duly translated by the interpreters into German, Italian, Belgian and Luxembourgese. This was to be the form at every time the course was addressed. A good grasp of English was obviously not high on their requirements for attendance! However, having an enjoyable time was, and to this end several social events were laid on. Included, were an English Pub night, a dinner night for the officers (revealing several diverse uniforms}, and a games night for the NCOs (revealing several diverse skills 'bottle walking' must be part of the Belgian Army' s basic training). The majority managed a weekend in London too, seeing the sights with our American friend managing to find the 'small corner shop called Harrods'! After three days of VP + AMF codes revision, their skills were put to the test in a 24-hour comms ex on Salisbury Plain. A mock battle was fought out over the air and to add to the realism, it was written into the instruction that the Italians withdrew, so to practise tearing down and setting up drills of course. The end of this exercise was also the end of the short course, and after a farewell buffet, the students went their various ways. However beforehand they passed on their appreciation to the Unit for laying on an unconventional exercise that went well and furthers our good relationships in NATO.

July 1985

244 Signal Squadron (AS)

Archway Express

With Bravo Troop off enjoying itself, Alpha Troop travelled to Turkey for an AMF exercise. Having despatched the vehicles by sea some 10 days earlier the Troop flew from Brize Norton to Istanbul, living on an airfield has some advantages.

Turkey proved to be a little outside the experience of most of the Troop but once we realised that the ever-present armed guards were protecting us and not imprisoning us, thing went well. During the early stages the Troop was involved in FAC training but found some time to visit the Black Sea coast and Istanbul. For most people, their first experience of bartering in the market proved great fun.

January 1986

249 Signal Squadron (AMF(L))

Exercise Archway Express

The camp in Turkey

Less than a week after the relay race, the advance elements of the Squadron were in Turkey providing a communications link between the various reception areas prior to the arrival of the remaining AMF. All ideas of deploying to a holiday resort were soon forgotten as the initial aircraft were surrounded by Turkish guards. After having successfully cleared the airport at Istanbul, coaches packed full of drivers completed a 'death ride' to meet up with the vehicles docking at a nearby port. The scheduled four-hour journey was completed in less than two by the cannonball style of the Turkish drivers. Vehicles were then moved along the few reasonable roads to the staging area, where, before long the whole force appeared. What was barren wasteland was gradually transformed into a heavily populated military area, surrounded by Turkish guards to keep away the curious.

This time proved to be the best of the exercise. The weather was hot, tempers were still kept under wraps, and for the majority it was a new and interesting country. However, as the novelty wore off, the dust started to grate on people's nerves, and the inevitable 'chuff charts' were started.

The exercise proper then filled the next fortnight leaving very little time for relaxation. During this period two of the newest vehicles in the squadron were rolled, one seriously. Although Sig Pete Gait was medically evacuated back to the UK, he was not seriously injured However. Shortly after the exercise phase, there were a couple days set aside for competitions and administration, prior to loading the boats for the return Journey.

Within 24 hours of Endex a Squadron team was crossing the start line in the defence of the NATO Challenge Cup. This Cup was last competed for, and won, by the Squadron in 1983. The competition consisted of a forced march carrying rifle and light order equipment followed by a simple shoot. The Squadron team of 26 led by Capt Frazer Grant performed exceptionally well on the march, beating all the minor units by at least nine minutes, and being beaten by only one major unit, the Ge Para Bn, by just 24 seconds. The shooting part of the competition was not so successful and although only marginally behind the leading team, the shooting tipped the balance. This left the Squadron holding the second place and unfortunately meant the loss of a cup from the trophy cabinet. However, the next day, was devoted to R&R and the majority of the Squadron were transported to Istanbul to see the sights. Although many presents. were bought, they were at wildly fluctuating prices, due to. the expertise of some hagglers. Many unusual incidents were witnessed, but perhaps the most outlandish was the sight of an Islamic extremist trying to persuade Cpl Petherbridge of the advantages of being a Moslem. Quite a difficult task from what we saw. Over the next few days all the Squadron were returned to Britain. Turkey started to fade into the background, as the prospect of another winter Norway loomed. Recces were sent to inspect their accommodation and training areas; meanwhile at home preparations started in earnest for another two months in the Arctic.

249's very own car wash

Volvo driver training - oops!!

July 1986

244 Signal Squadron (AS)

Exercise Hardfall and Anchor Express '86

Report by 2Lt 'Tiny' Coleman

With the Troop OC 2Lt 'Simon' Purser attending the Norwegian White shod course, it fell upon the large shoulders of 2Lt 'Tiny' Coleman to look after the Troop until 12 February, while being looked after himself by Sgt 'Terry' German. Force eight gales met us on deployment from Marchwood Military Port. Fine sailing weather! After an uneventful, but queasy crossing, the Troop arrived at the Brakanes hotel in Ulvik, co-habiting (that word again!) with 249 Sig Sqn. The one week's ski training proved trying for those of us who had not stood on 'NATO planks' before, the favourite downhill method being face first. The introduction of pulk pulling and wearing loaded bergens proving an additional hazard during the AST. The weather stayed reasonably cold and a good time was had by all.

The Arctic warfare training exercise provided a few amusing incidents, Sig Willy Wilson's impression of a human torch with a peak cooker being one. On being told to put him out Sig Woods tried to throw him out of the tent and not bother about the fire. A second incident was Cpl Douglas's local clearing patrol around the defensive position. It was out for four hours during which time it took out all the enemy positions for the other platoons. The other lasting memory will be of the 'flying' Doc, Capt Cade stitching a victim while standing up and with his skis on. The highlight of the hotel stay was 'A' Troop's victory in the 'Trivial Pursuit' competition.

21 February saw the Troop deploy north, a three-day cruise on board RFA Sir Lancelot, conditions this time being better than our previous trip. After the usual turmoil and confusion of docking and unloading we moved to the staging area south of Bardufoss. Deterrent ops lasted until 6 March giving time for practice moves for both TOCs. As we moved into combat ops the weather began to

deteriorate, mild with a lot of snow. This phase came to an abrupt end, due to the fatal avalanche on 6 March. The last few days were spent in Troop exercises. All in all, the Troop enjoyed itself with not too many 'Sophies'. Norway was an experience for a young officer to remember.

Right to left: Cpl Patterson, LCpl Hornsby, Sig White, Cpl Douglas, Sig Hawkins, Sig Jones

LCpl Adams - Engine Rider

November 1986

249 Signal Squadron (AMF(L))

Exercise Allegro Exchange

The Official View

This year's CPX "took place in north-eastern Italy. Every effort was made to keep clear of the tourist traps of Venice, the resorts and beaches, however, it was essential in the course of duty to travel via them on several occasions. The weather was more than kind to us for all but two days, and Sig 'Ugly' Richards relentlessly strove to prove his theory that clothing m excess of a pair of shorts was superfluous in such a clime.

We did, predictably, fall foul of the Italian drivers. Their habit of steering their vehicles and refusing to accept that anything could get in the way, is not compatible with the accepted manner of driving. Fortunately, the three accidents we incurred were all very minor. Cpl 'Nobby' Nevill glanced off a Fiat (the whole crew apparently woke with a start and answered a non-existent radio check), Rebro Reece suffered a Fiat to the wing with the 2IC Capt Andy 'No I was not driving' Higgs and Sig 'OK-I'll say I was' Edes on board. Lastly Sig 'Weeble' O'Brien disproved the adverts and did roll over, amazingly without a Fiat in sight.

The exercise was viewed by all as a success and was rounded off with an excellent barbecue run and attended by Support Troop. If the exercise was measured in the amount of kit 'traded' with our friends from America, then it was an all-time best. However, we have still to obtain the drivers manuals for the fleet of Chevrolets 'obtained'.

Exercise Allegro Exchange

The Unofficial View by LCpl 'Buck' Rogers

ALLEGRO 'Not-so-fair' EXCHANGE

'Twas peaceful in Italy, the night satin-smooth,
'til the crickets were drowned out by a scream 'Move-move-move'.
The farmer runs out to a terrible sight,

The British have descended on his corn fields by night.
He curses the flattening of the cobs he can't see,
not realising they've eaten the lot for their tea.
For with notional warfare, but genuine 'dets'
249 is out for the years CPX.
Armed with Chianti, Lambrusco, cheap plonk,
they observe ancient rites of Drive, Drink then Gonk.
Little suspecting the halcyon days
of sunshine and basking in Deterrence phase
would come to an end with a violent thump
as 'Combat ops' started when the Belgians got bumped.
The OC's tent blew up, a figure emerged
from the smoke, hair alight, shaking, bowels purged.
'Fetch me Sarn't Perry Quoth he 'within Five,
he reckons he's fixed it, but my gene's alive'.
An Italian colonel walked in thru' the smog;
'Haff you seen my driver? I t'ink ees called Slog'.
But Davey was sleeping at a different site,
blissfully unaware of his officer's plight.
The airwaves were buzzing, the battle was joined.
'Set up' meant 'Crash out' and locals annoyed;
for wherever they went, you could find them by dawn,
by following the trail of fields stripped of corn.
'Tis time' saith Vince Edes 'to prove we're not yokels.
to prove that we're cultured we'll drive like the locals'.
The 2IC gulped, his eyes showed his fear,
before he could speak, there was a crash from the rear.
A Mach Two Italian had spoilt Vince's plot,
and proved Iti' drivers are the worst of the lot.
At last came the order, 'time to stop play'.
Endex was called, it was back to UK.
Aeroplanes took off and Northwards they banked.
Italy raised its arms to the sky and gave thanks.
Except for the farmers who still get bad dreams,
in which they can hear the Satanic screams,
and they wake up still shaking from cardiac fright
if you shout 'Move-move-move' in their courtyards at night.

May 1987

249 Signal Squadron (AMF(L))

Exercise Hardfall (South) '87

During the months of February and March all the normal comings and goings in the Squadron ceased for the annual deployment to Norway. For many this provided continuation training and for the rest an introduction to Arctic training. This training was so intense that the continuation course was almost pushed out and replaced in the Hägglunds.

Ulvik

For the second year in succession the Squadron was based at the head of the Hardanger Fjord in the Brakanes Hotel, Ulvik. Although this is a small community all the locals were extremely friendly and helpful. However, it was disconcerting to find a Glaswegian Norwegian whose husband spoke with a Govan accent! South Wales and London were also well represented in the population.

Training

For the first two weeks YofS Terry Crosby was given the unenviable task of putting the Squadron onto skis. To help him he had a group of posey Military Ski Instructors, and to hinder him, NATO planks. For those individuals who excelled in the skiing, skins were presented, and for the 'Prima Donnas' snowshoes. The culmination of the ski training was the 10km Race and the 'Cook Pot'. The winner was YofS Terry 'The course setter' Crosby and the first novice was LCpl Terry Dowse who came in a very good 8th.

Now that the Squadron was mobile on skis and YofS HTB Elkan, Sgt 'Billy the Kid' Bull and Cpl Mick O'Brien had learnt to stand up, the Arctic Survival phase started. Lt Nigel Godbolt took Sgt Alec Sampson and Cpl Ozzy Osbourne (the video team) aside. The Squadron was then issued 100lb Bergens, a steep bill or two, and crash barriers to play with. It was at this point that the Squadron was renamed 249 Sig Sqn ASF (L-S), ACE Static Force (Land-Soft). During this all members of the Squadron, by Platoons, spent three nights out, sleeping in ridge tents, tent sheets and brushwood shelters. As an added bonus, three members of each Platoon volunteered for swimming lessons, wearing skis and carrying rucksacks. The next stage of the deployment was the Arctic Warfare Training. This involved the application of low-level tactics to the Arctic conditions and this was covered in two exercises. The first was an introduction to basic tactics, involving section battle drills, patrolling and the Platoon in defence. The final night of this phase was spent in a 'survival situation', in a real white-out living in snow holes and snow graves. Cpl Whacko Jackson and Cpl Dave Kennedy will verify the 'survival situation' after spending a frightening night watching the roof of their snow grave getting lower and lower as the safety patrols stomped around trying to find their entrance. The second exercise was Pronto Skirmish which allowed 249 Sig Coy to practise its newly learnt skills and fieldcraft and to provide Garibaldi biscuits for the visit of Maj Gen F Angioni, Comd AMF(L). It also gave Cpl 'Pathfinder' Waters the chance to create an amphibious snowshoe Platoon, which could cope with ice-floes on lakes in the dead of night.

The rest of the Platoon wish to stress that (L) stands for (Land). In order to qualify as Arctic Warfare Trained individuals had to compete a 20km Biathlon race for the Squadron's Richmond Trophy. This was won by Lt Mike Grimson, and the first novice was Sig Clinton from 244 Sig Sqn, closely followed by LCpl Charlie Challinor in 22nd place. On the last day of Pronto Skirmish Col C A Brown flew out to pay the Squadron his last visit as Comd I Sig Gp. During his tour he has given much time and attention to the Squadron and we are much indebted to him, and indeed to HQ I Sig Gp. Many thanks to all those who have helped us.

The final exercise of the deployment, Eagles Domain, allowed the Squadron a chance to return to the work of communications, and to provide an enemy Platoon for I Para. Over the five-day exercise in the area of Voss, the locals became accustomed to Heli-borne assaults, convoys of Volvos and the midnight para illuminating sun.

As well as the military training the Squadron also became involved with the local school, and a few other tasks. Shifting timber by Puma is a new sport and it has been heard that the Squadron clears a good area of brushwood.

Don't kick sand in my face!!

LCpl Tim Mackereth not even bothering to watch the 2IC Capt Wayne Coupland digging with an empty shovel

PR School Visits

During our time at the Brakanes Hotel the Headmaster and English teacher of the Brakanes School approached the Squadron with a view to helping out with their 'living English' lessons. Everyone backed off from the challenge except W02 (SSM) Gordon Shelley and Cpl 'Bob' Unsworth who visited four classes in all and had a thoroughly enjoyable time in the process. The format of each session began with a question-and-answer interlude and some of the questions proved very searching indeed!

What are the responsibilities of a Brigadier?

Do you like Norwegian girls?

Is the British Army food as bad as we have heard it is?

Can Mrs Thatcher ski?

Despite these the SSM bobbed and weaved and kept the party going explaining to the children that his job was to tuck up in bed each of the soldiers in turn and take them tea first thing each morning. After the classroom the children flocked outside and clambered over Cpl

Ian Crawford and Sig Jason Barsley as they sat in their detachment vehicle and queued for a ride in the Hägglund expertly driven by LCpl Annie Barker.

Don't Ask!!

September 1987

249 Signal Squadron (AMF(L))

Exercise Aurora Express

This year's southern option CPX took place in North Eastern Turkey in the Erzurum Kars area. It is a rugged, mountainous, inhospitable country, sparsely populated and with a very few roads or tracks. Despite the terrain and temperatures as high as 43°C, the Squadron once again excelled itself and produced excellent comms throughout the exercise.

Driver of the Exercise was a close-run competition, but Main Troop drivers were not found lacking, as they tried every way to win this award. Sig Vince Edes was at it again with Rebro Reece. On the first day he 'bogged' the vehicle (Yes, he really was driving this time), 9,000ft up a mountain and 25km away from the nearest village. After five hrs digging the vehicle was abandoned as he and the 2IC Capt Coupland walked through the night to arrange recovery. After some sleep the next recce mission was in a borrowed Land rover, which was returned the same day with a broken half shaft. After this offers of a Landrover were very sparse. Fortunately, 2Lt Bill Fathers was ready with a map and the LAD. In less than 24 hrs they managed to bog in two vehicles enroute and eventually recover the Rebro Reece vehicle from 'Death Valley'! The award for Diver of the Exercise must however go to Cpl Jim Brehner, for his route choice in difficult terrain. He bogged his Landrover Rebro in the middle of a fast-flowing river. The REME vehicle inspection later produced a list of 'A' jobs, not least of which as the comment 'remove rust from the dashboard!'. Well done Jim.

The locals were very friendly and showed us tremendous hospitality. However, there were a few notable incidents. Cpl 'Nobby' Nevill went missing with his Rebro for two days. When he eventually turned up there was some weak story of being chased by dogs and children. The efforts of Cpl Dave 'I'm posted soon' Anderson and his crew of 98C, LCpl Spick' Oldman and Sig Steve Cooke in fostering Anglo/Turkish relations were superb. They not only provided a 'Son et Lumiere' by allowing the local children to burn their cam nets, but they 'gave away' most of their kit. Guy ropes, respirators, magazines, webbing and shovel were all returned when a Turkish LO appeared a few hours later and threatened to punish the children!

Cpl Brehner's efforts win him 'Driver of the Exercise'

January 1988

249 Signal Squadron (AMF(L))

Kiwi Trophy

Avid reader of our news will know of the gruelling 20km biathlon held in Bulford every summer. Every fit member of the Squadron with 35lb Bergen and personal weapon for the coveted Kiwi Trophy. This year's competition in July saw a fine effort by most of the Squadron on a very hot day. Brig JOC Alexander, Comd Comms UKLF was present and presented the prizes. The overall winner with the fastest time and a very good shoot was Sgt Pete Gower.

Sgt Pete Gower is presented the Kiwi Trophy by Brig Alexander

NATO Challenge Cup

Report by Lt (now Mr) Nigel Godbolt

Once again, the Squadron entered a team in the NATO Challenge Cup biathlon competition this time held in Denmark. Following the success of winning the competition in Turkey in temperatures of 35C+ and 6,00ft up, the idea of entering the event in Denmark seemed relatively appealing. However, there were different Infantry Battalions competing in this one, including German Paras and Canadian Rangers.

With minimal training time but some promising shooting and zeroing figures, we entered a team of 40. From this list, the organisers trimmed off 14 names and gave us our final team list 24 hours before the event. The competition started 500m from a very unusual assault course, which the team completed in 11 mins with no penalties, we then continued immediately on the 15km run. Thankfully, it was relatively flat, enabling a good pace to be set and maintained. The team finished in 1 hr 18 mins, with everyone having given of their best. Top marks must go to LCpl Charlie Challinor for his facial contortions as he crossed the finish line. From here it was straight to the range which was controlled by an Italian section. Consistent shooting gave us a good score and high hopes of a favourable result.

At the prize giving the news was even better than we could have hoped for. Not only had we won the overall competition by a healthy margin but also the cup for the best team shoot. An excellent result by a minor unit not only beating all major units but all infantry units too. We are looking forward to defending our title in 1988 on skis in North Norway.

Cpl Terry Dowse appeals to heaven for assistance on the 'steps' of the Assault Course in the NATO Challenge Cup!

'Whose idea of a joke was this? WO 2 (YofS) Harry Elkan on the assault course

November 1988

244 Signal Squadron (AS)

Exercise Alley Express

by Cpl Andy Drummond

On Wednesday 7 September, five members of D Troop (MAOTs) deployed on this exciting and busy exercise taking place in European Turkey.

The five members formed two detachments, M8 and M10, the permanent AMF(L) detachments within the troop. The exercise was in four phases: deployment; deterrent ops; combat ops and having won the war, redeployment. However, when we arrived late at night at Corlu Military Airport, it seemed that the deterrent phase had been exempted and combat phase announced straight away. As we were all about co deplane, a warning was giving by a mover (everyone loves a mover) to watch out for snakes, scorpions, wild dogs and live marquee tent poles. Well, we all managed to survive the first night in the holding area all right, except for Sig 'Taff' Jones, who ran out of cigarettes through worry. There is an old saying 'never get separated from your kit'. Well, the next day saw us board a coach to join the Ship, which was bringing in our vehicle, and watch our kit go on a Turkish 4-tonner. It managed to find us four hours later. Units then deployed to the staging area for seven days of deterrent ops. D Troop MAOTs were kept very busy through this phase and not managing any R & R to Istanbul. Out at first light, to co-ordinate with the different nationalities, Turkish, American, German, Belgian, Luxembourg and others, in procedures for day and night landing sites.

Not only were they out on the ground with the troops, they also had to provide long range HF Comms back to A Troop at the HQ, VHF Comms to the patrols on the ground and UHF Comms to the AMF Forces Helicopter Unit. This provided some good experience to the new members of the Troop, Sig 'Pat' Gray and 'Liney' Cadman, who incidentally, because of his dark complexion was mistaken by a member of A Troop for a Turk when off duty. Some hard work by the lads went into the emplaning and deplaning of troops, and also with big artillery moves of three or four batteries of different nationalities. Not only were the detachments able to show off their helicopter handling qualifications, which they were taught by Cpl Andy Drummond before deploying, but for Sig 'Pat' Gray to practise his German, which he learned whilst at 202 Sig Sqn Paderborn. Seven days later, combat ops were called, and D Troop was still extremely busy. On one occasion, both teams were involved with a night move with 350 American Infantry by helicopter on a night LS, for the pick-up and drop off. Both sites were recce'd and set up by the two HHI Det Cdrs, Cpl Andy Drummond and LCpl Bri Ives. During this move, a surprise visit to both ends was made by a 4-star Turkish General, who was impressed by the efficiency of the move. There were three occasions when D Troop members thought they had done their job but ended up straight onto another.

Whilst returning from a fuel lift, M8 and M10 came across an RMP motor cyclist in a ditch, who was badly shocked after being run off

Apocalypse Now (Turkey '88) Sig 'Pat' Gray providing UHF comms

the road in a motor accident. Flt Lt P Kenned, Flt Lt K Whittaker and Sig 'Baz' Cadman attended him, whilst Sig Pat Gray called up the Italian Medevac Helicopter, which arrived within 20 minutes. During this time traffic was being co-ordinated by other members and a broken leg attended to by the three trainee doctors, who then helped to stretcher the cyclist to the helicopter.

Another occasion was when all members of the troop assisted A Troop with a firefighting team, when an American trip flare had accidentally set alight bushes.

The last occasion was when Sgt Barry Martin-Pitt from A Troop found the two dets with time to spare and gave them SA80 Drill under a cam net. The exercise flew by very quickly, the weather was hot except for Endex, when D Troop managed a morning at the Black Sea, no sunbathing here, force 8 winds, persistent rain and 12ft waves. Never mind.

November 1988

249 Signal Squadron (AMF(L)) Bulford

Exercise Ally Express

The squadron deployed to Turkish Thrace in September for Ex Ally Express. This was a chance to deploy for the first time with SA 80 and with our two new Mobile Satellite Ground Terminals. The following photographs reflect the Squadron during Deterrence Operations, Combat Operations and during R & R awaiting flight back to UK after Endex.

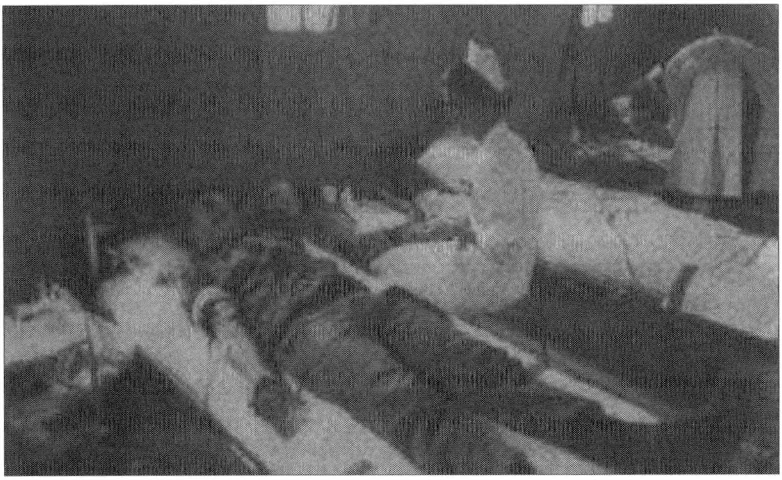

The Squadron responded well to a call for blood donors on the exercise. Sig 'Vamp' Evans seen here, nursing a private fantasy, donating a pint at the Italian Field Hospital

'The things that get left in engine compartments these days' . . . Cpl Tim Mackereth of the unit LAD keeps the vehicles going

The end of the run . . . Sig 'Happy' Phillips gives a triumphant salute or is it a Slope arms?

Sgt Jim 'Dundee' Weeks R Australian Signals, Sgt Steve Hughes, Capt Wayne Coupland and Maj Willie Bryant US Army prepare for a recce on the next location for Headquarters

The OC Maj Simon Kidner presents 'Jimmy' to the Comd AMF(L) Maj Gen Angioni to mark the General's last exercise with the AMF

'Get set! . . . Go!'. The Squadron team on its way to the third consecutive NATO Challenge Cup Competition, this time in North Norway. L to R: Sig 'Chalkie' White, Cpl 'Taff' Collinson, LCpl Harry Harrop and Lt Kim Evans

May 1989

249 Signal Squadron (AMF(L)) Bulford

Exercise Hardfall '89

To be absolutely frank, the Squadron never actually leaves Norway! The training year starts in March with the physical build up for the stresses and strains of Langlauf, and progressively increases throughout the summer. A short hiccup is experienced each September, albeit Italy, Turkey or Denmark, then it's into the final push and run-up for the Norway deployment period (January-March). So, the Squadron is either in Norway, just returned from Norway or gelling ready to go to Norway (or so it seems!). Once there, however, minds and bodies focus hard on ski training, BV206 driver training, military training and of course Arctic Comms training. Although it's not all hard work and no play, most of the members take their few R & R days on the downhill ski slopes of the Hangur in Voss.

LCpl Urquhart demonstrates the art of Arctic anti-gravitational training

May 1989

244 Signal Squadron (AS)

A Note from Sig Barker

I arrived at RAF Brize Norton on 15 August last year to be informed that I had been posted to Alpha Tp, AMF(L) of 244 Sig Sqn (AS). Several hours later I met my new roommate LCpl 'Billy' Taggart and received my first and probably most important piece of advice- 'Keep your mouth shut and eyes and ears open for the first six months and you'll be OK'! Next day I was woken rather abruptly at 0400 hrs (anyone who has ever lived approximately 100 yards away from an aeroplane runway will know why). After showering and finishing my block job – toilets - some things never change from training, I made my way down to Hangar 66, my new place of work. Remembering the advice I had received from LCpl Taggart I began my first day's work bright eyed and bushy tailed, being really polite and calling everyone by their rank, I was that worried about upsetting someone even the civilian electricians got addressed as 'Sir' or 'Sergeant' a couple of times. However, this was soon to end when I went to the Stores and Cpl Esson refused to acknowledge my presence until I called him 'Kev'. I enjoyed my first day in the Hangar and survived most of the practical jokes i.e., going to MT to get a hand generator serviced or to get a tin of patch paint. The next couple of weeks passed with me working in the Hangar and gradually trying to figure out the good guys from the bad (LCpl 'Tug' Wilson), whilst still trying to establish myself in the Troop. Then came my first test, a three-week exercise, Ex Ally Express 88 in Turkey. Another big difference from training, not having an exercise at Bishop Monkton or Catterick Training area. So, on 3 September 1988 I deployed on this very busy exercise along with my Det Comd, LCpl 'Slick' Simm and fellow crewman Sig Vera Duckworth. Over the next three weeks I was to learn a lot about the role of Alpha Tp in the AMF. It was interesting to see Dets and pieces of equipment at work that I had never seen in training, but perhaps most importantly I learned the rules of volleyball, which we seemed to play a lot in Turkey. Since Turkey the Troop has been busy having travelled a fair distance on exercise including Denmark, Norway and Italy - not one to be forgotten with such events as Sig Clint Barker getting run over and Sig Any Wiseman and Jase Moore getting arrested for a crime they did not commit - honest! Alpha Tp AMF(L) is a small Troop with only 24 people therefore everyone knows everyone else and it is a fairly close-knit workforce, which is kept in line in the single block by Cpls Andy Salmon and Mick Brown.

Exercise Hardfall 89 by LCpl Brynn Ives

January arrives again and it's time once again for MAOTs to deploy to Norway. LCpl 'Baz' Cadman to Brandset on an MSI Course. Cpl Gary Thomson, LCpl Pat Gray and Sig 'Jack' Frost to Ulvik for Arctic Warfare training. Cpl Andy Drummond, Sig 'Taff' Jones and myself to Bømoen for MAOT tasking. The deployment started slowly due to the distinct lack of snow but there was enough rain to cause Noah some worry! The MAOTs were used mostly in the training of other units and in PR exercises. One in particular stands out, using a Chinook to move a prefabricated hut for a Norwegian Biathlon. Spare time was spent by all downhill skiing at the hangar in Voss, under the expert guidance of LCpl Pat Gray, our very own JSDHSI. We all improved tremendously under his expert tuition. Once all the courses were completed it was time to turn our attention to the Brigadier's exercise involving all members of the AMF(L) British contingent. Unfortunately, due to bad weather the Hercules drop was cancelled, and the engineers bridge lift was brought forward and so the exercise passed quietly for the MAOT teams.

MSI Course - by LCpl 'Baz' Cadman

On 3 January, after an expensive Christmas leave, I was happy to be travelling out to Norway on a Ski Instructors Course. The flight out was up to its high standard of comfort on a Hercules (about 5 inches of leg room and almost sitting on the guy next to you).

We eventually arrived at Brandset Camp, a small Norwegian army camp out in the middle of nowhere, but at least it was warm and comfortable. The next day, we started on the ski training. A lot of skiing was done on flat ground which was tiring work, but we had a whole week of downhill skiing during the last third of the course (watch out Klammer). The course was shared with all the AMF(L) although most were RRF. I enjoyed it and was glad of the opportunity.

Arctic Survival Training (AST) - by Sig 'Taff' Jones

Day I: We set off bright and early from Ulvik and arrived at the training area around midday. We then skied up a large hill and had our first experience of the pulk. We spent the night in a 5-man ridge tent.

Day 2: We had another early start and we skied up yet another hill. We then saw a tent sheet demo, and yes, we then made our own tent sheets and had a pretty rough night's sleep.

Day 3: Back down to the bottom of the hill and then we had our survival night. This involved digging a snow shelter of some sort. Most people got soaked through to the skin, but we knew we were going in the next morning, so nobody cared. We then had about a week of ski training and Demos.

June 1990

244 Signal Squadron (AS)

Hardfall 90

On 3 January AMF(L) 'D' Troop deployed from RAF Lyneham by Hercules aircraft for Norway, expecting to meet up with our vehicles on arrival! However, they were 'lost' so LCpl Cadman, Sig Green, Sutherland and Wiseman were dispatched to look for them since 'they were definitely on the boat'! Ten days later they were found . . . at Marchwood Docks lined up and waiting to be loaded! After this delay, work began in earnest. Recces were undertaken so that helicopter night flying could take place in some of the remotest spots you could possibly imagine. The weather was abysmal which seriously curtailed night flying in the region so the two dets took turns in moving up to Hjerkenn in search of better weather and to assist the Force Arty in gun lifts. Sig Green was also detailed to provide safety comms from the site of a crashed Puma. The next move was to Granvin Docks to load the vehicles onto the boat for the Northern deployment. This time everything was going smoothly until Sig 'Wiz' Wiseman hit black ice which took his BV 206 (Vehicle) over the crash barrier and into the drink (Thank goodness they're amphibious!). In the North we joined up with other NATO allies and were soon busy working with German Huey's, Canadian Jet Rangers and British Gazelles and Pumas, although a lot of time was spent liaising with aircraft pilots. The redeployment went smoothly back to windy Blighty and everybody was happy to be home.

August 1990

249 Signal Squadron (AMF(L)) Bulford

Personalities

OC	Maj Peter Neale
2IC	Capt Jim Richardson
QM	Capt Bill White
SSM	W02 John McCaffery
FofS	W02 John Hoyland
YofS	W02 Pete Barron
Trg YofS	SSgt Steve Brant
SQMS	SSgt John Parrish
Ch Clk	SSgt (ORSQMS) Richard Warne

NATO Challenge Cup

The NATO Challenge Cup was a ski-biathlon in Northern Norway the scene of our previous victory. Our running and fitness had never been in doubt, beating all comers in Denmark and Turkey but shooting had been our weakness. The team was selected from over 50 volunteers.

The victorious NATO Challenge Cup Team with Comd AMF(L) Maj Gen Carstens

Came race day, we had 26 lean and mean Arctic Warriors. Starting fifth out of 17 teams we soon went ahead and were soon in third fastest position behind 2RRF and a Coy from an Italian Alpini Bn. In the shoot phase we gained 113 points out of 120 from 200m which gave us enough points to take the non-infantry trophy back to Bulford. Well done to all who took part.

AWT Course

After completion of the AWT last year, six members of the Squadron, Lt's Hill, Evans, Sgts Pollard, Waters, Cpls Ormerod and Kemp were selected to 'volunteer' for an Arctic Warfare Instructors course in Norway. The course was run by the resident AMF Infantry Bn, 2 RRF supervised by the Royal Marine Mountain Leaders. It soon became clear that this was no 'attendance pass' course. Powers of leadership, ability in map reading and instructional qualities not to mention physical fitness were needed here.

The course consisted of two weeks 'Dryshod' in UK and four weeks 'White shod' in Norway. The Dryshod phase was the classroom phases, being lectured and lecturing the order of the day. Success in this phase saw you on your way to Norway and Part 2 of the course. Happily, we all went on to Part 2. Tests started from the moment we reached our destination after a 24-hr journey, until the day we finished the course. During our time in Norway, we were given various tasks to complete and we spent nine nights out in the field in bell tents, tent sheets (still as bad as they were 40 years ago), snow holes and then finally a survival night (perhaps tent sheets aren't so bad after all).

December 1990

244 Signal Squadron (AS)

Alpha Troop

The year began once again in the frozen wastes of Central and Northern Norway. Throughout eight weeks deployment there were many notable moments, but none more so than the courageous efforts of the Alpha Tp Ski Team. Certainly Cfn Gaz Paterson, Sig CJ Barker, LCpl Jase Foulger and Lt Ade Clewlow demonstrated many new styles of Alpine Skiing.

Just home from the Arctic and many of the Troop flew to Cyprus for deployment in Air Support Communications. After extremes of Arctic and Mediterranean climates within a month, the Troop deployed to Baumholder. The location was a large training area and range for the 75,000 US Servicemen and dependants based in the town. Located south of the Mosel Valley, the Troop provided air support communications for Ex Ardent Ground 90, a NATO Artillery and Offensive Support live firing exercise.

Whilst there, the Troop discovered a life-sized statue of 'Jimmy' in the nearby town; held two barbecues and had five days R & R at the end of the exercise! One adventurous group, otherwise known as LCpl Hayes, Sig Chick, Deary and Cfn Gaz Paterson, went off to Amsterdam. The second team spent a more relaxed two days in Krefeld with 16 Sig Regt.

Sig ' Foxy' Clink, Will Dryden and Chris Clayton travelling north through the Arctic Circle

Never trust an ED to check your wheel nuts!

THE CHANGING WORLD 1991 TO 2003

1988 to 1995 - Clint Barker - 244 Signal Squadron (AS)

I joined the AMF(L) or 'Amesbury Muppet Force' or 'Ain't My Fault (Lads)' in 1988 as an 18-year-old, straight from training, and left in 1995 as a 25-year-old full screw. I was part of Alpha Troop AMF(L), 244 Sig Sqn (AS) which I had joined mainly on the advice of my brother who had been in the same Troop some five years earlier (deploying to the Falkland Islands). 'You won't find a better place to start your career' he told me - and he was right.

Within two weeks of turning up at RAF Brize Norton I was on exercise in Turkey and so began the whirlwind of exercises abroad.

At RAF Brize Norton

Within my first 12 months ticking off not only Turkey, but Denmark, Italy, Belgium, Germany and of course Otterburn training area. The exercises being 'Deterrent Operations' or 'Det Ops', essentially 10 days of wearing 'civvies' to show the host nation country that you were there to help them, usually by raising the profits in the local bars, and then moving on to 'Combat Operations' or 'Combat Ops' - the same as 'Det Ops' but with a Cam net!

Roughing it on the beach in Turkey

My first story comes from an exercise in Italy on Det Ops. The saying 'Time spent on Recce is often wasted', well sometimes the reverse can be true. Working at the time on a 3-man FAC det we were given a 'goose egg' to deploy to and set up comms – arriving (as is often the case) around midnight we found a decent spot with what was we though good vision looking out to sea to get 'eyes on' the fast jets as they came into the exercise area. We were woken about 10 o'clock the next morning (it was Det Ops!) by local police informing us that we had set up on a beached area approximately 400 metres down from a popular beach tourist area. They weren't bothered that we were there but were just checking that we were happy. We were, and we spent six days there with daily resupply of Pizza and Vino as our fresh rations.

Prior to going to Norway, we were 'encouraged' to use 'Pusser's kit' i.e., everything that you would need but wasn't yet issued as it was in subsequent years. The biggest outlay before a Norway trip was your ‘Cotswold Camping’ bill as you bought a load of kit - Helly Hansen 'lifa' undershirts, Yeti Gaitors, Ajunkalak Sleeping bags and so on.

Like many people who have been in the AMF(L) I still have a fondness for Norway and the Hardfall deployments, for me this is what being in the AMF(L) was all about. In total, I did seven Hardfall deployments to Norway, four of them ‘long’ ones moving ‘up North’ to Tromso and an additional two ‘Winter trips’, one to do my MSI course and one to do my AWI course – hunting the trophy of the ‘white balaclava’.

On my AWI course – notice the White Balaclava!!

The issued hat was the 'Hat Arctic ECW (Extra Cold Weather)' which was very effective, however, to stand out from the crowd all the AWIs wore white balaclavas, usually rolled up in a particular way to look cool. I have no idea if this was a direction from the Mountain and Arctic Warfare Cadre of the Royal Marines, who basically ran the show when it came to Arctic Stuff or if the AWI's did it just to look good. Anyway, it was a source of amusement winding up the AWIs who insisted that you had to 'earn the right' to wear the White Balaclava! - 'the right' being having attended the AWI course.

After my first Norway I attended my Military Ski Instructor (MSI) course which I successfully passed, and so my 'job' for the first 4 weeks of my next Norway was teaching the guy's basic skiing. On my course there were 3 other Signals guys, all from 249, and I think we decided (one night in the bar probably) that when we went to the next Norway that we would also wear the coveted 'White Balaclava' having completed the MSI course. We did this initially just to wind the AWIs up, and it worked. When we started wearing the white balaclava's the AWIs were not happy.... but it stuck!

A few years later I did my AWI course with a guy from 244, Ivor (Jim) Hawkins. There was already another AWI in the troop, Gethin (Taff) Thomas. He was a great guy and completely 'Norway crazy' and a bit of a Marine Groupie. Taff made it known that when we went to Norway, he was the 'senior' AWI. Jim and I were not fussed, but we decided to write up a memo on Royal Marine headed paper and even falsified the signature of the Mountain and Arctic warfare conducting officer at the time. Basically, we sent this letter to the 'Senior AWI of each unit (clearly we only actually sent it to Taff). The memo or letter laid out a long 'dress code' that AWI's had to adhere to including stuff like the white balaclava with the small metal rank slide pinned to it, mini temperature gauge attached to left gaiter. I think we even said that a white 'dot' had to be worn by the senior AWI on his jacket rank slide. Taff fell for it and the first 'parade' on the car park at the Stalheim Hotel he came out with all this paraphernalia hanging off him. It took him a while to realise he had been wound up!

During the Southern deployments of Hardfall I spent my first two years at the Ulvik Hotel, my next two at the Stalheim, the following year at Bømoen Camp near Voss, the next at Maurset Chalets and my last year at Hagatun. For the Northern deployments my time was split between Tromso Air station and Hjerkenn Ranges (apparently one of the Star Wars films was shot there).

The mandatory Emergency Ice Drills

A couple of light-hearted Norway memories. Firstly in 1992 I was helping out on a Nordic Survival Ski Course being run for 33 Sqn RAF, who provided the Puma Support Helicopter role. As part of the four-day course the RAF guys had to do one night in snowholes. One of my jobs was to do the rounds in the early hours of the morning making sure that all was ok and of course that someone in the snowhole was on 'Candle watch' those that know, know the pain of being on candle watch!

Happiness is a warm Snowhole

About two in the morning, I shuffle up the excellent tunnel that had been built in this particular snow hole to find pretty much as expected, four guys fast asleep (warmest night you'll ever spend, apparently) and one guy sat bolt upright reading his Arctic Aide Memoire on Candle watch, except this particular RAF chap, ever resilient, was on 'Cyalume Watch'. A few minutes into his shift the candle had run out, he hadn't a candle of his own and didn't want to wake anyone so had 'improvised, adapted and overcame' by using one of his Cyalumes, which he diligently stared at every couple of minutes. I asked him 'what did he think the aim of candle watch was' to which he replied 'to make sure at least someone is still awake and it gives you something to concentrate on', I guess he was half right but it didn't stop a quick run around the Snowhole area for him and his tent group!

A good example of how, on the Hardfall exercises, you would be constantly bumping into people over the course of the months you were there. I was, at the time, on a MAOT detachment with a guy called Mark Wyldes, laying out Helicopter Landing Sites all over the place. We were pretty much free running. This exercise was up North, and we were laid up for a couple of nights in a disused quarry (always seemed to be a disused quarry!). On the second night an old friend of ours turned up, Cpl Kev O'Neill. Kev had been my first det commander in the Squadron but had been posted and now worked on the AMF(L) TACP. Again, a free runner doing the FAC 'stuff' with his boss. After a quick chat with Kev, we helped him set up his five-man ridge tent and then he had to shoot off, working. About an hour later Mark and I got the call we were moving and had to be ready to go in an hour. We packed up in 30 minutes and had some time to spare. It seemed like a good idea at the time, so we decided to fill Kev's tent with snow as a little surprise for when he got back. 'What could possibly go wrong' we thought as we redeployed. What we didn't know is that Kev was getting bounced around all over the place that exercise, and after having been on the go for thirty-six hours, he returned with his boss to get a couple of hours kip before himself having to redeploy. Imagine Kev's surprise when he unzipped his tent to find a five-man ridge tent ...of Ice! Kev had to leave the whole thing there with his new boss not impressed by the childish antics of Kev's 'mates'. All we heard over the radio chatter for the next four weeks was that Kev was going to absolutely kill us when he got hold of us, and he did when he finally caught up at the movement centre at Tromso. We were about four hours from safety, but of course our VC10 got cancelled! We're all still friends. I could go on, but I won't!

I had the best of times and met the best of people, whom I still consider great friends today. Even now, if I bump into someone who I have never met but they were in the AMF(L) there are stories to be told and a shared experience......good times.

Turkey 91... this was the Forward Helicopter Unit detachment we had from A Tp

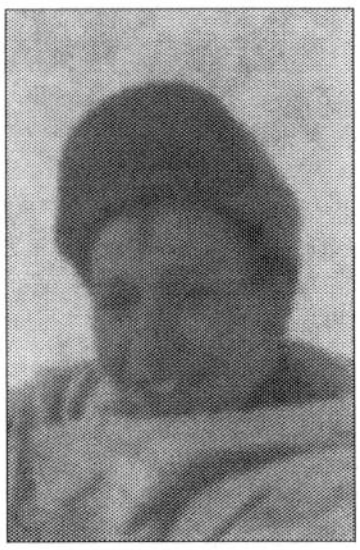

1989 to 1992 - Mark Haworth - 249 Signal Squadron

I joined the Squadron in 1989 and the Officers in the Squadron, that I remember were: OC Major Oldfield, Lt Duggan, Capt Hill, Capt Munro, QM Capt Bill White, FofS Bill Erskine and SSM Taff George.

In 1992 I took part in the Arctic Warfare Instructor (AWI) cadre course which was for experienced members of the squadron who were candidates for the AWI qualifying course. Two of the instructors were Sgt Dick Malt and Cpl Kev Read. The course consisted of 1 night in ridge tents, 1 night in tunnel tents, 1 night in

AWI Cadre Course 1992

tent sheets, 1 night in snow holes and 1 night in snow graves. Snow graves weren't a usual shelter for Arctic training, this was the first and last time I used this type of shelter. Everybody on the course carried a bottle of "Black" (Norwegian beer) for the last night. I have no idea how far we skied but we were fully loaded and traversing down a very steep slope with a frozen lake at its base, Stu Bull got fed up kick turning and traversing, turned down hill and got into the egg, he held it to the bottom where he instantly stopped as he reached the severe gradient change of the lake, he left a perfect impression in the snow. The last day saw -36 and evacuation off the

AWI Cadre Course 1992

Ski Race start 1991

hill by Snowcat.

Another story involved Paul Drysdale who got frost nip in both thumbs and both thumbs split and had to be stitched. We used to wear two sets of gloves as a minimum, contact gloves (we couldn't touch anything metal as we would likely stick to it and rip off skin} and thick mittens with trigger finger holes, additional gortex gloves were also used when needed. Hands and gloves needed to be kept as dry as possible to avoid frost nip and even worse frost bite. I am guessing his hands simply got wet and the rest is history. After a couple of days, the stitches came undone and fell out. Paul got transport to see the duty medic, he knocked on the duty room and explained about needing stitches. The bloke from the duty bunk cut some thread and Paul grimaced as the thread was pushed through the same holes. With this done on both thumbs Paul was asked "Do you know how to tie the knots?", Paul was confused and asked why he was being asked. "I'm only the duty driver the duty medic is at scoff". He was eventually sorted out by the medics.

Ice breaking drills were to simulate emergency action on falling through broken ice. Attached to a safety rope and with a bergen on

Ice Breaking Drills 1990

one shoulder we skied into the ice hole. The drill is to exit in the direction of entry as the ice here is known to be solid as you have just skied over it. In the ice breaking drills to ensure you are in the water for longer you are made to ski in, ditch bergen, recover skis, swim to the end, and then exit using ski poles. Then you roll in the loose snow to remove water and run to a warmed tent to change. By this time your legs are blue.

Noise and Light demo

Noise and lights demo's were carried out to demonstrate how noise and light travel at night. This is not specific to Norway as these demo's are done on numerous courses. However light especially is different in Norway due to reflection from the snow.

For this noise and lights demo however we were due to spend the night in ridge tents. We skied to the demo and once it was over we were told "your shelters have been destroyed by the enemy and you now need to survive for the night. We carried enough in our smock pockets to survive for 24 hours. This was the coldest night of my life huddled under a cornice out of the wind. That night was 'Beyond Cold'.

1992 to 1993 - Tony O'Toole - 249 Signal Squadron

I was posted away from 244 Signal Sqn (AS) early in August 1992 upon disbandment and was posted to 249 Signal Sqn (AMFL) at Ward Barracks, Bulford. I was allocated to Main Troop commanded at that time by Lt DJ Duggan and the Squadron Commander was Maj Oldfield. I was married at the end of August

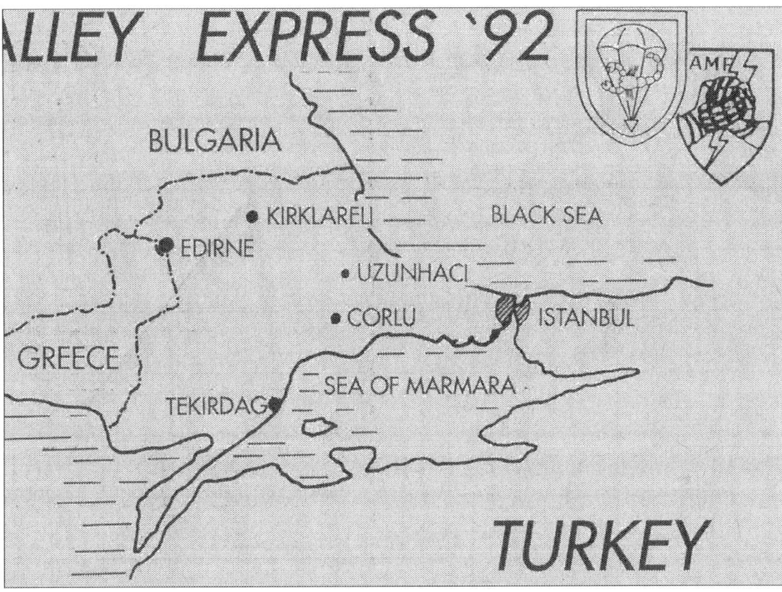

and then went to Turkey to take part in Exercise Alley Express 92.

During part of the exercise our two-man Key det, crewed by myself and LCpl 'Macker' were attached to the AMF(L) Support Helicopter Unit to provide force wide comms while A Troop of the old 244 Sig Sqn (now with 21 Sig Regt (AS)) were co-located with the RAF to provide their dedicated comms. Early in the evening of the 28th September 1992 I was manning the AMF secure force wide net when I heard German troops talking about a serious multi casualty accident on another net, describing how they had come across a serious RTA where a lorry had gone over and crushed a number of people. The Italians were providing medical cover for the AMF and had a detachment of ambulance dedicated Huey`s but they could not be raised on the net, we suspected because it was mealtime, so I went over to the RAF 33 Sqn AMF(L) detachment which flew Puma`s and mentioned the problem, asked if we could help and as an ex RAMC Combat Medical Technician I offered my services as a medic in the back. By now it was starting to get dark.... and they had no night vision goggles plus the maps were seriously out of date, especially regarding power lines etc, but despite their reservations, the RAF agreed to give it a go, so I got onto the net, told the German`s we were on our way, got their location and then boarded the Puma.

The crew of the Puma were an RAF Flt Lt and a Sgt 'Loadie' (who was an ex Royal Marine) and in the back with me was an RAF medic who had agreed to come too. Flying to the location at low level, night soon set in and we were all crowded around the cockpit with eyes out on stalks looking for power lines and helping with the navigation, we even passed over a motorway which was not on the ancient map but thankfully we were lucky with power lines and managed to spot them. Arriving at the RTA we were met by a scene of utter carnage! A German doctor and medic had triaged the most seriously injured and the RAF medic and I double checked them before loading as many as we could carry into the back of the Puma. The floor was slippery with blood as we worked on the casualties once airborne and one had a seriously crushed skull which felt like jelly. He continuously stopped breathing during the flight and I had to resuscitate him a number of times. The back of the Puma was pitch black but between us we dressed wounds and kept the civilian casualties as calm as we could despite the language barrier.

Upon arrival at the hospital the only place we could land was the car park but it was surrounded by tower blocks so we had to transition to the hover quite high up at around 500 feet and then descend down slowly. To help the pilot the 'Loadie' opened the side doors so that he could look out and spot any danger.... but upon opening the door one casualty got up, thinking we had landed and was just walking out of the door into the blackness when I reached up, grabbed the back of his belt and pulled him back! When he realised his mistake, he looked even more ashen than he already was! One thing which sticks in my mind about our descent, as we slowly dropped into a floodlit area between the tower blocks, was an old Turkish lady with a headscarf and peasant like clothing stood on her balcony, bashing the hell out of a dusty old carpet and not even looking at us as our Puma helicopter passed within what seemed feet of her!

Anyway, we landed.... we were helped by hospital staff to unload the Puma and we rushed them into the hospital... which I remember thinking at the time was white tiled and quite dirty and resembled an old public toilet!

Climbing back into the Puma, it was quite gory inside with blood-stained bandages and dressings and slimy with blood, but we were pleased that we had not lost anybody and had `done our bit'. The pilot and 'Loadie' were magnificent, their flying was outstanding, but we now had to return to base, so more 'eyes on stalks' in the pitch black as we map read our way back.

I was pleased that we didn`t lose anybody, but I felt mentally and physically drained afterwards, when the adrenalin rush wore off. When I crept back into the 9x9 tent on the back of our Landrover Macker asked how it went, and then let me get my head down on the camp bed for a few hours before it was time to stag on the net again.

Next day, the 33 Sqn RAF lads asked if I fancied going out with them for a few hours as a `co-pilot' for a treat and Macker kindly agreed to man the net while I was away. We flew for around 4 hours ferrying artillery, troops and conducting abseiling training for the Belgian Para Commando`s, all in all a trip that I will always covet, we even flew in formation with 4 German CH-53`s and 3 RAF Puma`s.

To finish off, the Turks threw a big party for the top brass and officials to celebrate the exercise and our crew were invited to attend at the top table as guests of honour! My crewmate agreed `again' to stag on and cover the net, but our SSM, `Taff' George, was not impressed with me... a mere Siggy... attending and tried to stop me going! Anyway, I went, had quite a bit of Raki as our glasses were topped up by very smart looking Turkish Army waiters every time, we took a sip and we had to eat sheep's eyeballs, a local delicacy which the crew`s pilot insisted that we had to eat as otherwise we would offend our hosts, arghh!

Back at Bulford, I was informed after a few weeks that my name was on South East District Orders as I had been recommended for an award by Alpha Troop and the 33 Sqn RAF AMF(L) Detachment. I duly received a Commendation awarded by the GOC South East District. I would like to say that I received it in person, as you used to see in Soldier magazine, but for some reason the Squadron would not allow me to travel to Aldershot to receive it in person and I was duly handed it on a Monday morning works parade back at Ward Barracks instead. The lads were happy for me but the Sqn hierarchy did not seem very happy about it at all, all very strange? The RAF Pilot sent me a lovely letter from the officers' mess at RAF Odiham congratulating me on my award and I received some letters from the top brass, which was nice too.

I was involved in another Casevac during the Lanyard Trophy in Wales which involved calling in a Sea King for one of our lads who fell off a mountain in a Landrover when his wheel hit a rock and tipped him over! His Rover, which we had just got out of, rolled over off the track and rolled down the mountainside, spinning in the air as it went with bits flying off everywhere! He was thrown out half way down but I missed him at first and ran right past (there were lots of parts flying off like the doors, wheels etc) as I chased the wreckage until it finally landed in a stream! After climbing in to see he wasn`t there, I stated running up and down the steep debris field until I eventually found him sans a few fingers and with his neck broken! By this stage I was injured too as my knee cap had dislocated! Anyway, I got a lad to run to a phone box and get help. Using my previous Combat Medic experience, I sorted his neck out by splinting it using a map and some clothing as a neck brace and then the Royal Navy Sea King thankfully arrived to take us to hospital at Abergavenny, having heard there was some bother on the radio net. Afterwards I heard that the injured lad, who needed emergency surgery following my first aid, had a metal framework drilled into his skull and neck!

Despite being recommended for promotion previously at 244 I still wasn`t recommended for promotion in my next Troop Commanders report mind you. Ah well, it`s nice to be appreciated! In the summer of 1993, I was posted to 19 Mech Bde HQ & Sig Sqn at Catterick.

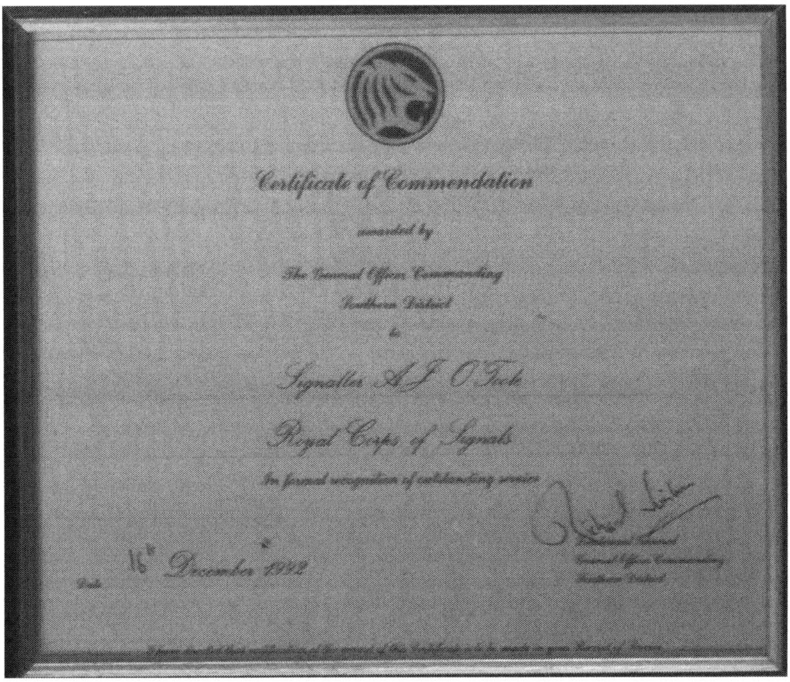

002-GOC'S COMMENDATION
SIGNALLER A J O'TOOLE R SIGNALS

The GOC commends Signaller A J O'Toole 249 Signal Squadron AMF(L) for his actions on 28 Sep 92 when on exercise in Turkey.

He volunteered his services to assist in the rescue and air evacuation of five Turkish civilians who had been seriously injured in a traffic accident. The evacuation took place at night by PUMA helicopter in very difficult conditions. Without Signaller O'Toole's initiative and care, at least one of those rescued would probably have died before reaching hospital.

The GOC directs that an entry be made on his documents in accordance with Queen's Regulations Chapter 5 Annex H.

(Ref: 200702 MS)

Tony O'Toole - Turkey 1992 the day after the Casevac and now ready for the `Jolly' flight.

1995 to 1998 - Rich Simpson - 244 Signal Squadron (AS)

I started fresh out of training as a Radio Telegraphist, Tele Op Tg, and was posted into Alpha Troop, 244 Signal Squadron, 21 Signal Regiment (AS). I served in the Troop from 1995 to 1998 and was 22 years old when I was posted in. I was employed initially as a basic signaller within the FHU and ended up after 3 years as a LCpl Det Commander of MAOT 1.

The garages were a mixture of the old series 3 petrol Landrovers and 110s that were winterised, though one I remember wasn't and that is the one I was given. Obviously, the Hägglunds Hotel vehicles were what was drawing my eye. I would have to wait a while before that would become my detachment. Painting the wagons was a pretty standard job, we had to put a hefty dose of kerosene in with the paint in order to give it a good shine, which I thought defeated the idea of camouflage! However, that is what the Cpls wanted, especially 'Wooden tooth Scotty'. Scrubbing the vehicle and trailer springs wasn't one of my favourite jobs. I remember getting bollocked for probably being cheeky and sarcastic, I had to pick up a turf-winch and hold it above my head whilst running around the hangar. The SNCO's were bastards! I knew after that to keep my distance from them. However it wouldn't be the last time I got beasted.

We spent a long time learning the Arctic safety rule (act like natives always stuck with me) and ways to spot cold weather injuries. Every year we would go to some hideous training area to practice arctic warfare drills before heading out to Norway on Ex Hardfall and onto the full-on AMF exercises. One year, in preparation, we went to Dartmoor and the first night navigation was disastrous. Out of the back gate from that camp on the moor, it was raining hard and it was quite misty too, we were doing okay then I think that one of the blokes, Matt Lavender I think, walked into a puddle but it was so deep he had to be dragged out! Shortly after at some random craggy area we were ordered to get into any shelter and get into our bivvy bags, by now we were all pretty wet and cold and getting into the bags wasn't questioned. Not sure what was going on, whether someone was missing or what, we were in our bags a long time, it was warm and when the order came to get out and crack on it was not welcome at all.

Wet tents and eventually water flowing through them, as we were told where to pitch them rather than choose ourselves, meant that a nearby stream swelled and went into our tent, I remember turning over and then spluttering on the freezing water. Not good.

Getting to Norway was amazing, first time on skis and I was doing it on army planks. Skiing with webbing (had to get ourselves a chest rig) bergen and rifle was not easy. Then we had to drag pulks. Going uphill was okay but going down was suicide as none of us could snow plough effectively enough to slow it down and so the call of 'you're on your own!' meant that a very heavy pulk was about to run over the top of you or, at best, whip you around and make a very uncomfortable end.

I remember digging in the section tents for what seemed like all day. We were mostly happy with that as it kept us warm. Then came digging the comms trenches and fire positions. Stag-on, standing on bracken that was supposed to insulate our feet (still in leather ski-march boots) from the wet snow and ice. Stagging-on was quite hard, we only did 45 mins, I think, so that we didn't freeze to death, but it did mean that sleeping in the tents was always disturbed with people shuffling in and out of their doss-bags. We were all highly drilled in tent admin, and took a bit of grief from the Cpls, but we all became a slick team. As a sprog I had to stay up to prepare the hot flasks and then get up early to heat up the flasks and get the brews on first thing in the morning.

Arctic safety training was great! I loved doing the snow shelters, using the gollock knife to cut bracken and ice blocks and to pretend to shave with. The actions on avalanche prone slopes was something that I was worried about. In our somewhat extensive pocket contents we had to tie about 20 metres or so of red para cord, then put in overhand knots getting steadily closer together as they are closing in on my jacket, the reason being is when skiing across avalanche prone slopes the order to 'deploy av-cord' would be given and so the cord would trail behind us. We would be at least 20 metres separated and if we were to be swept away by an avalanche, not a problem as we would be found in a jiffy by merely locating the prepared cord! Absolutely not convinced about that whatsoever. Nowadays of course we are all issued with electronic transceivers. I do know that some soldiers were told to wear every bit of clothing they had, get sandwiched in between two roll mats so that we could try to find them with our av-probes. This took ages and the unfortunate individual (normally one who was on a biff-chit) must have been so cold. That must have been cold but not as cold as survival night. On our training we spent a good bit of time digging a Quinzee shelter, a day or so later during our training we had our bergens taken off us and told that we were now in a survival situation and that we were told to stay in this area for 24 hrs. Our pocket contents were now all we had to survive on for that period of time, along with our gollock. So for a relatively short period of time we were okay whilst cutting bracken/branches for insulation. We had our candles (edible too apparently but I never did trust them) for us to do candle watch whilst inside our shelters. It was the longest, coldest night ever! Our survival blankets didn't hold much heat, these were the old fashioned type, basically a huge clear bin bag. Staring at the candles, watching each one burn out and pathetically trying to get heat into our hands, exercise extremities (another one of the rules that stuck with me) all the time. We took turns to go outside and see if daylight was appearing. It seemed like a week before the sun made an appearance but when it did, it did spur us on a bit, but only a bit, we had to wait for an age for the DS to turn up and give Endex.

From that we went into the 8-man tent, luxury! The naphtha Coleman cookers went on, the naphtha Coleman lamp went on and the heat was amazing! Next morning 'Pull Pole'! We were already on our packed bergens and burst into action, packed away the kit and bungled it into vehicles to Voss and onto the lake to conduct the ice breaking drills. Plenty of views of that, we had to slide into the freezing water and swim to the other end, dunk our heads, answer questions then drag ourselves out using our ski poles. I remember my fingers being too cold to clench and take the cam whites off, I had to get the helper to do it for me.

We were given the next day off to recover, the duty rumour going around was that doing the ice dunking takes days/weeks/years off your life so the Army was being really generous by allowing us a day's grace! More skiing ensued, night skiing was always an amusing affair, the instructors saying that we should stay close and to simply follow his red cyalume attached to the back of his pack. He would say count to three then set off after me, we would then watch into the darkness this little red light bobbing up and down through the Norwegian wilderness to ultimately disappear out of view, a few soldiers went off, then a few more, then myself only to end up seconds later in a pile of mangled bags, skis, legs, arms and weapons in a frozen stream bed. So frustrating but also insanely funny at the hopelessness of it all, the instructor was not happy having to retrace his ski tracks to find us all in an entangled mess.

We did eventually get to grips with the skis and arctic warfare skills and became quite a satisfying way of soldiering, keeping warm was the main issue but at least we were clean. Temperate soldiering was always a filthy affair digging in mud and forests etc but in snow, it was fine. We were able to patrol and set up ambushes, conduct recce's, live and survive in pretty inhospitable terrain.

After the arctic training we moved onto the actual comms support for the annual Hardfall exercise. I spent the first couple of years in the Force Helicopter Unit (FHU) as a basic Siggy. We actually started the radio nets using just morse code, insecure RaTT then eventually onto voice nets. The comms for the training serials down south Norway were always pretty comfortable as they were in proper buildings with comfy chairs and heating with good scoff. I always remember listening to the radio schedules from the 249 Sig Sqn boys stuck up somewhere high up, sounding freezing in their trailer dets, "really cold here, tent has rips...oh can we get more bog roll?" Oh, how I laughed when we had to tell them that the weather window had closed and the next flight wouldn't be for a couple of days.

I had to laugh when one day I went back to my room, which I shared with Chris Bradshaw, to find that all my kit, bedding, chair...everything was taped to the ceiling and walls! Brad was always good like that!

The move up to north Norway was excellent. It was a fairly short drive to the port of Ulvik. We then boarded the boat which looked like a full-on cruise ship, only to find that all carpets were covered over, all the shops and restaurants were closed and more drastically all the bars were closed too. All that we had was a two can rule and the TV's playing constant videos, Independence Day was all that stuck in my mind so must have been 1996. Outside though the views were stunning as we had a free cruise up the Norwegian Fjords. It did get rough though for 2 or 3 days before we stopped at Narvik up north and got the vehicles off. I remember still staggering around on dry land with my body still thinking that it was still on the rocking boat.

Driving to the exercise area where the FHU would be exciting. The RE had bulldozed down to permafrost for a flat area for the FHU tents. Pallets were put down, coconut matting on top of that then the 18x24 tents with the thick white insulation liners on the inside giving a bright feel to the place. It was still freezing though sat on the detachment chairs for your 8hr shifts. I do recall the day when the RAF brought in a gas heater but instead of standard gas, they used aviation fuel, wow, that thing glowed red hot, it was amazing for about a day when we realised that the permafrost was melting rapidly and the pallets were floating around. So, we had to turn it off and went back to freezing for the rest of the exercise.

During the hours off we did have to take turns on stag, we dug our positions through the high snow walls that were surrounding the FHU site. This tunnel inspired us to create our own crew room, so we spent a good deal of time digging out a sizeable area in the snow bank, chiselled out shelves for cyalume sticks, carved out individual snow thrones to sit in. It was quite luxurious actually and great way to spend the spare time.

Not a great way to spend time was when we had to pack everything up. The mast pegs frozen solid into the ice took forever to take out.

The tents were frozen solid and so ended up folding them up like cardboard. Oh, and then there was the crypto, this secret equipment had been collected up, all accounted for then put into a large metal cage which perfectly fitted into the back of a GS Landrover. It took a few of us to lift it up and guide it into position, just at the very last second of it going into the rover we were told to stop while some more kit or paperwork was put in, I had to shuffle around to get comfortable while it was unlocked and opened, my hands were freezing, I did have contact gloves on but they weren't doing much. Anyway, the order was to pick the cage up again, I poked my hands through the cage with my middle and index fingers on top of the cage, at least I thought it was the top of the cage until somebody dropped the cage lid, letting it slam down on top of my fingers! Searing pain went through both hands, both fingertips felt like they were broken. I dared not take my gloves off. It was an accident, lots of apologies then told to crack on. I then had to drive my Landrover back to the port, jump on a bus to Bardufoss and wait for the military flight home. All the time my fingers throbbing with pain. Eventually in the ramshackle waiting area (where we spent a couple of days it turned out) I decided to see what the damage was to my fingers. The nails were bulging sickeningly out, glowing red with the blood underneath. No med cover was available as it was the end of the exercise so after several hours of deliberation, I decided to self-treat. I got my Leatherman out and pierced the skin under the nail. It was like a horror scene, especially with the blood splattered on the inside of the white tent, but the pain relief was instant. More amusingly, I then spent the next month or so with blackened nails being able to flick the 'V's up at the rest of the troop with all their micky taking of the incident.

During the summer season we also deployed to the southern flanks of Europe. The first trip out was to Turkey. This was most exciting, not necessarily because it was as far as I was naively aware, a holiday destination, but more the fact we would be issued 'Trops' Clothing for Tropical environments. Lightweight cotton DPM but so much cooler looking.

It was a lot of effort getting the kit and vehicles to Turkey, usually started a good couple of months before, removing the arctic tyres for normal tyres and getting the vehicles to the port at Marchwood. Getting them bolted onto the ship was always a nause and a dirty job. Getting the dreaded crypto cage on board and the lucky devils who would then stay on board and escort the kit for the month or so journey.

I remember the deployment day; really early start and I think we flew out from RAF Lynham on a crammed Hercules. Sat on the netting with our knees crunched under our chins because of the baggage in the middle of the craft. As soon as the plane had reached cruising altitude, we all unclipped and jumped on the top of the gear and spread out.

I had no idea, other than Northern Turkish coast, where we landed and it wasn't far to the port. Our vehicles had already been taken off and were parked up. I was the driver, fairly sure it was the full-screw Scotty who was the vehicle commander and possibly the packet commander too but that was above my head back then, all I knew was that there was a massive, multi-national convoy and we were among the first to head off. It was great to see the other nations in different DPM uniforms rather than the bland white and olive green that was all I had ever seen previously.

Our vehicles were heavily laden with kit, fuel and water for the long journey towards Erzurum then onwards towards Pasinler in the NE area of Turkey. Driving through the towns and villages it must have been something of a spectacle as lots of people were lining the streets and watching and clapping. An hour or so inland we trundled into another town, I remember it clearly, half-built houses with a hillside made up of dusty looking farmland. Again, people out looking on at the convoy, not as many people now but still supporting the AMF(L) soldiers driving by their homes. Now in the distance I spotted a farm dog sprinting down the hill full-pelt, I initially didn't think much about it but as I continued so did the dog, time and distance and speed estimations didn't need the brains of a physicist to work out that we were on a collision course. I said to

Scotty about the dog but he said to keep on going. The dog was still running at great speed and I was still trundling along on my only route option. I spotted what must have been the owner turning around towards his dog, he opened his arms to greet it but it just ran straight under his legs, onto the road, right in front of me. I swerved but felt the awful bump of dog against front wheel, followed by the rear wheel then a very awkward bump of the trailer wheel. The owner of the dog now had his hands on his head in disbelief. I cried to Scotty what to do next, he told to me 'just keep effin' going Simmo!' I was mortified with the thought of pretty much the whole of the AMF(L) convoy going over the top of that poor dog.

Pasinler itself was a small town, the FHU was just on the outskirts on the edge of some hills and farmland. Not very inspiring and far from being a holiday destination. The next few weeks were spent just doing our comms job. Starting off with morse code, insecure RATT then eventually onto secure VHF and insecure HF voice and data. The RAF and Germans turned up in their helicopters, landed on the fields just by us and we were instantly covered in what turned out to be human fertilizer giving me severe case of the 'Deli Belly' for the rest of the exercise! I was very poorly equipped for the trip, I had no camp bed, only a roll mat to lie on the semi-desert soil. I ended up using the vehicle seats to lie on instead to give a bit more comfort. It was insanely hot during the day and keeping the radios cool was critical, didn't matter that I was losing weight drastically and melting in the heat.

I did get a few driving trips out to visit the rebro sites, even though Eastern Turkey was quite barren, there were some stunningly beautiful parts out there too with a stunning reservoir full of amazing looking water.

Going for a run was somewhat perilous as the Turkish army seemed to have trouble working out who were friendly forces and who were terrorist PKK, there were incidents where personnel were being mistaken and shot at, fortunately the conscripts are dreadful shots, nevertheless it was a good enough deterrent not to go for a jog!

Towards the end of the exercise the helis did a massive fly past before landing, really impressive and created a really impressive shit cloud too just to cheer me up. That night a clandestine attack from us in 244 Alpha Troop decided it would be a good idea to 'zap' the helicopters with our Sqn stickers. Turned out not to be the best idea in the world as even though we thought they had been stuck in an innocuous area, they had been spotted by the crews. We got a jerry can beasting for that, thought I was going to faint with my weakened, emaciated state and with it being at around 5500ft high the air was a good bit thinner.

After the beasting we were told to start removing the tent pegs and prepare to pull everything down the next day. Now all exercise there had been blazing sunshine and hardly a breath of wind, that night however the Law of Sod occurred. I was still on radio stag during the night and I felt the tents starting to shake, increasing gusts making the FHU tentage lift up and down, then suddenly a huge gust lifted off one half and blew it over the top of mine. Aircraft crews were running around like headless chickens to tie down their helis. People everywhere trying to untie mangled tentage, paperwork of goodness knows what classification being scattered into the countryside. I was then alerting people of the dangers when a tent blew away in front of me revealing a startled RAF officer on his camp bed shouting where the fek has his tent gone! Absolute chaos but also highly amusing as all of a sudden, the heli zapping seemed irrelevant now.

After all the commotion had calmed down and the RAF weather forecasters had received their bollocking I received some very sad news in that my Nan had passed away. With that, even though the exercise was finishing, I was driven to the military airport and took off. Only to find out there was a problem with the aircraft and that we had to land in Ankara. I remember getting into a minibus and being driven through the city and parking up outside the Ankara Sheraton Hotel. For the first time in weeks, I felt the wonderful feeling of air-conditioning, then walking through the grand foyer listening to the string quartet playing classical music. I distinctly remember looking at myself looking extremely dishevelled, patting myself and dust falling off me. Walking into the dining room and the range of fruit, cereals and an amazing wall of honeycomb to put onto fresh bread was an absolute shock to my eyes. The dirt floor was replaced with an air-conditioned double bed with ensuite.

A bitter-sweet end to an extraordinary exercise.

The Wire Magazine 1991 to 2003

Over this period the role of AMF(L) was under review post the fall of the Berlin Wall and the demise of the Soviet Union. Emphasis was still on specialist training for all members of the unit but by the late 90's, the expansion of NATO to include previous Eastern Bloc countries placed extra demands on NATO which led to AMF(L) taking on additional roles as can be seen by the later deployments.

The Wire – June 1991

249 Signal Squadron (AMF(L)) Bulford

EXERCISE HARDFALL 91

This year the Squadron divided into two separate courses of three weeks duration. It was the first-time novice students underwent the new Novice Ski and Survival Course (NSSC), covering mobility over snow, navigation in Arctic conditions, health and medical subjects in cold conditions and Arctic survival. The latter involved learning about avalanches, avalanche rescue, ice crossing and breaking drills and improvised emergency shelters including the infamous snow hole.

This year the Squadron went into the wilderness and stayed at the Maurset Hotel chalets, miles from anywhere. Snow conditions were good, and this combined with a team of excellent ski instructors headed by W02 (YofS) Pete Barron, the standard of skiing this year was noticeably higher. Even the Gurkhas under Lt Dorje Tamang seemed to have a great time despite sometimes bitterly cold conditions.

All members of the Squadron (Jess non-swimmers) participated in the Ice Breaking Drills, an experience most would probably not wish to have again! The two ski races produced some impressive results with Sig 'Alfie' Alford winning the best novice prize for the 10km ski race and Cpl Kev Read winning the 20km biathlon in an excellent sub two-hour time. The new Sqn Comd Maj Paul Oldfield proved to be a dark horse, but he did admit to some previous langlauf experience! He certainly surprised the younger members of the Squadron as he screamed past them in the races!

Most of the novices seemed overjoyed to complete the final exercise, after the last night in survival shelters using just a shovel, survival bags and roll mat. To balance the work there was some rest and play, mostly downhill skiing in Voss, Geilo or on the hotel's own slopes. All in all, a very successful Ex Hardfall 91.

The Wire – December 1991

249 Signal Squadron (AMF(L)) Bulford

EXERCISE ACTION EXPRESS

During September the Squadron was shipped and flown to the sunny shores of Denmark to take part. in Ex Action Express 91. It is the ACE Mobile Forces temperate climate annual training exercise and took the form of a nationwide deployment throughout the three main islands of Denmark. The first of the RATT detachments left in the early hours of 6 September and began to build the communication network on the island of Zealand, closely followed by the majority of the Squadron's vehicles travelling by sea.

After a long and picturesque journey from the port, the Squadron made its home in a crowded Ringstedt Barracks. The deterrent operations phase of the exercise then began, with lots of flag waving and the building of good relationships with the host nation. The vehicles and their crews left the main base with their Key companies and HQ's, shifting, eventually, into the combat phase of operations. During these procedures Capt Bill White came to the forefront and visits to 'Ech' always resulted in 'yet another' bag of bread. A notable highlight of this phase was the capture by enemy forces of Sp Tp Comd Capt Bob Munro, not once but, twice! (The Squadron does not hold it against him for passing information, namely grid locations, to the enemy after interrogation!) Sgt

'Tommo' Thompson and 2Lt Richard Deans also managed to get a ride in the back of a vehicle but not of their choice! They are understood to have greatly appreciated the cigarettes and Pepsi!

During the break between phases the Squadron retained the minor units NATO Challenge Cup. Sig Robson was the man of the hour and collected the trophy from Commander AMF(L) Maj Gen Carstens (GE Army). Well done all those who took part. After rest and recuperation in Copenhagen it was redeployment back to blighty and sunny Bulford.

The Wire – June 1992

249 Signal Squadron (AMF(L)) Bulford

EXERCISE HARDFALL 92

The main event of recent months has been the Squadron's deployment on Ex Hardfall 92. Feelings varied from the extreme enthusiasm of the seasoned 'Arctic Ninja's' who relish their two months Arctic deployment, to sheer fear from some of those new to the Squadron. Inevitably tall stories of skiing 50km a day with 100lb rucksacks towing 70lb pulks and living in snow holes did little to allay fears.

The deployment went smoothly with the usual 'Hurry up and wait' syndrome courtesy of the Army's sleep deprivation centre (alias 50 MC Sqn RCT). The Squadron took Alpha Tp 244 Sig Sqn (AS) under its command and was split between two locations but married up for excellent training on the Hardangervidda. The mandatory Novice Ski and Survival Course occupied the first three weeks and covered an intensive few days on skis followed by survival training. The ski training can be highly amusing to onlookers and competent skiers, but for the uninitiated the idiosyncrasies of the military ski can be a severe test of one's sense of humour!

After a weekend's R & R the Platoons dug a tactical campsite. There was an excellent noise and lights demo courtesy of Sgts Bob Goode and Dick Malt. On return from the demo the Platoons were informed of the recent notional mortar attack on the campsite. The students were told that all their equipment had been destroyed and were therefore in a survival situation. Many strange and unusual shelters were constructed but the tent group with WO2 (SSM) Martin 'The JCB' George spent a comfortable night in rather palatial snow cave.

The 20km ski race was won with a fine performance by Cpl Kev Read and this was followed by Arctic Warfare Training. However, due to horrendous weather (akin to skiing with a pillow case over one's head) the final attack had to be abandoned. After a period of Squadron radio training where Cpls Bart Storey and Ted Stuart claimed to have seen the tops of their antennas glowing purple (precipitous static or emptied hipflasks?) the unit deployed on Ex Arctic Hook, the Commander UK element AMF(L)'s exercise, to provide control comms. During this Capt Bob Munro led an enemy Platoon against 1 DWR. A series of disasters, including collapsed bridges and poor map reading in a white-out meant that any contact was avoided until the last couple of days. A strong defensive position proved too much for an exhausted 1 DWR so upon instructions from the umpires, Capt Munro led (from behind!) a death or glory snowshoe assault, uphill to allow I DWR to win.

This marked the end of another successful Hard fall deployment and the Squadron returned to the, by now, welcome sight of sunny Bulford.

2Pl led by Lt Dave 'Silva' Duggan

Sgt Chris Martin struggling to survive

The Wire – October 1992

249 Signal Squadron (AMF(L)) Bulford

EXERCISE ALLEGIANCE EXPRESS/ARDENT GROUND

The Squadron deployed on one of the AMF(L)'s less glamorous deployments-In this case Otterburn Training Area in the north of England! The Squadron settled into its various deployment areas and then set about breaking down the language barriers with our NATO allies. Despite our best efforts some found the 'Geordie' dialect more difficult than Italian! The exercise followed a familiar format with the high-profile deterrence ops being followed by the more tactical combat ops phase. Communications were no problem and breaks in the exercise schedule provided the opportunity for walking along Hadrian's Wall as well as the highlight of abseiling out of Huey helicopters, courtesy of the US Army.

FIELD FIRING

At the conclusion of Ex Allegiance Express the Squadron travelled direct to Sennybridge for an extensive field firing and training exercise. A superb training package was provided by the Training Staff which included section in defence and live section attacks as well as FIBUA training. All this enabled us to refresh old skills and learn many new ones. A section competition added a competitive edge to the training with sections trying to outdo each other. The highlight of the event was the live firing section attack under extremely realistic conditions. The eventual winners of the competition were 2 Section led by Cpl Rickey Taylor.

The Wire – June 1993

21 Signal Regiment Colerne

ALPHA TROOP – 244 Signal Squadron

HARDFALL '93

January saw the first exercise deployment of the year to Norway. This annual visit to Hardfall South was once again centred around terrible accommodation in the form of a 5-star hotel. Some 25 members of the Troop were having an awful time in plush surroundings whilst the remainder stayed in Bømoen Camp, known as the coldest hole in Norway. But at least they had a main town on their doorstep. Elements of the Troop, FHU and FOB, were operational from day 1 supporting 33 Sqn RAF. This was carefully controlled by Sgt Mark 'Tipsy' Tivey, a suitable name given by 33 Sqn Hierarchy. Cpl Dave 'Dodgy' Birtle took 1st place in the Golden Blanket award with stiff competition from LCpl Dave Longstaff who managed second this year. At the hotel, early phases of the exercise took the form of mandatory lectures given by the Troop's resident Arctic Warfare instructors Cpls 'Scouse' Johnston and Taff Thomas. LCpl 'Sonney' Lambert realised that Comms on his mobile phone were going to be just a little ZGN. Ski training again proved that there are more ways than one for a soldier to wrap himself around a tree.

Most of the Troop were novices at skiing, but thanks to the perseverance of a couple of the Troop's Military Ski Instructors, Cpl 'Harry' Harrison and Sig Mark Deary, they were able to achieve excellent results with five members obtaining a bronze award. Pats on the back must go to Sigs 'Zag' Latham and Dave Aitken on proving their potential by attending their MSI course. Sig Dave Aitken receives congratulations on taking 1st place in the 10km novice ski race organised by 249 Sig Sqn.

OOPS! Driving instructor Cpl Harry Harrison showing how not to do it

The weather was mild which played havoc with the training, due to danger of avalanche; nevertheless, training objectives were achieved. Senior members had the pleasure of entertaining Brig Wood (Comd Comms UKLF) at a dinner night. Many thanks to Brig Wood for answering the many questions put to him and for visiting us in the field. Thanks also to LCpl Kev Murphy for organising an excellent meal. Other social occasions included a Sgts v Cpls games night and a Regimental dinner night. A three-day visit by the Sqn Comd Maj Bob Holt proved fruitful for LCpl Holroyd who received promotion to Cpl, well done.

Thanks to Linemen Sigs Lee Berry and Danny Rudman for all their help and support. Finally, congratulations must go to Sigs 'Fossy' Foster, Chris 'Tap Off' Clayton, Jim '4ft 1' Petrie and Mark Deary for achieving 6th place in the UK force downhill ski race. Seven cold weeks later, the green grass of Colerne never looked so beautiful as it had the day we left.

The Wire – June 1993

249 Signal Squadron (AMF(L)) Bulford

EXERCISE HARDFALL - CONTINUATION PLATOON

During Ex Hardfall, the usual 'Demo Platoon' was renamed Continuation Platoon. This Platoon consisted of the more experienced members of the Squadron, i.e., those who had been to Norway previously, passed the Arctic Warfare Trained course and were competent skiers. While the novices were taught the basic skiing and survival techniques, Continuation Platoon undertook several different activities. There were several 'recce' type expeditions to explore the surrounding area in an attempt to find the best locations for the Novice Ski Survival Course and the Arctic Warfare Training. Due to a series of unfortunate accidents and poor weather conditions several of our BV206 over snow vehicles became bogged down, requiring further excursions to recover them! At one stage a BV206 seemed almost unrecoverable when, after becoming bogged down in deep snow the team were forced to abandon the vehicle due to the danger of avalanche. Thankfully, the vehicle was recovered several weeks later by a very determined Q Tp expedition led by the Quartermaster. It took some 15 hours digging and the help of a tow from the AMF(L) Workshop Recovery Section before they managed to recover the vehicle. Even after three weeks of being completely buried under snow, the vehicle started first rime.

The continuation training continued with some downhill skiing during which a member of our intrepid house staff Cpl Stu Bull dislocated his shoulder. If that was not painful enough the RAMC medic rolled the Landrover with the pair of them on board on the way back from the hospital, ouch!

During the Arctic Warfare Training (AWT). Continuation Platoon acted as the enemy for the novices. Three days were spent digging in, patrolling and finally the 'grand' final attack. The display of pyrotechnic which caught an unsuspecting 2 Platoon napping would have made even Guy Fawkes happy!

L to R: Cpls Dave Coussons, Chris Lloyd, Kev Reid and LCpl John Chamberlin in a snow hole

Following the successful completion of the AWT the Troops were reformed for a PACE, which was followed by a Squadron Comms Ex. Despite the inhospitable Norwegian terrain some excellent comms training was achieved. The Squadron Ex preceded the Commander's exercise designed to test the UK Infantry Battalion. The squadron provided umpire communications for this FTX which passed off with very few hitches.

SUPPORT TROOP

The Troop deployed from Bulford to Norway on 4 January. After landing in Norway, we travelled to the Stalheim Hotel, 32km North of Voss, this was to be our home for the next nine weeks.

We were introduced to our first taste of Cheese Cake and the Troop then split into Platoon orbat for the Novice Ski and Survival Course (NSSC) and the Arctic Warfare Training (AWT). A rude introduction to the perils of Arctic training swiftly followed when the instructors carried out an equipment check and found suitable punishment for those with vital arctic equipment missing. On completion of the Novice Ski and Survival Course and the Arctic Warfare Training course, the Troop engaged in its first R & R. Two generous days were granted to enjoy the ski slopes of Voss and the local nightlife. They then deployed to a Squadron Communications exercise providing the RRB's and various echelon detachments. With the exception of a few wheels missing from vehicles the Troop performed well during this phase. On return to the hotel, we found that someone had decided the hotel was haunted and that Main Tp had seen a ghost. (Informed opinion suggests the 'ghost' was YofS Leaning after a particularly strenuous R & R!). A few days later we again deployed to the field to provide umpire comms for the Infantry FTX. Once again this proved to be a challenge, but all our objectives were met by Endex.

The Wire – June 1993

21 Signal Regiment Colerne

ALPHA TROOP – 244 Signal Squadron

EXERCISE ACTION EXPRESS 1993

Midway through September Alpha Tp, in support of the AMF(L), deployed to Denmark. Having only just arrived and this being my first exercise with the Troop, I was unsure of what to expect. I'd heard about the excellent command and control within the AMF(L) from other members of the Troop, the initial deployment put me in the picture. How five hundred vehicles and trailers were loaded off of the ship and expected to fit into the area of a basketball court was a truly amazing task. A special thank you goes to all the movers and loaders for their delicate handling of our vehicles.

Ignoring this slight upset, the Troop set about its mission and by the end of the second day were well into the smooth-running routine. A few highlights (or lowlights} of the exercise; many congratulations to Sig Jim Petrie on actually turning on his sets and we hear he even managed to pull up a mast, though this may only be a rumour. A thankyou to Sig Danny Adams on his excellent wiring that melted the generator lead.

After the fifth consecutive day of rain, shouts and groans of dismay were heard from the FOB detachment on being told to move, LCpl 'Geordie' Longstaff wanted to stay longer and wait for the rice in his paddy field to ripen. I've been warned not to mention SSgt Steve Davison's mishap with the generator and kerosene and also his off-road driving course, so please ignore all the above.

Towards the end of the deterrent phase the chance of a day's R&R surfaced so a posse led by Lt Graham Fletcher headed for the bright lights of Copenhagen. A big thanks to all the Techs, Cooks and REME personnel attached to us for all their hard work and enthusiasm. Also, to Cpl Paul Parkes on loan from India Tp and Sig Treena Taylor from Juliet Tp. We hear she is trying to rewrite the challenge and reply procedure for the AMF(L) whilst on sentry duty. The two weeks generally went well but I'm sure the grass of Colerne was never greener than it was when we got home.

The Wire – December 1993

249 Signal Squadron (AMF(L) Bulford

EXERCISE ACTION EXPRESS

The Squadron deployed to Denmark on 12 September 1993 on Ex Action Express; the RATT dets had deployed a week earlier. From our arrival in Denmark until we left it rained ... in fact the daily weather forecast was rain, mixed in with occasional showers and floods.

Deployment Ops ran very smoothly. With Main Tp being the 'backbone' of the Squadron, it was no surprise to see a large number of the Troop competing in the NATO Challenge Cup team led by Lt Mannings and Sgt 'Johno' Johnston. The team succeeded in winning the overall competition and turned in the fastest run and assault course time ... if only we also had SUSATS! All in all, 26 teams from the multi-national force entered, of which 249 proved to be the fittest. A big thanks must go to the fitter members of the team who 'encouraged' everyone else.

Elements of the Troop also took part in the Observers' Day Parade demonstrating an Arctic Stand. The parade was attended by hundreds of civilians as well as many foreign soldiers. LCpl Gluba was very impressive as the 'Snowman' for the day. On the parade that followed the NATO Challenge Cup team collected the trophy and their medals.

Combat operations ran very well, but everyone was glad when Endex was declared. Overall, it was a very successful exercise and we were praised for our efforts. Unfortunately, there proved to be little time for R&R, but most managed at least one night on the town.

The Wire – June 1993

21 Signal Regiment Colerne

ALPHA TROOP (AMF(L)) – 244 Signal Squadron

EXERCISES HARDFALL AND ARCTIC EXPRESS 94

A Tp AMF(L} has now returned from Norway. at last, to a welcome from the squadron. The annual three-month arctic deployment was an extremely successful and fun packed experience, especially for Sig Matt Dorling who showed himself as potential future Olympic skier. After completion of the Novice Ski and Survival Course and Infantry Arctic Warfare Training, the Troop moved on to special-to-arm training and trial exercises. Meanwhile the Force Helicopter Unit detachment under the steady reins of Sgt Mark Tivey fitted in the odd downhill ski session, despite the workload. The Troop Mobile Air Operation Teams continued the motion!

Notable successes were the deployment of two four-man manpack RRB by helicopter to mountain locations led by Sgt Steve Davison and Cpl Ian Johnston. A fantastic third placing in the force downhill ski meet led by Sig Stu Foster. A successful defence of a bridge during AWT by the entire Troop.

Thanks go to 249 Sig Sqn AMF(L), Regimental and Squadron Ops team and the Force RMP Det for their valuable support during Hardfall. After completing the move North, A Tp set about the serious task of providing SH and OS comms for the AMF(L) within the Arctic Circle. Joined by the Sqn 2IC Capt John Norris, the Troop again managed to complete the task with flying colours. Sigs Dave Horton and 'Harry' Harrison (attached from 237 Sig Sqn) gave lesson in ballroom dancing and the dark hours were spent watching the northern lights and reminiscing in the Tp Comd's tent.

The dismounted Rebros about to be inserted

Cpl J O'Neill, our FAC man on what he thinks might be his last deployment in Norway!

Cpl 'Taff' Thomas and Sig Mel Jones enjoy the comfort of their BV

A Tp--Lt Graham Fletcher tries to walk on water. The Yeoman finds it easy

The Wire – October 1994

249 Signal Squadron (AMF(L) Bulford

EXERCISE CLEAR VOICE 1994

Over the period 20-24 June the squadron hosted 28 officers and SNCO's from eight nations within the AMF(L) for Ex Clear Voice. The aim of the exercise was to leach the students (many of whom spoke little English) the use of Joint Voice Procedure currently used within the Force, a major task. The course was directed at staff officers, watchkeepers and radio users to ensure a commonality of both procedures and language. The exercise proved to be a great success, thanks to the hard work and preparation of all the instructors and of course the students themselves, most of whom had some knowledge of communications. It was good to see attendance from Norway and Spain for the first time: hopefully the association will continue next year.

The Wire – April 1995

249 Signal Squadron (AMF(L) Bulford

EXERCISE HARDFALL '95

249 Sig Sqn (AMF(L)) deployed for their two-month Norwegian 'skiing holiday' at the beginning of January with elements from 2 Sig Regt, 602 Sig Tp (SC) and 609 TACP joining us for the ride. January was to see some hard training but was particularly demanding for the newcomers to the squadron on the Novice Ski and Survival Course (NSSC) which took place from 14-30 January. The course was run by Capt Keith Mannings with the able assistance of Lt Gareth Marsh, Sgt Johnston and Cpls Million, Chambers and Redstone. For this phase of training A Tp, 244 Sig Sqn joined the Squadron and also provided three Arctic Warfare Instructors of their own. Cpls Thomas, Hawkins and Barker. Three training troops were formed and one of them found itself with a last-minute substitute as Troop Commander. Sgt Frank Gainey of D Tp tells 'the rest of the story'.

The following is a personal overview of D Tp experience on NSSC. It should have been otherwise but it's amazing how critical voices can disappear when asked to put pen to paper. The NSSC course consisted of three phases: novice ski instruction, practical living in the field and further ski training and finally tactical training.

The novice phase went well, instruction in the morning followed by free skiing in the afternoon, combined with plenty of falling and many living snowmen, soon turned 28 sets of 'Two left skis' into budding Franz Klammer's. It was at this stage in training that such phrases as 'You don't need your Gortex on' and the old-time favourite ‘never hang around in the Arctic' were learnt.

Phase two was four days practical living in the field and began in earnest on 21 January at 0901 hrs with 'You’re late. You owe me. To the BV and back. Go!' Okay it was a fair cop, but if 'You never hang around in the Arctic', how do you get 28 men to appear instantly on parade at 0900 hrs without being late or early (which was equally punishable?). On deployment to the field the troops dug in a harbour positions for five-man tents. It's at this stage that you learn to dig your tent hole to exactly the right size, thus avoiding digging three ton of snow instead of two. That evening the troops did a night ski which is an incredible experience. The senses are sharpened to a fine degree and you feel that you are going down a helter-skelter with six-foot planks strapped to your feet to the cry 'Man down' echoing round the valley every 30 seconds.

The second day started with a very impressive avalanche drill and rescue demo, produced by the Norwegian advisor (Lt Bade) and a member of the Norwegian Avalanche Rescue Service. The highlight of the display was watching a search dog identify, within minutes, two separate locations where 'willing' volunteers had been buried under two metres of snow hours earlier. The low point of the display was that it took place in a blizzard with wind chill bringing temperature down to near minus 30. ('You don't hang around in the Arctic'). That night everyone slept in snow trenches. An experience made interesting by the blizzard raging outside that constantly filled up the entrance with drifting snow and threatened to entrap the occupants.

Day three commenced with 'You don't need your Gortex on it's not wet'. (Oh no? Well, what's snow when you fall over in it and it melts on you?), followed by practical skiing carrying ‘green sacks of pain.' After digging in the platoon position, this time using four-man tents, there were demos on cam and concealment and tactical harbours. Then back to the tents for tea and medals at 1600 hrs. In the evening there was a noise and light demo. This was followed by a thunder flash and 'You've been attacked. Your position is destroyed.' (Not that old chestnut)! ‘You're in a survival situation.' Having found a suitable snow bank, we dug in as a section, producing an array of survival snow holes from caverns to cubby holes.

The final day saw a move to a new location and, at parade time, a surprising 'Get your Gortex on lads.' Not bad advice. The day's accommodation was a tactical snow hole dug to the correct specification. Plenty of potential there for a very wet day.

The interlude between phases saw two very interesting events. The first was Ice Breaking Drills (a practice on what to do if you go through the ice when crossing water). Having watched the video, it all seemed very simple. Ski to the hole, slide in, throw your bergen and skis on to the ice, then use your ski pole to claw your way out. All over in 40 second without getting your hair wet. Not so. 'It wasn't like this in the film' I told myself as I took four strokes to resurface to find that I had one ski pole to get out with and the other was lost under the ice. The second interesting event was a 20km biathlon, except that the range was closed and, after completing the course, it was alleged to have been 28km Jong.

The final phase of training was conducted with a tactical scenario. This started with the war being put on hold and the QM demanding that the peace time location be given a quick clean before hostilities were permitted to recommence. An hour later troops were moved by BV to the Jordalen valley, where after drop-off, troop commanders recced and established their own tactical harbour positions. Nine hours of digging later the harbour was established and patrols were on the ground. Following a series of recces, patrol and OPs, a plan of attack was formed. The attack against the enemy, A Tp 244 Sig Sqn, was to go in on the early hours of the third day. D Tp were to provide the attacking sections, E Tp the fire support and illuminations. Fire and movement in snow holes is a really fun aerobic activity recommended to all readers (who needs Mr Motivator). The deed was done, and the battle won (what else), and war stories were told in the BV's on the way home. This ended what was regarded as a demanding, informative and enjoyable period of training.

The Wire – June 1995

21 Signal Regiment (AS) Colerne

ALPHA TROOP AMF(L) – 244 Signal Squadron

NORWAY 1995

by Cpl G Scott

On a cold winter' night in January, the Troop and a few selected attachments deployed to the snowy surrounding of Norway on Ex Hardfall. On arrival we collected our vehicles from the port and split into two group. The old and belted disappeared to Hagatun and Bømoen to do continuation training under the guidance of Sgt Steve Davison and Sgt Stu Seddon. Us novices went off to Stalheim Hotel to get some snow under our boots. Under the control of our AWI's Cpls 'Ivor' Hawkins, 'Taff' Thomas and 'Clint' Barker and with our MSI's LCpl 'Jasper' Marritt, Sigs Norm Addison, Danny Adams, 'Mel' Jones and Dave Horten to guide and steer us, we embarked. On learning how to stay upright on army planks with some memorable moments particularly from Cpl Penrose and Sig Bargna. Sig Dave McKay was presented with the winter warrior for winning both the 10km and 20km ski race. NSSC proved to be a laugh, well it was if you managed to stop falling over, as you attempted to haul a 501b+ bergen up and down hill on two planks. This included staying out for four nights living in various now shelters which you had spent several hours building and few minutes destroying. This concluded with the notorious 'ice breaking drills' or throwing yourself into an ice-cold lake just so that you know what it feels like. Thinking along those lines Cpl John Penrose decided to shoot himself in the leg on the next range day.

Our training finished with us deploying as a platoon, digging for England and defending against 249 Sig Sqn (AMF(L)).

The Wire – June 1995

249 Signal Squadron (AMF(L) Bulford

EXERCISE STRONG RESOLVE

Ex Strong Resolve was a major NATO FTX held West of Trondheim, Norway, over the period 16 February - 13 March. The aim of the exercise was to practise the deployment and operation of a Combined Joint Task Force (CJTF); for the Squadron it was the culmination of its build-up training further South in Norway. As usual, movement to the exercise area was far from uneventful and resulted in the odd night or two in the AMF(L) holding area for personnel waiting for their vehicles to arrive. Weather conditions were good with relatively dry conditions for the majority of the deployment.

The exercise passed relatively uneventfully and was a complete success for the squadron. It was even rumoured that the Yeomen were happy with comms. Some people, however, were rather confused about the exercise's Objectives after observing the frantic activity around the Norwegian Mobile Bath Unit. The USMC was unable to secure this vital installation which seemed to become the focus for the entire exercise. Rumour that it was now part of the Squadron Echelon were later denied by the Quartermaster, Maj P C 'Shower King' Bawden.

The squadron sends special thanks to the members of other units who joined it for both Ex Hardfall and Ex Strong Resolve; Sigs Williams, Roachford, Withan and Hansford from 2 Sig Regt and Sig Broom from 602 Sig Tp (SC). See you next year!

Sgt Cook about to leave Sqn Echelon

Sgt Castle and Cpl Concepcion enjoy the arctic sunshine at Log Base

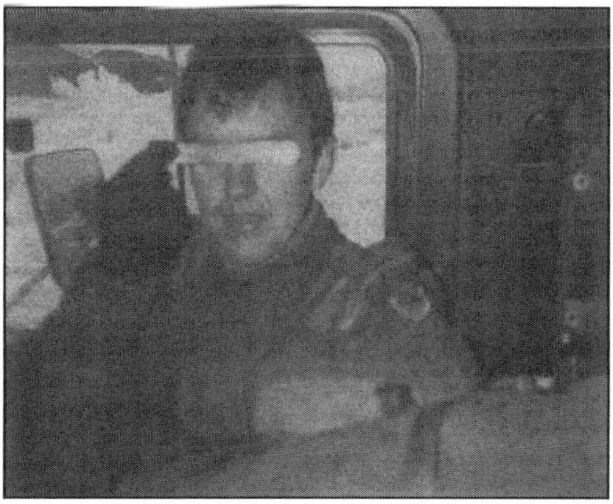

W02 (ROMS) McNab during a BV206 mounted roving acquisition

The Wire – April 1996

249 Signal Squadron (AMF(L) Bulford

EXERCISE DRYSHOD - PRE ARCTIC-DEPLOYMENT TRAINING

by Cpl Swanston

This year Ex Dryshod was held on Salisbury Plain Training Area, 15-22 January 1996. For those who are not familiar Ex Dryshod is the compulsory training required by all 'non-arctic trained' personnel prior to the annual Arctic deployment on Ex Hardfall in Norway.

The exercise was conducted in three phases. The first phase, which lasted three days, was spent in the classroom being bombarded with information on how to survive in the Arctic and use the specialist equipment. The instructors, Lt Gareth Marsh (AWO), Cpl 'Chas' Chambers and Cpl 'Tug' Wilson tried desperately hard to excite us with their knowledge of subjects, such as mountain and arctic warfare safety, avalanches, cold weather injuries, snow shelters, patrolling in the arctic and even the arctic ration pack (good stuff!). It wasn't until I had coped with the hundredth view foil that I began to feel the strain, despite the professional use of computer graphics. I must admit though, the midday PT sessions were well timed, and yes, the 'hill' sessions were also very demanding. No one complained though, we were being mentally and physically challenged, what a fine balance!! Ex Gilbert Gutbuster (the name speaks for itself) was the deployment phase of Ex Dryshod. The aim of this phase was to enable us to put into practice what we had recently been taught and get familiar with the equipment: furthermore, to allow us the privilege of carrying excessive weight! (We all carried between 65-80lb Bergens, depending on who volunteered to carry the radio and spare batteries.) We deployed in section on to Salisbury Plain where we were to start a two-day navigational exercise. At the end of the first day my section had completed 20kms and had arrived at our predetermined campsite. Spirits were high and thing were going well, even though the stove and lamp refused to light, nothing to do with the Anny's bright idea of swapping Kero for the 'proved-for-years' Naphtha!!

The next day, however, complacency crept in. My section was late, and we had forgotten some of our 'tent group routine' (drills). After being given the mandatory attitude adjustment period we were sent off on our second days mission, a 30km tab. That day everybody in my section took it in turns to map read in between check points. Although the weather was cold and there was thick fog, my section did not get lost ... although for about half an hour we were unsure of our whereabouts (by the way I'm a map reading instructor!!). That evening we were all exhausted and our feet, although suffering, had done a good day's work.

The final phase was the exam, which all but three, successfully achieved first-time passes. All in all, it was a challenging and intense Ex Dryshod 96, but we can all look forward to deploying to Norway, on Ex Hardfall 96, for the real thing and the chance to earn and 'bathe in the warmth' of the coveted Squadron belt.

The Wire – June 1996

249 Signal Squadron (AMF(L) Bulford

EXERCISE HARDFALL 1996 - NORWAY

FEBRUARY/MARCH 1996

The Squadron deploys to Norway every year as part of the UKs contribution to the AMF(L). The AMF(L) has various deployment options of which Norway is only one. The UK Element deploys early each year in order to complete some in-theatre training before joining up with the rest of the multi-national force for the Commander AMF(L) FTX. Every soldier in the Squadron is required to complete the Arctic Ski and Survival Course (ASSC) followed by Special-to-Arm training in order to gain the mandatory Arctic

Warfare Trained (AWT) qualification and wear the extra warm Sqn belt.

Sig Clubb demonstrates how warm the Squadron Belt is whilst teaching how to Skijor behind a BV206

The Squadron run a training programme which accommodate soldiers' three or four year posting cycle. In the first year they complete the ASSC and Special-to-Arm training to gain the AWT qualification. Those Signallers and LCpls who show a natural skiing ability get selected to attend the Military Ski Instructors (MSI) course to instruct on the ASSC in their second and third year. The Cpl and Sgts that excel on the course get selected for the Arctic Warfare Instructors (AWI) course and are involved in the planning and instruction for DRYSHOD (pre-Arctic training) and on the ASSC course. In their second-year students go into demonstration troop responsible for giving all the demo to the novices which include snow holes, ice-breaking and battle drills. In a soldier's final year, they move to Continuation Troop where they take part in expeditions onto the mountain ranges, skiing with heavy loads, practising survival techniques and possibly live firing exercises.

SKI TRAINING 9-19 FEBRURY 1996

After the mandatory lectures on survival in the Arctic.'46 Arctic virgins prepared to don skis and face the rugged Norwegian terrain. Within minutes of starting and under the guidance of the military ski instructors (MSI) several people were 'dobbing' in style. Whilst attempting to master the art of the diagonal gate and double polling. By the end of the day MSIs Raine and Wragg led the way on a downhill ski jump competition in which 2Lt 'Man Down' Seymour won 'Dob-of-the- Day ' with a 180-degree forward roll whilst kissing his skis.

The course was then split into ability groups with Capt Foulkes and Sgt Ward showing off their previous skiing ability by rarely dabbing in. Many complete beginners at skiing picked it up very quickly including Sig Milne and Sig Harding, others worked hard including Cpl no style but its fitness that counts' Wilson. Para trained Sgt Lothian was desperately advocating the use of snow shoes to go up hill instead of herring-boning.

As the course became more proficient ski tour were embarked upon building up to 20km over the mountainous terrain which was quite impressive.MSI 'hat' Hill who led group two seemed to be on a personal mission to go up any mountain he could find in Norway. Groups four, five and six instituted the ‘no fear’ club which seemed to involve adopting the egg ski position on every downhill slope. Sgt Turner ignoring the rule of staying in single file soon realised the error of his way when he skied over a six-foot cornice into a snow bank and could not move.

ARCTIC SKI AND SURVIVAL COURSE (ASSC)

Once proficient at skiing the next stage was a practical course in living and surviving in the Arctic environment. The first morning was a demonstration of brushwood shelters. At the end Lt Marsh, with an evil glint in his eye, informed us we were now in a survival situation. A rather stunned group were led up to an area and left to survive. The day was spent building brushwood shelters and mountainous wood piles to keep the fire going at night. During the day spirits were high as people got stuck in. As the light began to fade fires sprang up around the areas as the temperature dropped.

Sgt Greaves and Cpl ‘Needermyer' Chambers, brought provisions in the form of raw fish which provided everyone with a culinary challenge. Although it was cold everyone survived in good spirits.

Moving above the tree line and to deeper snow, we then set up the five-man tent. Soon the Coleman lamps were blazing, and the tent became surprisingly warm. That evening the groups did a night ski which proved to be almost easier than skiing during the day. LCpl Love, who by day was a ‘dob’ specialist, proved to be a most proficient night skier.

A move the next day with heavy bergen proved tiring and then into another harbour area. Problems were made worse by the wind building up. In the afternoon the group climbed 700ft on skis which pleased MSI Hill and then saw the snow shelter demo given by the small but perfectly formed Sgt O'Neil. The return journey down the mountain looked like the retreat from Moscow as people dobbed in everywhere and even a few MSI fell, much to the amusement of everyone else. Tent groups were soon learning who the tent rhino was. In one tent group Sig Lawrence unpacked all his equipment looking for his poon, only to find he had lent it to Cpl Ferrer the day before.

The next day the groups found themselves in near whiteout conditions. A decision was made to cut the ski tour short and with great speed the harbour area was erected. Tents were blowing in the wind and in temperatures of -25C the training paid off. That evening the group practised recovering an injured person off the mountain. Capt Marriot used his medical knowledge to get his group off the hill in quick time, winning the competition.

The final day dawned glorious as the groups went into the set routine of dismantling the harbour area in the Arctic known as 'pull pole'. Within twenty minutes the whole site can be packed away and ready to move. The final day was a ski tour with bergens before a return to the Stalheim hotel and a well-deserved monster meal.

ARCTIC WARFARE TRAINING

Loaded up with even more equipment the two platoons, Delta and Echo deployed on this three-day tactical exercise. The move out to the area was by Puma which was piled high with equipment. Once out of the helicopter it was a tactical move into the harbour location. Once there it was shovels out and start digging and keep digging for the next 24 hours. Once the sites were complete, they were surprisingly hard to see.

Patrols were sent out to recce a bridge that was currently held by the enemy. Both initial patrol teams were captured, although Lt Smalley managed to escape by hiding in the now for an hour. Sgt Rowe on the other hand was happy to be a PoW, as it meant sitting in a heated vehicle drinking hot brews. Cpl Grassick then took out a recce patrol which thought it was going to be captured and was all for attacking the bridge with his five men. While all this was going on Sig Harding awoke to find his sleeping bag on fire and the rest of the tent trying to find the fire blanket cunningly hidden under the radio.

The final attack was planned at dawn the next day with a sweeping attack up the valley floor on to the positions. The first move was at 0330hrs by vehicle to a drop off point where snow shoes were donned. The move to the fire support position and line of departure were hard. At H-hour all hell broke loose as two vehicles drove on to the position throwing out smoke. Fire support opened fire with everything they had, ably led by Sgt Ward firing shermulies like they were going out of fashion. Then as if they were going 'over the top' at the Somme the assault troops appeared from the riverbed. With much taunting from the enemy, the assault troops closed with the enemy and destroyed them. With the only casualty wounded pride, the good guys had won again.

ICE BREAKING DRILLS

The final hurdle of the course was the infamous ice breaking drills on the Opheim Lake. Each man had to enter the water with skis and bergen on and recover them to the side before clawing their way out with their ski poles. As always, a demo was needed and ably supplied by the OC. Sig Cresswell, on entering the water decided that it was far too cold and leaving his equipment pulled and kicked with all his might to get out. Sig William's aiming to dispel the myth that the 249 stable belt keeps you warm in all weathers entered the water wearing his plastic belt and was heard to say it kept him just as warm. Once out of the water everyone made like Linford Christie back to the vehicles to warm up.

Brig J H Griffin enjoyed watching this spectacle during his successful visit to the Squadron during Ex Hardfall 96. In conclusion the three-week course had turned Arctic virgins into 249 Signal Squadron elite Ski-Borne Arctic Warriors.

The Squadron holds its breath hoping that W02 (SSM) Barnes completes his ice-breaking drills without harm

NORDIC SKI RACES 1996

Each year in the Nordic deployment of the Squadron it is customary to hold two ski races, both using the classic style. The aim of the races is threefold; to test all the Squadron novice skiers, to test all the Squadron skier and finally the 10km and 20km races form the first two parts of the competition for the Barrie Trophy (for the best all round individual performance by a Squadron member over the year).

The 10km race is open to all members of the Squadron but is primarily aimed at the novice skiers, for which it is compulsory. The course is specifically designed to test the ability of the new novice skiers. This year the race was held in the Jordallen valley and took part on a previously unprepared track. The course proved to be extremely challenging due to the varied terrain (hills!) and the poor condition of the snow.

10 km Ski Race Results:

First	Capt Talbot	57 min 35 sec
Second	Sgt Greaves	1 hr 2 min 13 sec
Third	Lt Marsh	1 hr 4 min 7 sec
Fourth	Capt Foulkes	1 hr 6 min 13 sec (Novice Champion)

The 20km race is compulsory for all Squadron members. The race takes the format of a military patrol and relevant weight and military equipment is worn and carried by competitors to simulate this. The venue for the race this year was the Myrkdalen FIS biathlon course. This provided a stiff test with a lot of short steep climbs to be negotiated, quickly followed generally by even steeper and more hair-raising downhill to try and stay upright upon.

20km Ski Race Results:

First	Capt Talbot	1 hr 21 min 05 sec
Second	Sgt G reaves	1 hr 34min 37 sec
Third	Lt Marsh	1 hr 36 min 20 sec
Fourth	Capt Foulkes	1 hr 40 min 30 sec

SPECIAL-TO-ARM TRAINING

After the rigours of ASSC and AWT, the Squadron embarked on Special-to-Arm training. This training, as in previous years, took the form of a comms theory day, a comms practical day and concluded with a Squadron level exercise.

The theory day concentrated on core subjects with particular emphasis on differences when communicating in the Arctic. The practical day was a ski tour around a series of demonstrations. Following a Troop maintenance day, the Sqn moved to a concentration area in Bømoen and deployed out on Ex Winter Link. This exercise simulated a standard AMF(L) deployment covering the four phases: deployment, deterrence operations, combat operations and redeployment.

3 PARA LIVE FIRING EXERCISE

The 3 Para FTX commenced 15 March and followed a peace support scenario. It began with three company group clearing separate routes and culminated with live firing company attacks. The comm support to the exercise was unconventional in that it required the Squadron to provide the RRB infrastructure for 3 Para's VHF Command net and at the same time provide the Force VHF safety/enemy/umpire net both of which were insecure. In addition, the Sqn provided an enemy ski-borne section as part of the OPFOR and a civpop party to act as casualties and refugees. A four-man team was also provided to augment the permanent range team who provided safety cover during all live firing.

During the exercise the Squadron were visited by the GOC 3 (UK) Div, the Director of Military Operations and the Norwegian Army Winter School. All in all, the Squadron have had an extremely busy deployment and look forward to some well-deserved block leave after which we will turn our attention to Ex Dynamic Mix in Turkey in September 96.

The state of RRB at 1411m, temperatures below -50°C, with wind-chill

The Wire – August 1996

21 Signal Regiment (AS) Colerne

A Troop 244 Signal Squadron

EXERCISE HARDFALL 1996 - A PERSPECTIVE ON THE DEMANDS OF ARCTIC TRAINING

by Cpl Frazer McCarthy (A Tp 244 Sig Sqn)

The thought of living in Snowholes, Ice-breaking drills and stagging on whilst the temperature drops to -40c for some reason never really appealed to me, but in January of this year I found myself as one of the new boys in A Tp, 244 Sig Sqn and as we were only four weeks away from deploying to Norway, I felt it better to get on with the job then than to do the traditional 'Schimpf'. Who knows, I might even enjoy it. A soldier in the AMF(L) needs to be able to do many things in the Arctic but above all he need to be able to survive, and during the initial six weeks, I was going to learn just that.

The move out went well, with the Advance party consisting of the 'Arctic Warriors' of the Troop, settling in nicely with the RAF and FHU. The remainder of the new boys moved north to Scheverheim Lodge and we prepared ourselves for the first week of ski-training. Even though we were being expertly trained by our MSIs, it is no easy task skiing on Army Planks and by the end of day three we had lost Cpl SI 'Silver Streak' Rogerson and Sig David 'No Fear' Marlor through injuries. We were soon introduced to skiing with particularly heavy bergen and at the same time pulling pulks, a pulk being a sledge that is pulled by two skiers and contains all the sections tent kit. This may not sound too difficult but one of the most difficult pieces of kit to master and pulling It can reduce a man to tears, something Sig Simo Simpson could probably tell you about.

'May the force be with you'

By week three we were considered to be good enough to carry out the AWT, which consisted of staying out five days and four nights in varying shelters from snowholes to five-man tents and carrying out various tasks, all in a tactical scenario and of course, carrying those very heavy bergens. Having been put into a Platoon and then being split down into three sections I found myself I/C of section three which consisted of Sigs Stoves, Lavender, Glasspool, Lindley and

Horton with my 2IC Cpl Grant 'Moral' Campbell. Over the next five days we were inserted by Puma and then ski marched 5km to our defensive location which we guarded with our lives, during which we were attacked and became attackers ourselves.

At times the weather was very harsh with the temp dropping to -30c and the wind picked up causing the windchill factor to cause even more trouble. Finally, after five days and under the guidance of SSgt Stu Cousins we returned to our drop off point and were picked up by Puma and returned to base.

Sgt Morton finding this particular swimming pool 'a touch chilly'

Unfortunately, to be Arctic Warfare Trained, there is one final test that you have to carry out, Ice breaking drills. This involves a very cold lake with a big hole cut out of it, a soldier on skis and a couple of AWI's on the safety ropes. The soldier shuffles up to the side of the hole, slowly, but under control sinks into the water. He then throws his bergen to one side and swims to the far side and removes his skis and despatches them out of the water too. Then, coolly and without panic he turns around, swims to the point of entry and claws his way out with his ski poles that he has retained from the beginning. Of course, this all sounds very good on paper but there were some particularly funny moments especially when Sig Lee 'Pavarotti' Porter decided that his legs no longer worked, and the safety rope came into action.

All the survival training now complete we were able to concentrate on comms, but not before Cpl Harry Harrop planned a perfect R and R operation to Bergen in which all missions were completed, especially the one Sig Paul Dearden was set, but that's another story.

The Wire – December 1996

249 Signal Squadron (AMF(L) Bulford

EXERCISE DYNAMIC MIX '96

On Saturday 14 September the main body of the Squadron left Bulford Camp for the start of Ex Dynamic Mix 1996, in Turkey. Considering the fact that this was the first AMF(L) deployment for 18 month and a large proportion of the Squadron hadn't been on an AMF(L) exercise before, expectations were running high.

On arrival at Trabzon Port the Squadron spent the night unloading the vehicles from the boat and grabbed a few hours' sleep before an early start the following morning on 'The Mother of all Convoys' to Erzurum Airbase (12hr), where we were held for 48 hours before completing the final leg of our journey to the Staging Area at Horasan. Once all the detachments had deployed to their relevant Company and Battalions the Squadron carried out a period of Comms Testing until the TOC was up and running and the exercise scenario took over. Cpl John Hilton managed to provide the Comms Ops crews with the first real good laugh of the exercise after informing us that he had 'something bigger than a dog' snooping around his location and 'did we know what it could be?' After Sgt 'Joker' Crabb had dished out some sound advice we received the reply 'I'll get my crewman to do that now', ha ha, unlucky Clubby!!

Rest stop during 12 hour convoy to exercise area in Eastern Turkey

As the Exercise ground on, the NBC state seemed to fluctuate more than the temperature, but Sig 'Dizzy' Driscoll managed to keep everyone's morale up by 'warming up' his dog tags on the peak stove, and then getting them stuck around his head. The resulting burns weren't bad enough to require medical attention although they did make him look like an extra in a cheap Sci Fi movie!!

249 Sig Sqn in Turkey

As we moved into Combat Ops the TOC became miraculously NBC proof in it's overground 'underground bunker' and Cpl 'Grass' Grassick managed to get himself included in the final assault by driving right through the Belgian Para Commandos Heli Borne Assault, his appearance amongst a column of Turkish TS2s must have raised a few eyebrows among the assembled VIPs too.

Endex was marked with a few beers and a curry back in the staging area before the long drive back to Trabzon and the flight home to a well-deserved week of ATD training modelled around becoming NBC proof.

SATCOM COBALT, CORALICE, BOSNIA.

Between the last week in May and the first week in June the former crew of Cpl 'Andy' Egan, LCpl 'Mo' Pay and Cpl 'Adam' Wright-Mcarthy handed the detachment over to Cpl 'Taff' Baynham, LCpl 'Adam' Hughes, LCpl 'Two Can' Mulheran and Sig 'Mick' Collins. The new crew were inexperienced to say the least, none of them had previously worked on SATCOM and they only completed the SATCOM course at Blandford a few weeks ago.

249 Sig Sqn in Bosnia - Sig Collins looking slightly confused

After a few weeks of the deployment, we were beginning to climb the steep learning curve through the many and varied problems we encountered. We can honestly say that after just three weeks we were all thoroughly competent at operating the VSC 501 det. LCpl 'Two Can' Mulheran really enjoyed himself with all this new equipment to take apart and now that he has mastered the 30 Sig Regt demand system, we are sure that the stores in Donnington will run out in a very short time indeed. (The SQMS at 30 Sig Regt remarked upon receiving his demand list that it was the biggest tech demand he had ever seen).

The Camp at Coralice had very little to offer. The Canadian Bn we are supporting are having a 'Dry Tour', but where there is a will there is a way. LCpl 'Adam' Hughes has appointed himself as the det entertainment and refreshment officer. The things he gets from the American PX must be seen to be believed! The French Canadians have just taken over and have already improved the facilities no end by erecting a punch bag. Now we finally have a way of venting our built-up frustration.

Finally, we would like to thank our sister detachment SATCOM Brown at Kupres for putting on a barbecue for us recently, unfortunately they could not keep up with the pace. We look forward to handing over our detachment and returning to the Squadron in time for Christmas.

SATCOM BROWN, KUPRES, BOSNIA.

On 13 June 1996 we took over the detachment from the outgoing crew. Many thanks to them for their excellent handover and for the condition of the detachment. We trust you all had a good leave upon your return to the UK. Life for the new crew, Cpl 'John' Swanston, Cpl 'Villa are Crap' Nowosielski, Sig 'Danny' Pearson and Sig 'Paul' Richardson has been pretty hectic, the learning curve has been somewhat steeper than we were led to believe it was going to be. It is really cold here at the moment, it was as cold as -42°C this time last year apparently, and it certainly is getting toward that level again. But don't worry back there, we have all got our Squadron belts with us and that should do the trick. The detachment is providing a PSB for 1 GS Regt, who are certainly suffering with the effects of the cold. They have tried on our Squadron belts, but it does not seem to work as effectively. Never mind, a few seasons under their belts will soon remedy that situation. The crew are very much looking forward to returning to the UK for Christmas leave and have the following message for their replacements. 'Don't forget your Belt's, as it's freezing!'

The Wire – April 1997

21 Signal Regiment (AS) Colerne

ALPHA TROOP (AMF(L) 244 Signal Squadron

EXERCISE HARDFALL/ADVENTURE EXPRESS

Alpha Tp, commanded by Capt Bob Lovett, have been in Norway since the beginning of the New Year, making the most of the arctic conditions out there. Two women signallers with the Troop sent us the following article on their training.

ASSC WITH ALPHA (AMF(L) TROOP IN NORWAY

by Sigs Mackenzie and Haine

Since our arrival in 244 Sig Sqn and subsequent placement in Alpha (AMF(L) Tp, Norway was mentioned quite frequently, though not always by us, we hasten to add. After four weeks in Turkey on Ex Ardent Ground and Ex Dynamic Mix, things soon calmed down and before we realized it.

Ex Hardfall 97 was rapidly approaching. Five months later-voila! much night skiing. Over those four nights, we spent three in tents and one in a snow hide, this latter night being our survival night. We even managed the impossible task of having four hours' sleep in it! We ended the course by doing ice-breaking drills, from which we received the stark realisation that the water at home in Scotland was no comparison to that of the Arctic in terms of coldness! The course finally ended that night with a drink or three(!) to celebrate our successful completion.

In conclusion, as the two of us 'crewbirds' passed the ASSC in style, there is absolutely no reason why there shouldn't be more female 'Arctic Warriors'.

Sig Mackenzie about to take the plunge!!

The Wire – December 1996

249 Signal Squadron (AMF(L) Bulford

EXERCISE ADVENTURE EXPRESS 1997

by Sig Chris Noviss

In early February after a month of intensive training in the Arctic Ski and Survival Course, Arctic Warfare Training, Special to Arm training and the food deprivation phase of Continuation Training, the Squadron prepared for and deployed north into the Arctic Circle. This was for the three-week final exercise of the deployment, Ex Adventure Express '97. After a week-long exercise in Hjerkenn with 3 Para and the Force Arty in temperatures reaching -30C it was a relief to step off the ferry into what could almost be described as 'warmth'. I deployed on REBRO C, commanded by Cpl Nav Elliott and Sig Phil MacDiarmid. As usual the Rebros were expertly guided into location by 'The No Fear Club' or Rebro Reece. Day in, day out Sgts Rowe and Turner risked life, limb and the Sqn Comd to get onto the mountain in their BV without mashing eggs in the fresh resups. As the exercise progressed, the AMF(L) moved out of Deterrence Ops and into white cam for Combat Ops as 3 Para, the Dutch Marines and the Italian 'Alpine Bn', amongst others, bravely fought the Whiteland Forces back over their borders. As usual life was busy, and the radio nets were crammed with frantic messages in broken English as the 7 NATO nations fought both the battles of language and the war. As usual operators were deployed to all major units and on redeployment many tales were told of the pros and cons of Italian, Dutch, German, Luxembourg and Norwegian ration packs.

Exercise Adventure Express

Life on the RRB's was not without incident. W02 (SSM) Barnes attempted to fit in more flying time than the actual helicopter pilots in his effort to visit as many det as possible. A German Huey managed to mistake an HF Dipole for a HLS, hovering feet above the braid we cringed and prayed that the pilot would discover his mistake and move before we had to contend with two broken masts. LCpl 'Mick' Raine decided to try and perfect his Guy Fawkes impression, however Sig Dave 'Leading Fire-Fighter' Nix put a stop to Micks' 'burning' ambition. Luckily without major incident, the exercise ended, the AMF(L) rightfully victorious and the Squadron prepared for redeployment back to the UK. It was a pleasing sight to see the green of England after two and a half months of pure white as we touched the ground at RAF Lyneham on the 17 March.

ARCTIC TRAINING

by Sig Samuel

Ex Hardfall is an annual exercise for 249 Sig Sqn, which is held in Norway. There, the Squadron prepares itself to fulfil its role within the AMF(L) to carry out duties in an Arctic environment. A large part of the exercise is given over to training new member of the Squadron to work, fight and survive in the Arctic. This is done chiefly through the Squadron run Arctic Ski and Survival Course (ASSC).

The First section of ASSC, namely ski training is where all the new snow sprog were introduced to a wonder of modern technology, the 'Army planks', on which we were expected to be fully capable of transporting ourselves on by the end of the course. It also gave many people the opportunity to audition for the next winter Olympics freestyle ballet team. However, before we started skiing, we had to be transported to the various suicide slopes. This was done primarily by BV 206's, tracked articulated vehicles, and the Ayrton Senna driving award must be awarded to Sig John Spooner who managed to roll his leading BV on the very first day. The consequences of this were that from that moment on it was always a race to get to the BVs, since the slowest people were the ones who ended up inevitably with ‘Spooner'.

One of the first things we learnt was the graceful art of 'Dobbing' where your skis go one way and your body attempted to go in a completely different direction. This move was soon perfected by everyone, some more so than others. By the end of the first day everyone was ready for a well-deserved recovery session in the bar. The next couple of days were very similar to the first, with exhausting, and sometimes painful sessions on the slope, followed by evening PT sessions in the bar. By the third day confidence had grown, and more than once 'death before snowplough' was heard being shouted across the slopes. Unfortunately, ski training had to be postponed for a couple of days, due to the poor weather conditions (most of the snow melted!!), with conditions back in the UK being more suitable for skiing than those encountered in Norway at the time. When training resumed, we started the survival section of the course with us having to construct brushwood bivvi's to spend the night in. It was during this period that most of the people wished they had perfected the art of fire starting before being deployed. We were also warned of 'midnight choppers' of which there were more than a few. It was during this evening that Sgt Russ Ezard's section managed to misplace their 'pulk', allegedly stolen, although the section in question were seen to have quite a roaring fire at some time during the night. In the morning a replacement pulk was soon brought out, much to Cpl Adam Wilkies dismay, since he would be one of the people pulling it. Pulks looked and weighed like concrete filled coffins, and are used to carry extra section equipment, these improvised torture devices usually being pulled by the stronger members of each section. It was from now on that people seemed to be careful about how quickly they improved, since to become too good on skis inevitably meant you ended up on the pulk.

Sig Shore going for an early bath!

Sig Dodge perfecting his dobbing technique

The rest of ASSC consisted of climbing steeper and steeper hills, carrying heavier bergens and pulk, with a final night spent in snowholes, until they collapsed, when it was back to the safer tented accommodation. The conclusion of the ASSC was the 10km ski race, which was strenuous, exhausting and at time exhilarating, with the SNUT's on attachment from 11 Sigs surpassing everyone's expectations and being branded downhill speed gods, namely Sig Andy 'Doris' Day and Chris Whitely. We look forward to seeing you being posted in at the end of trade training lads!!

After ASSC came Arctic Warfare Training (AWT) but not before it became necessary to send a search party out to find W02 (SSM) Barnes, Capt Foulkes and Cpl 'Tug' Wilson, who did not return from a recce for an event later in the exercise. They claimed they knew exactly where they were, and that it wasn't necessary to have sent a helicopter out just for them. Although it did help boost the morale of all the other people who had been finding it hard to tell the difference between one pile of snow and another when looking at their maps.

The AWT phase was the tactical phase that seemed to be digging trenches and building now walls. Then watching as Mother nature decided not to play along as a temporary thaw set in and walls came tumbling down. To finish off the initial training phase it was necessary to carry out the infamous ice breaking drills, skiing into and then subsequently exiting from a hole in the ice, on one of the local lakes. It was here that most photos were taken since there was a lot of new facial expressions (as well as verbal) being exchanged. It also gave Sig 'Graffe' Clubb and LCpl Marty Quinn the chance to volunteer to have a go, but this was only so they would not have to have a bath for the rest of the deployment (allegedly).

Sig Clubb enjoying Ice Breaking Skills

With training now complete, and all of us were meant to be competent skiers, the Squadron was able to organise another ski race, this time 20km, with bergen. It was during this race that the Squadron found out it had a budding David Bailey amongst the ranks, namely LCpl Dave Howe, who used every opportunity to take photos to send back to his wife, instead of racing. The big problem was he usually stood in the middle of the race-track to take the photos. The end of the ski race also saw the end of the ASSC. But any recovery periods were short lived since most people went onto continuation training, but like I had been told before I joined the Squadron, 249 like to work hard and then play hard, and this was certainly true on Ex Hardfall 97.

FIRST IMPRESSIONS

by 2Lt J C Fraser

When I received the joining instruction for my Pre-Troop Commanders attachment to the squadron for Ex Hardfall '96 I had an idealized picture of what the Arctic environment would hold in store. Far too much time watching classics like 'Where Eagle Dare' at university instead of working distorted the reality of life in sub-zero temperatures. The condensed Dryshod package gave you an idea of the many complicating factors which effect decision making at all level in the Arctic Environment. Two things are plainly obvious, ultimately the weather is the boss, you have to work round him. The other point that struck me was how on earth do you get all the kit that is required into an issue bergen. I would soon find out.

We deployed to Norway on the 6 January to be greeted by a sudden thaw. The weather in the UK it seemed was far more suitable for ASSC training at that stage than the Voss area of Norway. Never the less we donned our army issue planks and headed for the hills to learn the art of Nordic skiing. The first lesson was on how to get up after a fall or 'dob'. Seeing our skiing ability two weeks on it still remained the most important lesson. Although none of us Arctic virgins managed to emulate the display of telemarking or the alternative Arctic dress of LCpl Macgregor, we did start to master the art of survival skiing. None more so than Sigs Abbott and King who seemed to lead charmed lives. The weather forced a reshuffle of the programme and ski training was put on ice. (I should say slush) I was to get a rapid first-hand look at the squadron's communication role and how it deployed and worked.

I thought whilst in training that the letter codes that constituted army speak were numerous but speaking to Signallers about their equipment is like listening to a never-ending stream of Batco. I have however managed to ingest the basics of what the squadron does! The detachments are scattered to the four winds of the AMF force providing comms for the entire force in a specialized and unique configuration not seen elsewhere in the Corp. The standards of the Signallers are very high by necessity and the one thing that comes across is the self-sufficient nature of the squadrons dets. However, there was one dilemma that seemed to perplex Sgt Castle at Echelon. Should we try and fix the calor gas heaters or go with the cutting edge of kerosene heating technology.

By week three the weather had changed in our favour and the ASSC returned. The course, 49 strong, took to the hills again to try and batter the Norwegian landscape flat in an endless series of high-speed wipe out. As we tried to improve our skiing new challenges in the shape of pulk and bergen materialised. With new centre of gravity and the problem of regaining your feet with weight on your back we began to see our limitation. in terms of movement in the Arctic. We also had to learn the basics of survival. The Norwegian Forestry Department need never worry about thinning or weeding its forests again. Give the army a forest for its brush wood bivvi's demo and watch the wood clear. The improvised shelter saw many variations on a wigwam theme. From Cpl Wilkies brushwood igloo to LCpl Strachan's mixed corrugated iron and brushwood thatched condo. These shelters with a fire burning were very warm. However, the forest did seem to have a peculiar tendency to spout huge naphtha induced flares periodically throughout the night. By the end of the ASSC we had slept in five and four man tents, brushwood bivvi's and a brief spell in snowholes all demonstrated throughout the course by Sgt Hawkin's Demo Troop of veteran Arctic warriors. BV's however seem to prove more comfortable.

With this completed the next phase was to put the skills into practice in a tactical environment, the AWT. With a first troop of 49 I soon found out that reality is very different from training. The Arctic is a very unforgiving place and command at rimes is a very lonely experience. The exhaustion of the course began to take its toll as the exercise continued and the Norwegian Independent Telemark Society in the shape of the Squadrons' ski gods conspired to prevent anyone getting any sleep in our tactical camp site. With the exception of two luckless members of a replen party who were kidnapped and forced to spend the night in a BV with their sleeping bags. By midnight on the second night the weather again let us know who was the boss. Rain poured down collapsing all the snow

defences that had been the main effort over the last 24 hours. Despite a valiant, if not self-defeating, exercise in damage limitation there would be only one winner, the weather. Despite the brief threat of survival night to finish, we returned home exhausted, to thaw and dry out and reflect on the previous two weeks of life in the Arctic.

The last month with the Squadron has taught me a great deal about what life in the field army is like. The learning curve is a very steep one for anyone, but at 249 you need crampons. However, the experience has far greater reward and the lessons learned certainly stick. The level of experience within the Squadron is vast and as an introduction to the Corps it is second to none. I have certainly learned a lot both good and bad both about the army and myself.

The Wire – August 1997

21 Signal Regiment (AS) Colerne

ALPHA AMF(L) TROOP 0N EXERCISE ARDENT GROUND 97

by LCpl Lutkin

Ex Ardent Ground 97 took place in Northwest Turkey and comprised of elements from eight nations. These included seven Gun Batteries, six Mortar Platoons, 11 Support Helicopters and three Fast Jet Squadrons. In total, 2,500 troops took part in what was to become the biggest Ex Ardent Ground yet. Our advance party deployed to Turkey on 27 April I997. Our Troop supplied communications for both the Support Helicopter Force and the Offensive Air Support Cell. The offensive air support side of the exercise became the busiest for several exercises, and as a result the Troop Forward Air Control (FAC) detachments soon disproved their reputation as the '20-minuters'.

As the exercise progressed, LCpl 'Squirrel' Lutkin and Sig 'Au Natural' Cogram were soon having to cope with up to 20 sorties a day from three nation’s Air Forces and spent a considerable amount of time deployed as a direct link between the multinational FAC team and the aircraft. On the whole, the exercise was a valuable boost to Troop training, whilst also providing the opportunity for some interesting cultural visits.

The Wire – August 1997

Back cover

249 Signal Squadrons' Lanyard Trophy Team enroute to winning in fine style.

The Wire – December 1997

21 Signal Regiment (AS) Colerne

ALPHA TROOP – 244 Signal Squadron

EXERCISE DYNAMIC MIX

Some thoughts from a new arrival.

As a recent arrival at 21 Sig Regt (AS) straight from a 2-year apprenticeship, I was happy to discover that my Troop exercised in different parts of the world around the year. During my first week, I was told that the Troop were deploying to Sardinia on Ex Dynamic Mix 1997.

We left RAF Lyneham on a cold and wet September night, arriving to be met by a hot Mediterranean sun. The Exercise was a CPX and once the initial set-up was complete, we established an Ex-routine, which included 'cultural visits' to the military beach - the suntan competition was started on day 1!

The Force Helicopter Unit (FHU) once again got the better deal by being accommodated with the RAF in an air-conditioned, all-facilities building, whilst the rest of us roughed it on the Ex-Area. The Troop Mobile Air Operations Team (MAOTs) had a quiet time apart from one night when Sig 'Simmerman' Simpson, aided and abetted by Sig '12 year' Lavender decided to bury their Land Rover in the sand and, much to their embarrassment, had to be rescued by colleagues. The rest of the Troop distributed their very heavy workload at the Tactical Operations Centre (TOC) by working 24-hour shifts. The weather stayed warm throughout the Exercise with temperatures up to 35 degrees Celsius, which proved too much for Sig 'Ruthy' MacKenzie, who, whilst on the convoy to the airport, forgot that the Italians drove on the wrong side of the road and got involved in a minor accident. Overall, I thoroughly enjoyed my first exercise with the Troop and look forward to Norway next year. Finally, Alpha Tp sends its thanks to all the attached personnel, namely Cpl Spencer, LCpls Graham and Pendleton and Cfn Noon for keeping the show on the road.

The Wire – June 1998

21 Signal Regiment (AS) Colerne

ALPHA TROOP (AMF(L)) - 244 SIGNAL SQUADRON

Without doubt, the winter is the busiest time of the year for the Troop with December taken up with preparation for Norway and January in Norway. With many new faces in the Troop this year the Arctic Ski Survival Course (ASSC) was the first priority.

ARCTIC SKI SURVIVAL COURSE

The newcomers to the Troop adapted well to the conditions and arduous training with Sig 'Bee' Hebden achieving a commendation to return for the Military Ski Instructors (MSI) Course. There were, however, a few minor casualties. Sig ‘Snowshoes' Daniel fractured a fingernail and was driven off the hill in a BV 206, while Cpl ‘Andy' Conley strained his knee but ‘iron manned' il to the end of the course. Sig 'Comms’ Torode deserves special mention for her excellent recovery. Having injured her knee, she returned to the UK and was seen dancing the night away down town that very night. Well done the Medical Centre. Finally, a big well done to Sigs Bradshaw, Marlborough and Simpson for passing their MSI’s course. With the Troop now fully arctic survival trained we moved onto Continuation Training.

CONTINUATION TRAINING

This year the Troop was lucky enough to join forces with 249 Sig Sqn for extra training. An excellent package was put together by their staff and the Troop learned a great deal, especially the first-year students. With the comms training complete the Troop prepared itself for deployment. In between the CO visited. He was very keen to get some snow under his boots, having already served as OC 249 Sig Sqn, in a previous life. Unfortunately for him, Sig ‘I’m a cockney' Cogram was his driver, and after trying to wipe the CO out, with some fancy BV driving, we eventually made it to the training area. That night the guys from 'The FHU' came up to the training camp and we enjoyed an eventful ‘Back to Front Night', with the CO leading. Three days of R&R followed; some of the Troop made it up the slope for some serious down-hilling. With morale on the up, we prepared ourselves for the move north and Ex Strong Resolve 1998.

EXERCISE STRONG RESOLVE 1998

After spending three rough days on the boat, we arrived in Narvik only to find that the vessel with the vehicles on was another three days sailing away. Unfortunately, those without vehicles had to stay in a top-class hotel while the rest of the Troop roughed it in the field, with temperatures reaching minus 25°C.

The Exercise started with a bang when Cpl ‘Evil Knievel' Conley crashed the Tp Comds Rover, with the Tp OC sat next to him! Both were thankfully unhurt, but the Rover was a write-off. Communications this year proved to be difficult and much engineering was required. Why is it that comms always drop out just when a Staff Officer wants to send a message - don't you just love 'em? Once again, we had the Squadron Rebros deployed: with Sig 'Rebro King' Stoves and Sig 'Chubby' Crossley on one and the ever-amusing Sig 'I want to be like Capt Lovett' Scully and Sig 'Strawberry Blonde' Barter on the other. Both teams were outstanding, especially when Sig Scully decided to put all of his petrol in his BV, leaving none to run his generator - what a guy! The highlight of the Exercise was, without doubt, the visit of the King of Norway, closely followed by the MRE bomb, which gave the Tp OC, Capt 'Steve' Abram a new hairstyle.

Sig 'I've got A Levels' Day on Rebro 21B during Ex Strong Resolve

The Wire – June 1998

249 Signal Squadron (AMF(L)) Bulford

ARCTIC SKI AND SURVIVAL COURSE 1998

(The Soldier's story) - by LCpl 'Nick' Cooper

Mid-January this year saw the Squadron leave Bulford for the annual deployment to Norway. For most of the Squadron, being 'Snow Virgins', we first had to get stuck into the Arctic Ski and Survival Course. The ASSC is an arduous two-week course aimed to train soldiers in Nordic Skiing and Arctic Survival. The first phase was lo train soldiers in the fine art of 'Dobbing' whilst attempting to get from A to B on a pair of army planks. Many times, members of the Squadron ended up face down in the snow, muttering profanities! As part of the course, it is mandatory to spend a few days under canvas and living in a snow hole. Leaming to live and carry out personal admin in a cramped tent is a test of patience if nothing else, particularly when you have to share a tent with 'tent rhino's'! After the tent phase it was time to construct and live in a snow hole spending a good few hours sweating, again muttering profanities, whilst building our 'home in the snow'. All course members were a little dubious at the prospect of the impending ice breaking drills. The thought of going into a hole cut into a frozen lake does not appeal to any sane soldier. The course was hard but with our humour and morale intact we all got through ready for the move from Voss in southern Norway to the frozen wastes of the north.

For the Squadron ED's, Sgt 'Bas' Ward, Cpl 'Si' Robinson, LCpl 'Taff' Cooper and Sig 'Gregg' Hardman the first six days were very busy. All were constantly being called out on Gene repairs, mainly cold related faults. The Squadron MT were busy on resups, with the occasional minor accident involving Sig Paul 'Rolly' Kemp whilst driving the squadron OC. Better luck next time Paul! The MT Cpl, Cpl Dave 'Ginger' Atherton, was often seen in the local Esso Garage consuming their entire stock of hot dogs, claiming he had missed meals in the cookhouse! The conditions we were working in tested morale at times, but thanks to two 'Morale Officers' from the power section, morale was maintained daily. Few people escaped from being victims of the morale officers, even the SSM, W02 (SSM) Dave Cummings had his pace stick held to Ransom: 'Bend to our demands, or the pace stick gets reduced to pencils'.

This was my first Norway deployment and it was a real eye opener. However, by the end of the exercise phase the entire Squadron were very eager to return home to see their wives and girlfriends. My Memories of the squadron deployment to Norway are good ones and even such events as the dreaded ice breaking drills were not as bad as I first thought.

ATTACHED IN NORWAY

The Officers Perspective - by 2Lt Chris Preston

No sooner had my feet touched the ground in Bulford than Arctic kit was issued, explained, demonstrated and played with. All with varying degrees of success. My first taste of the Norwegian winter was about to come, and I didn't even know what the majority of items were for. All of us had to get our basic Introduction course out of the way before re we were allowed to work in the arctic environment. This course is all about learning how to ski and as I had done a fair amount of down-hilling in the past I found it relatively easy. This course was centrally run for all UK Units within the AMF(L) and as a result there were well over 100 on the course.

The Mountain Leader heading the course had an obsession with pocket contents, a collection of safety items that seem pointless until you hit an emergency. Every morning he would have the entire course parading with individually waterproofed candles. The same instructor also showed a transvestite streak by demonstrating the ice breaking drill in a borrowed female swim suit. As we had never seen the guy smile, people had discussions about whether or not it was a triathlon outfit or was it a joke.

Maybe he was simply a pest! The ice breaking was not as bad as expected. Anyone who has capsized a canoe in near freezing conditions and experienced brain numbness need not worry. Of course, the water temperature is almost always well above the temperature of the air and as such could be regarded as a refreshing dip! That is not to say that your voice and parts of your body do not take a vertical leap! Having completed the snow hole phase on ASSC I was invited by my OC, Maj Peter Holliday to jump into another one.

The last two weeks of the 249 Sig Sqn Arctic Warfare Instructor Course would prove to be my continuation training. This course proved to be physically demanding and I lost half a stone in the fourteen days – some would say I needed to! The Survival week included three types of snow hole and the same number of nights out on the mountains, time spent in the snow trench left Cpl Bell and me homeless and decidedly unhappy.

My thanks go to Cpl Bell for not losing his rag as the previous two hours work collapsed at our feet. Ice Breaking 2 allowed us to practice speaking whilst in the water. The demonstration of the swim is difficult to do as it is hard to stop the voice 'yodelling'. The top prize for coolness under pressure went to an RAF Flight Lieutenant who made the water look warm. I found that the extra time in the water turned my thighs blue! The survival week finished with a brushwood bivvi night. This proved to be one of the most cold, wet and miserable nights of my life. Whilst Sgt 'Jack' Hawkins slept in his warm BV206 we erected an improvised wigwam and huddled around the fire. Unfortunately, the frozen stream that we did not see melted, flooding the shelter and swamping the fire. Undeterred we moved and started again. The next shelter proved to keep out only part of the persistent rain and eventually when it set alight, we abandoned the bivvi entirely and walked about until dawn.

Next came my Arctic Warfare Instructors course run by 3 Para! We started by going downhill skiing. The Force AWO proved his insanity suggesting we jump from the cable car to the powder snow. I assumed he was joking? Moments later eight of us bad followed like stupid sheep to the slope twenty feet below. Meanwhile other members of the course were still 'Rising from a Fall.' The four major exercises of the course kicked off with man-packing the large ten-man tents in pulks. This is hard work and a number of teddy bears flew at an early stage. Once at the destination for the day the DS insisted on a night navigation exercise as well that lasted a further four hours and removed valuable rest. Night skiing is a bizarre combination of feel and sight. Often your eyes tell you that you are moving, and your feet say otherwise. The survival phase of this AWI course was yet more snow-holes, My eighth in two months. Sgt Howley went one better and was buried as part of an avalanche demo: Unfortunately, a visiting photographer stole his ski poles and he had to ski the downhill run next day with a bergen but no sticks. Fortunately, he was the best skier on the course.

Although this was an Arctic Warfare course, the warfare section lasted only 36hrs. A round robin of Fire positions on skis, extraction drills, snowshoe assaults and an Op lesson was the only instruction we were given before receiving orders to go and fight. The following night we deployed at 1800 hrs with full bergens and a rifle attached to our sides. The tab in was immense. In eight hours, we covered no less than 6km. The steep slope and the dense forest reduced our speed to a snail's pace despite working hard enough to stay warm in only a thermal top and smock.

Having reached the position, we dug the tent in and kept eyes on the enemy, who had been thoughtful enough to leave their vehicle indicators on. Fortunately, the following day allowed most of us to catch up on sleep as we stagged on. The Assault the next morning very nearly went 'pear shaped' as the enemy were found to be stood-to. This was simply because the DS were on the net and we retreated back to the FUP like startled rabbits. Eventually we found our way down a covered approach and took the position. I narrowly missed diving headlong into the toilet trench as I ran through on the assault, but it was the best available cover! The final phase was a long-distance unsupported tab that tested my resolve to the extreme, particularly as I spent a considerable period 'mono-skiing' after breaking a ski!

For a first winter in Norway, I had a 'Baptism of Fire'. Whilst most do a course a year. I had spent three months under-going training that finally gained me an AWI qualification. Bizarre as it may sound, as I enjoy skiing so much, I would do it again next year and if I am lucky enough to be posted back to 249 Sig Sqn (AMF(L)) maybe I will!

The Wire – February 1999

249 Signal Squadron (AMF(L)) Bulford

EXERCISE CO-OPERATIVE ADVENTURE EXCHANGE 1998

SLOVENIA

On 14 November at, 'oh my god o'clock' the main body of 249 Sig Sqn (AMF(L)) left Bulford for the snowy scenery of Slovenia. The flight was on time and all appeared to be going rather well until it was discovered that. in the hectic collection of vehicles at the port, one lone Land Rover appeared to have been left behind. So, the recovery party set off on the 5hr drive to the port. However, on reaching the Rover it was discovered that the keys for the fuel tank remained in the pocket of Sgt (YofS) Gaz Currie. But SSgt Ken Marsh and Sgt Jase Raybould didn't mind the drive (much).

The Squadron was dispersed to all four-comers of the Exercise area, the two-principal locations were the echelon at Cerklje airfield and the Radcon element, as part of the TOC, at Brestinica. In addition, the main part of the squadron was deployed to CP and RRB locations to provide full communications facilities for the exercising Troops.

It seemed as if we had been in Slovenia for a week before the exercise had even started but that is because we had! SSgt (YofS) Gaz Currie had been particularly busy attempting to teach other nation's watch-keeper (AMF(L)) voice procedure. He also convinced himself that he was the reason that the girls from Alpha Troop insisted on doing day shifts.

As the Exercise progressed the voice procedure did improve especially after Sgt Ady Simms (I am putting weight on honest) realised that in fact he was not the GOC! LCpl Johnny Whitrow managed to convince the German NBC Platoon that the blown-up bridge was just exercise play!

Meanwhile Sgt 'Saddam' Marsh shared his culinary knowledge with the Americans, as his new Friend Marty insisted on his advice for the banquet for the visit of the Belgian princess. We managed to top them serving Brussel sprouts. As Marty was so generous with his chocolate and cereal donations, SSgt Ken Marsh didn't have the heart to tell him that he was not in fact the Squadron's Head Chef.

What better way to finish an Exercise than with a march and shoot competition? The NATO Challenge Cup this year was over a distance of between 8.5 and 9.2 miles (allegedly) and, during the team briefing, the event was likened to a CFT. Some CFT! The route included sections going up waterfalls and down near vertical slopes and in total took approximately five hours. The whole team worked extremely well, but a mention must be made of Sig Adam Rudge and LCpl 'Buzz' Bury who both did good 'crazy leg crane' impressions - some people will do anything to get rid of their Bergens. The team finished in third place overall and a sterling effort was made by all with everyone who started completing the route and it was with smiling faces that we received the results and found that we had beaten many infantry units, including 3 Para!

The Wire – April 1999

249 Signal Squadron (AMF(L)) Bulford

EXERCICS DRYSHOD

by Sig Gaingee and Sig Smith

On the 4 December the main body of the Squadron departed from the familiar confines of its compound to Okehampton Camp, Dartmoor, for Ex Dryshod. The Exercise is designed to give the newer members of the Squadron an insight into life in a cold weather environment prior to deploying to Norway. The week was split into two parts. The first three days were spent in the class room, absorbing the endless but important stream of survival techniques (along with the occasional horror story) needed for the squadron's annual cold weather deployment. The skills taught included how to dress in a cold weather environment, how to treat cold casualties, numerous lessons on pocket contents and, most importantly, not to touch your ski pole with your tongue because it will not come off again (somebody manages it every year!).

The second phase was spent out on the rough, unforgiving hills and tors of Dartmoor. This began with a night navigation exercise during which the terrain proved treacherous to inexperienced hill walkers, such as Sig 'I can drive' Bailey and Sig Gallager, both of whom would frequently disappear up to their waists in mud. Sig 'Don Juan' Beat accompanying us from 21 Sig Regt (AS), managed to launch himself over a wall and dropped head first into a pool of stagnant water. This was a source of obvious entertainment for the rest of the team and thereby caused a great increase in morale. The next morning, after spending a comfortable night in our four-man tents and hearing tales of Norway that all began with 'in Norway', we set off on another navigation exercise. This time it was somewhat less hazardous, as the bogs were easier to negotiate in daylight.

We were split into five teams, each carrying 70lbs plus comms equipment, and covered over 20kms during the day. Most teams did arrive by the time night drew in, cold and wet but with high morale, ready for the final day. The final day began with simulated casualty evacuations. We were tasked, with the aid of 'helper sledges', with carrying several of the larger members of the Squadron such as Sgt 'Small Piece' Ashman, Cpl 'Haystacks' Hurst, and LCpl ' Blobby Bob' Abbott to an evacuation point via a swamp, a stream, a fence and a hill! But the grassy hills of Dartmoor proved a little more difficult to manoeuvre the sledges over, than the snowy slopes of Norway. Casualties were dragged through, rather than carried over the water, thrown over the fence and bumped up to the evac' point! After this we returned to camp where many a tired, cold and numbed brain attempted the closing written examination, in which LCpl 'Tech Burly' Longworth achieved top marks. In all it was an informative and thoroughly enjoyable week, one I would not hesitate to repeat, especially if the weather was a little more forgiving.

EXERCISE SNOWHOLE 1999 - NORWAY

Ex Snowhole 1999 was a training exercise conducted by the UK's AMF(L) contingent in Norway, in order to train personnel in the skills required to operate in a cold weather environment. The Exercise consisted of three separate, but concurrently running parts. The Cold Weather Warfare Instructors course (CWWI) and BV 206 Instructors Course (BVI) were run from Brandset Camp, while the Novice Ski and Survival Course (NSSC) was run from Bømoen Camp, Voss. In addition to being excellent individual training, the purpose of all three course was to ensure that the UK contingent retains its collective ability to operate in a cold weather environment. Next year there will be a longer, full squadron deployment to Norway, which will culminate with an AMF(L) FTX in Poland.

249 Signal Squadron in Norway 1999

The first NSSC started like many others in previous years - late. Due to problems with the RAF aircraft the course finally arrived at Bømoen Camp 12 hours later than scheduled. The course started the following day with various mandatory lectures and lessons in basic skiing techniques. The course is physically demanding and requires a high degree of personal skills. Its main aim is to teach soldiers how to survive in a cold weather environment and, of course, to stay upright and move on skis. As with any such course there are many highlights, most of which are at the expense of others. Two are worthy of mention; firstly, Sig Russ 'Son of Kev/fingers' Wellburn who managed to sustain a cold weather injury (frostnip) after only 30mins on skis. Secondly W02 (YofS) Tac 'Robin Cousins' Bartlett, who managed to injure himself on the Saturday night Car Park ice skating gala, needless to say he was the only contestant!

The finale of the course was the Cold Weather Warfare Training where, apart from digging in company harbour areas, the main source of entertainment was the OC, Maj Jim Foulkes, who whilst playing 'enemy on skis' with the instructor's course, was viciously attacked by a four-man tent pit resulting in him sustaining a nasty nick to the forehead. The course finished in the same way it had started - late. This time the aircraft managed to be 30 hours late, however, any animosity that might have been felt was quickly assuaged by the sight of the next course arriving at the airport.

SWISS TECHNICAL AVALANCHE COURSE, ANDERMATT

by Lt Preston

Whilst working hard with the Staff Officers of Heidelberg and their Norway training, I was offered the opportunity to attend the Avalanche Course in Switzerland. This course is run by the Swiss Army for any NATO countries and lasts two weeks. There had been no British Army attendees thus far and I joined Capt Crossman RLC, as the first two British Officers on the course.

Andermatt is two hours train ride from Zurich and is 1445m above sea level. The population is 1450 people and depends on tourism and the military for income. The Course centres around the Mountain Combat Training Centre and the Barracks which have existed since 1967. Three local mountains dominate the valley. The largest is the Gemsstock which stands a lofty 2963m high and provides excellent downhill opportunities. Smaller but with the ski lift just outside the back door of the school is the Gutsch (2344m). This was the location for much of the training. The course being multi-national uses four languages. German, French and Italian are the three national languages of Switzerland, whilst most people peak good English as well. The opening address given by Lt Col Gnos was in each of the four languages, an impressive skill. Once into the course the different groups were split up into language groups as hearing the same information four times rapidly became tiresome.

Lt Preston after a more spectacular fall

The opening days covered avalanche principles the Swiss way. We examined many factors in great detail, including the size of individual snowflakes, snow temperature, humidity and stability of each layer – this becomes in-depth science very quickly. The medical side of training was taught by the local doctor, resident in the main hospital of the area and experienced in treating cold weather injuries. The emphasis was on sharing the experience of the mountain rescue team members on the course. The big areas of debate were 'after-drop' and 'CPR'. The after-drop is the effect of moving a casualty after they have suffered the initial effects of hypothermia. The body pulls the warm blood into the core of the body leaving the extremities cold. The important areas stay warm as long as the blood does not move around too much. Excessive movement will reintroduce the cold blood to the heart area and will kill the patient. CPR is often given at the scene of an avalanche accident. However, if you start CPR then you must be able to continue treatment all the way into the hospital. This may slow down the evacuation and the patient may benefit from remaining in deep freeze until they reach the hospital where the Swiss now practice open heart massage and a gradual warming of the blood. Another aspect of the course which scared both of the British officers attending was the explosives section. Plastic explosive is used to stop the build-up of snow on steep slopes, initiating the fall of snow before it can hurt anyone. The Swiss having more relaxed regulations than the British would happily prepare explosive charges in the classroom. I am no expert on the British regulations, but my ATO colleague assured me that detonators are not usually allowed inside without extra precautions. Even more worrying was the method of carrying the detonator and fuse cord around the neck to avoid dropping it! Once on the range the excitement continued. The charge was prepared by adding an initiator or small percussion cap device to the end of the fuse wire. This needs both hands and so the student crouches forward to keep the charge dry with 100gm of plastic explosive between his knees. Once the charge is attached to a retaining cord it is thrown into the avalanche prone area, grenade style. The student then makes a hasty withdrawal and puts his fingers in his ears. Health and safety at work hasn't reached Andermatt yet! The course awarded each student with a diploma from the Mountain training centre and gifts a plenty. It is an excellent course which shows Norway trained personnel the alpine way of doing things and offers a wealth of new information.

EXERCISE WINTER LINK

The Squadron deployed to Norway this year in two halves. Whilst one half were cold weather training SSgt (YofS) Currie had the pleasure of running Ex Winter Link for the remainder back in Bulford. Ex Winter Link was designed to train the new operators to the squadron and revise the 'old and bold' on some of the equipment, procedures and skills required to provide effective communications within this unit's unique role. The first phase of the Exercise was classroom based with instruction on a wide array of subjects, including Communications in an Arctic Environment, the data entry device 'Kipling', AMF(L) Voice Procedure and the PRC 320 (which many operators claim never to have seen before) to name but a few. Once the theory was out of the way the 'students' were let loose on Salisbury Plain where they practised and were tested on what they should have learned in the classroom.

Over the next four days not only were their communications skills tested but the map reading and driving ability of the Squadron's finest were put to the test. Students were given the grids of stands which were strategically placed across the length and breadth of SPTA where upon arrival they were given practical demonstrations on how the unit provides communications for a truly multi-national force. They were then practically tested on what they had been taught throughout the week by the squadron's more experienced 'gurus'. The students were particularly impressed by the Kipling stand, where LCpl 'Johnny' Whitrow made them run around a field several times before testing them. Says LCpl Whitrow 'It's all part of a realistic scenario'. Really!!

The Exercise proved to be a huge success with not only the newer arrivals, but many of the more experienced operators learning some new and varied skills, skills that are particular to this units' unique role as the AMF(L) Radio Squadron.

The Wire – June 1999

249 Signal Squadron (AMF(L)) Bulford

ALLIED OFFICERS WINTER WARFARE COURSE ELVERUM, NORWAY SKYTE - OG VINTERSKOLE FOR INFANTERIET (SCHOOL OF INFANTRY, NORWAY)

by Capt Alistair Fawcett

This six-week course based in Elverum, Norway is designed to teach Officers and NCOs, from across NATO, the basics in military skiing techniques, minor tactics in cold weather condition and survival. The course is primarily aimed at the infantry and had students from sixteen different nations taking part. With fifty on the course the British had the largest contingent taking part. Of the fourteen from Britain six were Marines, four were from 22 SAS, one from the Special OPs RA, two from CSS Bn AMF(L) and myself. The other students came from as far afield as USA and Estonia, which did present a number of language problems during orders sessions as well as on the social front. The majority of them were from their own countries Special Forces, for example, my section consisted of a Greek, a Spaniard, two Danes, a German, some Americans and a few British.

The course tarted with the usual rounds of briefing and kit issues which were necessary prior to the start of the training itself. In order that every student had equal 'benefit' from his equipment the only kit we could use was that issued by the Norwegian Army. This meant no Gore-Tex, no thermal lined Alico ski-march boots, no bivvi bag, no expensive tent and wooden skis. The Norwegians are quite open about the standard of their kit, but with their experience in the Arctic climate they know what is necessary and what is sufficient. Their equipment is mainly made from natural materials such a cotton and wool, simple but functional. We don't know how lucky we are!

The skiing was the first important skill to crack, and this had to be done in a couple of days prior to the start of the first Exercise. Many of the students had no experience with military skiing and therefore it paid to have a sense of humour. Having never skied before I was concerned over my ability to a similate the required skills before the start of the Exercise. After a week of skiing, we deployed into the local training area complete with bergens, webbing, an AE-3 issued rifle, pulks (sledges for carrying equipment), carrying radios and on skis. The average pace of a proficient section on skis should be approximately 4km per hour. We didn't quite manage this, but everyone was impressed with our progress. It is not easy patrolling tactically on skis and yes there were a lot of falls. The learning curve was immense and by the end of the first Exercise we were skiing at night, while navigating, pulling pulks and in wooded locations.

The weeks progressed and individuals became better at skiing the distance and moves became further (up to 35km at a time) and the exercises became more tactically based. The temperature rarely went above -5 and on occasions dropped as -38. This proved difficult when in the mountains and while on sentry duty at night. The entire way you operate is dictated by the weather condition, but you soon learn what you can and can't do. Many students were from Scandinavian countries and were excellent at operating in this climate. They could generally ski very well but by the end of the course the majority of the other Students could keep up with them. The final Exercise had possibly the hardest start with a long 24hr infiltration ski, followed by setting up Op on various targets. This is very time consuming, as it is very important to leave no sign of your presence. The final task was a platoon ambush on a BV mounted Coy HQ while on the move followed by a rather long and quick exit ski march. The course itself was excellent. The Norwegians have a totally different attitude to working in Arctic condition and try to use it in their favour rather than let it dictate to them. The course was well structured with weekends being free, a number of Mess functions and a lot of good laughs, but ultimately it was testing both mentally and physically. An interesting aspect of the course was working with the other nations. After each Exercise, lecture, ambush or attack, for example, there would be the opportunity to discuss how each nation would have carried that particular aspect of the training. Generally, there were similar methods, but some details were wildly different. I would certainly recommend the course to any willing volunteer, but as we are the only squadron who can load officers and NCOs on to the course you had best get your posting preferences sorted.

Sig 'P' Perkins and those first faltering steps

THE COLD WEATHER WARFARE INSTRUCTORS COURSE

by Cpl Foster

It was a cold Saturday night when we touched down at Bergen, Norway. Ahead lay the Cold Weather Warfare Instructors Course, six arduous weeks of skiing and ski-touring. We were to be based in Brandeth Camp, approximately 20 minutes from the town of Voss. The initial three weeks consisted of giving lessons to and providing demonstrations for the Arctic Ski and Survival Course (ASSC). For the first two weeks we assisted the course run for the staff from HQ AMF{L) in Heidelberg. Many of whom were from differing NATO countries. It was during this phase that my accent came in to its own when I managed to confuse not only the students but most of the instructors a well. The culmination of this course was the survival phase, in which many chickens met the big chicken in the sky by way of the cooking pot.

On the third week we had to give a penetration demonstration to the members of the first Arctic Ski and Survival Course from UK. Included in this was the concurrent activities of section attacks and skijoring. Skijoring, my lesson, consisted of a lot of laughs as personnel were towed behind a BV at speeds of up to 25km. Needless to say balance was frequently lost, and many spent their time digging themselves out of snowdrifts. The section attacks were hard and Sgt Phil Render quickly realised that attacks in deep snow with snowshoes are pretty difficult. The final night of the course was an attack by our course against those on the ASSC. The ensuing battle looked very much like the opening scenes from 'Saving Private Ryan', nevertheless it was both enjoyable and a fitting end to the week.

In week four the course began the serious ski touring in the mountains of Voss. The going was good until the course ran into difficult weather. Visibility was virtually zero and we had to find shelter in a mountain hut. This weather did not clear and four days later we had to come down from the hills. It later emerged that many had been blown off their feet while attempting to get down. This was all part of the build-up to the final week, a mammoth ski-tour of 137km, during which temperatures dropped as low as -37. Fittingly the ski-tour ended at entertainment establishments of the town of Geilo. At the end of the course Sgts Phil Render and Chris Trowbridge gained their Cold Weather Warfare Instructor qualification.

EXERCISE ADVENTURE EXCHANGE 1999

The squadron saw a quick tum around post Norway ready for the AMF(L) annual cold weather deployment. This year's Exercise was based in north-east Italy in the regions of the Camil Alps and Friuli Venezia Giulia. The Exercise itself was part FTX and part CPX and involved five battalions including NATO's newest members, the Hungarians, Polish and Czechs. The deployment based on an Article V Scenario lasted approximately two weeks and saw the progression from deterrent operation to combat operations. The squadron deployed ready for adverse weather conditions with the

BV 206 over-snow mounted RRBs carrying ski equipment, white cam nets and sufficient rations should the weather have closed in.

Each individual carried cold weather equipment including cam whites and the SOP kit list for any cold weather deployment. Upon landing at the APOE we soon realised the initial weather report had been woefully wrong and only the highest peaks were snow-capped. The temperature was well above zero and at time reached into the twenties. Only the detachments on the highest features were in the snow line, but most still required 'careful' siting by the more experienced det comds.

RRB C and D carefully sited

Geographically the region is very mountainous with a number of valleys crossing both west to east and north to south. This presented a number of 'problems' for communications but the Command Net, and squadron main effort, remained consistent throughout. Both headquarters were in place with the alternate HQ providing the real-estate for the GOC, Maj Gen Reith, to trial a prototype battlefield integrated IS system. The prototype is a complex command and control facility designed to fuse information from the various staff cell databases and present it on a virtual screen. Still in its early development stage it did have a number of teething problems, but it has highlighted the way forward in many respects. The Staff had to work double time updating both the physical bird table and the virtual bird table, but Rome was not built in a day. This trialling did, unfortunately, mean the Exercise was relatively static with the change of control between HQ occurring only twice.

Deploying with the squadron were a number of personnel on their first Exercise. Sig Johnston, a case in point, arrived from Blandford on the Monday and was in Italy on the Thursday. A sudden realisation that he was no longer in Radio Group at 11 Sig Regt but providing communications for the Force Helicopter Unit (FHU). At FHU LCpl Daz Walker had the unique opportunity of providing communications from the air, in the back of a command-variant Blackhawk, whilst flying with the GOC. In addition, we had four augmentees from 35 Sig Regt, who managed to cope with the arduous 'arctic' conditions experienced and provided much needed operator support.

LCpl Daz Walker - Comms from the air

As with any major deployment the Squadron role of honour is long and distinguished and a few individuals deserve a mention. Capt 'The strawberry blonde' Stokoe after dealing with one DAMCON incident managed to play a number of games of football and reach level 10 on 'Quake' (oh how hard 2ICs work). W02 (YofS) 'The Gun Slinger' Bartlett managed to shock all in G6 with his sudden posting but promised everyone the Squadron would be getting a full-sized grown-up Yeoman as his replacement. Sgt 'Saddam' Marsh proved again that he wears the trousers in his Troop (right under his pinny) by producing a fine display of Indian cuisine throughout the Exercise. Cpl 'Mountain Goat' Upcraft will again never deploy without sufficient cigarettes as he almost had a heart attack carrying out a personal resup. LCpl 'I'll just remain in bed until Brig Radcliffe arrives' Douglas for demonstrating the professional nature of the Squadron's JNCO's by remaining true to the motto 'a good soldier sleeps when he can' despite Comd AMF(L) UK Element's visit being imminent. Last, but by no means least, Cfn 'Starksy' Hardy for demonstrating his defensive driving skills at the SPOD. A big well done to them all.

The Wire – October 1999

21 Signal Regiment (AS) Colerne

ALPH TROOP (AMF(L)) - 244 Signal Squadron

EXERCISE ADVENTURE EXCHANGE 1999

At the beginning of March, the advance party from Alpha Troop departed Colerne for the Winter Exercise of this year Ex Adventure Exchange. With our arctic kit firmly packed, we left under the steady leadership of Capt 'New Boy' Graham (Sqn 2IC) and SSgt (YofS) Scott Logan. After many delays at South Cerney and some companionable socialising with Force Arty in the NAAFI, we assembled at Brize Norton for the flight out to Italy. On our arrival on Italian soil, we speedily departed to the coast to collect the vehicles under police escort – flashing blue lights and sirens wailing. The journey to location was long and laborious but the locals managed to lay on road-side entertainment for the lads all the way. As always, Alpha

Tp soon came to grips with the extreme weather conditions which were encountered. With constant sunshine and temperatures averaging 25 degrees every day, the skis and mitts soon became redundant. Award for the best suntan was judged to a dead heat between Cpl 'Wills' Williams and Cfn 'This is hard work' Cooke. At Main and Alt, Villa Santina, much hard work was undertaken with our international counterparts, the Americans, Canadians, German and Italians, to name but a few. Sigs Kerrie Haines and Ruth Mackenz1e, enjoying their last exercise with the Troop, braved the Italian rail system and spent a pleasurable day in Venice. This exercise was also our final goodbye to Sig John 'Tabs' Marlborough and LCpl Neil Cogram. A final farewell to 2Lt Martin Willis, who has endured a SSLC posting to the Regiment, the Troop would like to thank him for his efforts of the past ten months in what has been an eventful posting and wish him well as he moves to Leeds University to embark on his degree course. Last, but by no mean least, the Troop says farewell to SSgt (YofS) Scott Logan who has endured almost a year with the Troop. Having eaten all the pies, he leaves to take on the equally demanding role of YofS for 220 Sig Sqn, when they reform at Colerne later this year. Welcome to Capt Andy Arthurton who takes over the reins as Troop OC as Capt Steve Abram moves over to become the 2IC Squadron for a well-earned rest having spent two years in command.

The Wire – October 1999

249 Signal Squadron (AMF(L)) Bulford

OPERATION AGRICOLA - 501 COBALT

Since the beginning of the NATO deployment and the increase of tension in the Kosovo region a detachment from the squadron has been deployed providing satellite Communications in a variety of roles to different headquarters. Deployed on the detachment has been Sgt Pete Eden, Cpl Gareth Howell, LCpl Gaz Prydie and Sig Russ Taylor. They have been ably assisted by two personnel from 30 Sig Regt. LCpl Puslikar and Sig Scott Cooper.

DEPLOYMENT DIARY - by Sig Russ Taylor

On initial deployment we were based in Kumanovo, Macedonia. Here we were attached to 7 Sig Regt providing a theatre COMMCEN and a Standby Ptarmigan link to the Corsham Hub. Life was very much static and routine as we waited for the decision to be made over possible move into Kosovo. During the two months we worked hard at honing our pizza eating skills, with Sgt Pete Eden emerging as the most superior. Most importantly we managed, against all odds to win the 30 Sig Regt Five-a-side football competition. On the day of the competition the bookie had us at 40-1 no hopers but the team consisting of Sgt Al Ironside, Cpl Gareth Howell, Sig Scott Cooper, LCpl Phil Hughes and myself managed to overcome all challengers to claim the prize. What tipped the balance was the cheerleading capabilities of Sgt Phil Eden, who was forced to sit the competition out after forgetting his trainers (Admin!!). When finally the move into Kosovo came it was quite an event. After closing down all links at 0600hrs on the morning of the move we had to push quite hard in order to be ready for the first packet leaving at 0700hrs. The French vehicles at the front were the first to move and the Whacky Races began. What followed was quite humorous as three lanes of traffic bound for Kosovo and one lane leaving attempted to make headway along a road that could be classed as a country lane. This meant that it took us 11 hrs to reach our final destination, the town of Mitrovica. In that time, we had travelled just I39km. Driving through the villages and towns enroute there was nothing but devastation as most areas were completely destroyed with rubble strewn everywhere. The people were out in force lining the streets and singing pro-NATO songs.

On reaching Mitrovica it was much the same story. The town was gutted and virtually deserted. We are now firmly entrenched in Mitrovica providing a Ptarmigan Satellite Bridge and eagerly awaiting our end of tour in September. During this time the Squadron has also had soldiers deployed on Op Palatine and in Albania on Op Spooner.

The Wire – April 2000

249 Signal Squadron (AMF(L)) Bulford

NOVICE SKI AND SURVIVAL COURSE - by Cpl 'Loddy 'Jones

On arriving in Norway for the first time my worst fears were realised. There was snow everywhere, I was freezing, and I really was going to need the mountain of equipment I had been issued on joining the Squadron. Thoughts like 'It can't be too cold, can it?' soon dispersed as I found myself severely underdressed in just a smock and T-shirt. Well, you live and learn.

On arrival at Mjolfjell Camp, our home for the foreseeable future, we were issued with yet more kit and these very long items I now know to be skis. The next day myself and my fellow non-skiers met our Military Ski Instructors (MSI). Cpl 'See its easy' Samuel gave us an excellent demonstration which had me thinking 'Well, that doesn't look too hard'. WRONG! I soon wondered why I was sat on my butt in the snow after trying the seemingly simple manoeuvre of standing up.

Sgt 'Tony' McBean - On the skis, now try moving

It was not a total disaster and as the week progressed our skiing ability improved - well sort of. We could now stand up for a short period of time anyway. Moving on from that to a night out was a step up again. Deployed in four-man tents, or should I say very small man tents. It was here that we came to understand the phrase 'Tent Rhino'. Four people dressed as 'Michelin men' trying to do their admin in a tent designed for pygmies would test the most organised of field soldier. Following our cramped accommodation, we moved to the comparative luxury of a ten-man tent. This mini-deployment was topped off by ice-breaking drills the next day. Cold doesn't even get close.

Cpl Si Upcraft feels the shock of the cold

Redeployment back to camp and a night out in Voss followed. Sunday brought the issue of yet more kit and preparation for the second deployment phase. A night in the pygmy tents was followed by a night in sow-holes. Basically, digging all day and all night to sleep in, if you don't mind enclosed spaces. Then, in order to qualify for the second 'S' in NSSC we moved onto the survival night. We had everything demonstrated from fire starting and brushwood shelters to sheep slaughtering - not popular with me as I'm a Welshman. Essentially all the skill required to survive in the Arctic. It was not that cold as building the brushwood shelter and cutting the wood to keep the very large fire going was enough to keep anybody warm. No sleep and little food meant that everybody was pretty tired by the time we returned to Mjolfjell on Friday morning, as if that wasn't enough, we had to take part in a 12km ski race on Saturday. 6km uphill, followed by a mad 6km descent: it was not for the faint-hearted. This was followed by an apparently obligatory toga party at Mjolfjell on Saturday evening. As I write the course has not finished as we are deployed on the Winter Warfare phase of it. I can say that the course has been immensely enjoyable and a worthwhile experience for all.

COLD WEATHER WARFARE INTRUCTORS COURSE

by Sgt Raybould

The CWWI course is the highest cold weather qualification that any rank can attain whilst serving with 249 Sig Sqn (AMF(L)) and for our sins (or are we just lucky?) myself and Sgt Pete Lawn were put forward to be the chosen ones. Once qualified we would be expected to advise the OC Sqn on all matters of cold weather operation and training. It also allows us to run the Sqn Novice Ski and Survival Course (NSSC) which is required by all members of the squadron to enable them to deploy to the Arctic and carry out their role. Having been brought back from Bosnia early to attend this course it had already got a big tick in the box from Pete and myself. That initial euphoria was short lived, as when we arrived in Norway there was no snow and things didn't look promising for our course. After ten days of struggling by the DS to stick to the programme, they decided to move us to a glacier near Jondal where we would be guaranteed snow and therefore be able to achieve the training objectives to gain the qualification. Once there we had more snow than you could wish for, however, we then had to put up with winds sometimes in excess of 60 knots. It all seemed a bit like 'out of the frying pan and into the fire'. However, after spending many nights out and every possible chance on skis we had not achieved all the objectives which left everyone concerned in a bit of a dilemma. It was therefore decided to bring the whole course back on 9 January 2000 to complete the remaining objectives such as ice breaking and snow holes and I was pleased to say everything went very well. Sgt Pete Lawn and myself are now qualified CWWI's and looking forward to our first challenge, which will be the sqn's NSSC in February 2000.

The Wire – April 2000

21 Signal Regiment (AS) Colerne

244 SIGAL SQUADRON - ALPHA TROOP AMF(L) - by Cpl Paul Annetts

The normal beginning then for the usual WIRE notes routine, let's say goodbye to a few members of the Troop: In no particular order then, seeya's to SSgt (YofS) Scott 'Pieman' Logan, deserting the Troop to be Sqn YofS, 150 yards up the road at 220! LCpl Daz Daniels who's off to the sunny delights of 14 Sig Regt, on promotion, Mr Dave Marlor who by now will be skipping down civvy street, and finally to our illustrious backbone, Sgt Tim Tomkinson off on his, cheers easy crypto and then YofS course, hats off fellas. Into the Troop fold we welcome LCpls 'Elts' Eltringham from JCUNI, 'Spud' Evans from 16 Air Assault Bde, Sig 'Blodwin' Owens from the factory and finally Sig Matt Simpson from 15 Sig Regt.

Well, it was back to Earth with a bang after the habitual self-abuse of the New Year and the anti-climax of the Millennium......no bugs in sight. We were greeted on the first day with a briefing from the CO telling us, that due to health and safety regulations, we could no longer work in the asbestos filled, rain leaking, electrically shorted, unheated and badly lit hangars, as we had been doing for a number of years. So, although the order from the CO not to do any work was greeted by some with whoops of joy, with only three weeks remaining until we deployed to the barren Arctic wastes of Norway, Alpha Tp felt the heat turning up! The same decision a few weeks later and we would have probably found us cart-wheeling down the streets of Colerne, but in good old Army tradition we adapted and overcame - (worked like stink when our kit was de-contaminated really!) and deployed in a ready state.

Thanks go out from all the novices to Sig Andy Day who, when as courier stopped their pocket contents from swelling. Whilst doing a unit pickup at Donnington for 100 Recco Reflectors (Avalanche locators - about 8cm long) was almost palmed off with Rover reflectors – Land Rover Reflectors!! Well spotted Andy, obviously the Lance Corporal in you trying to get out - MCM Div take note.

Exercise Hardfall 2000, is the UK element's Cold Weather environment training exercise. Starting on 30 January 2000, two courses were running concurrently, one with the AMF(L) Log Bn on which the lads from the Troop were participating and one run by 249 Sig Sqn, on which I was fortunate to be instructing, with the females and attached personnel on this course. With different levels of success, everyone was qualified to deploy north. A special mention must go to Cpl 'Scouse' Alston who completed the I2km ski race well ahead of all other novices and beating myself (resident MST!) by a margin of approximately one minute. Personally, I blame it on the fact people didn't like the idea of a Scouser where they couldn't see him so allowed him in front so they could keep an eye on him, not that I'm one to whinge! Another mention must go to Sig 'Taff' Charnley who was awarded a certificate for most morale on the course! It didn't stop there as he got frost nip where only 'Taff' can ......due to the lack of pants in temperatures of-14°C.

Although initially sharing accommodation with a fellow Corps unit, when 249 Sig Sqn had their main body arrive, Mjolfjell a small hamlet East of Voss was not big enough for the both of us. The Troop acquired a hostel a few kilometres down the road where it was possible to accommodate the Troop in its entirety. With mountains, snow and blue sky the continuation training days were enjoyable, not mentioning the real log fire, piano and a couple of cases of Double Ice that ensured the evening debriefs were cosy.

Finally, a short anecdote on how not to cut hair. As word spread around the tight camp at Mjolfjell of the Troop barber, my room seemed to take on the look of a down trodden hair salon. I, Cpl 'Vidal' Annetts, resident hair guru (not!) had the boss, Capt Holbrook, and the Troop Staffy, SSgt Daz 'RQ' Sheerin MBE, (who has just been selected for promotion), arrive for, 'Just a trim please.' Successfully completing the Troop Staffy's hair, a practice, for the man who writes my CR. I was engaged in lots of banter on how I would screw it up and cut too much off - I reached for the scissors. Whether it was all the skiing, I'm not sure, but I ended up cutting a little too wildly. Seeing the funny side, the boss allowed me to use the clippers on a No. 4. In the low-lit room, I inadvertently picked up a No.2 guard and only realised after the second stroke... oops. Thinking things could get no worse I decided not to tell Capt

Holbrook and continued. It was the boss who informed me 30 seconds later that the guard had fallen completely off. I had dealt one monk making, Rabi resembling, unguarded clipper blow to my boss 's head!!!!!- right on the crown- I felt sick. The accommodation block was rocked by laughter, none of it was mine or the bosses. Four days later he met the new Comd of AMF(L), Maj Gen Holmes and DCinC Land - only a three star! - he wore his hat on both occasions. By the way I'm writing these notes from the Army Correction Centre and I'm on course for a F4 CR. The Troop will be in Hungary on Ex Ardent Ground 2000 by the time you read this ...... it's a hard life!

The Wire – June 2000

249 Signal Squadron (AMF(L)) Bulford

EXERCISE ADVENTURE EXPRESS 2000 - by Lt Preston

This year's northern deployment was quite an epic: live EW, man-pack RRB, FFR skidoos, on board with Dutch Marines, Very High RRB Sites, working with Czech Helicopters and searching for the perfect meal amongst multi-national ration. We also hosted our fair share of visitors including D C in C (Land).

During the Field Training Exercise, we played the role of a hostile force attacking NATO over a dispute about the Senja Oil Fields in the north. the scenery in the entire area is harsh. Mountains loom out of the fjords as triangular peaks that would look more at home in the Himalayas. The mainland has huge streaks of water cutting through it, making movement from one side to the other a time-consuming task. On one occasion Rebro Bravo, under Cpl Walsh, was resupplied by boat. To make matters worse for communicators, the deep valleys used up Rebros very quickly indeed and in order to bring in the furthest location, the Log Base, Cpl Kenny was dropped off on a feature the height of Ben Nevis. Throughout vile conditions he managed to keep his trailer rebro on the ground until the tent broke and the antennas began blowing away. To make matters worse for communicators the EW teams were out in full force. The American direction finding, and Canadian intercept team provided great assistance and then coordinated a particularly effective false 'Endex' call which resulted in ninety per cent of the enemy going home early. On the Jamming side the Norwegians gave the Headquarters a difficult day which spooked the younger members of the team but the combination of the second in command's brief and the experience from former EW operators prevailed to ensure the command net was never dropped.

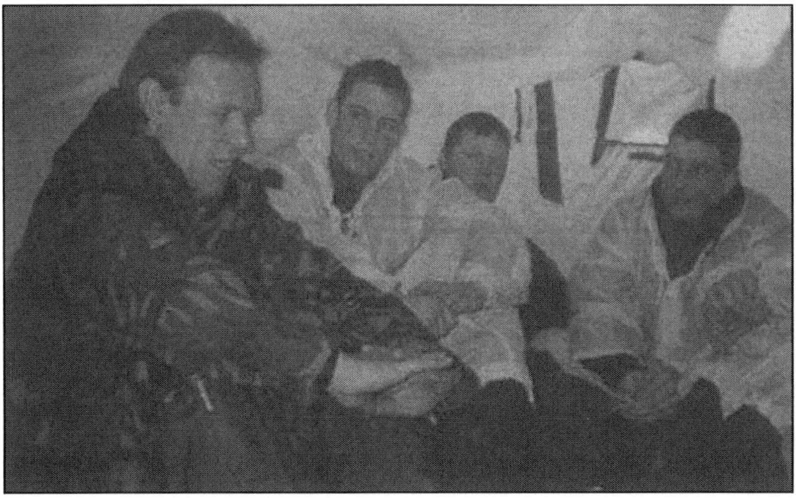

The Deputy Commander in Chief discusses Pay 2000 with Sigs Gould, Whitelaw and Patterson

The final mention should go to the Foreman who had an interesting exercise attempting to establish Satcom links above the 69th parallel: an impossible task. Having requested extra help from the far end and been turned down, he eventually travelled one hundred kilometres to the south and proved the equipment. As soon as he returned even the best location wouldn't work. Never mind. However, a notable victory as they manfully struggled until testing data over VHF worked perfectly. Is this the future for AMF Comms?

TRAILER REBROADCAST 82H - by Sig Gould

On 9 March 2000, Cpl Kenny and Sigs Gould, Hasset, Ward, Cook and Lawson deployed onto a mountain top at 1089 metres to provide comms for exercise Adventure Express. We were dropped in by helicopter at about midday to dig the position in and bridge the distance to Log Base, the most remote station. On arrival we quickly started digging and soon found that the position had a thin covering of snow on top of solid rock. As we couldn't dig down any further, we began building snow walls. After a quiet first night without any snowfall, we noticed that the wind strength was beginning to build and that the extra help brought to establish the Rebro could not be flown out due to poor flying conditions. Over the next two hours the weather deteriorated further, with high winds and heavy snow. The Pilot now decided it was too dangerous to fly. During the night we all crammed into a four-man tent and a trailer 'nine by nine' tent and got little sleep whilst the site was gradually destroyed by the wind and snow. The following morning the site was rebuilt despite the poor weather and the repairs we made were strong enough to survive the next night. Fortunately, we managed to regain some rest as the evening calm set in. However, the lads were beginning to speak their minds. Sig Cook provided the classic quote, 'This is worse than Survival night,' referring to the long night during the basic ski and survival course.

Our situation began to improve when after an hour of waiting, the extra men were flown off back down to Echelon and we settled into some kind of routine. Now down to just three people, everything started to run smoothly with each of us knowing our job. This continued until day five when power started to become a problem. On the fifth day the first generator broke down. Initially we thought this to be just a minor problem as we had two spares. Unfortunately, the others had also suffered in the weather and we couldn't start either of them. After twelve hours of hand cranking generators and a few blisters, we had still failed to start any of them, and the weather deteriorated once more. Now the wind was blowing so hard that we had to hold onto the tent to prevent it blowing away. The nine by nine had turned into a huge kite despite the fact we had dug it in. Going outside had now become too dangerous in the wind that made standing up very difficult. Once outside in the blizzard we got disorientated in seconds and found it impossible to find the antenna.

Further orders told us to break the Rebro and send a sitrep every hour, on the hour, and get as comfortable as possible. This is easier said than done in a nine by nine with three generators, three blokes and all their kit. Cpl Kenny was starting to look extremely concerned by now and was even less happy when we were told to stay put until we ran out of rations. Aller a mentally tough night the wind once again died, and we could inspect the damage done. The EVHF whip section had snapped off during the night and we had greater difficulty with tents. The four-man tent had suffered three snapped poles and the angles on the nine by nine had broken. We continued to call in reports and hoped the helicopter would come sooner than later. Fortunately, before we knew it the Czech pilot had braved the conditions to come and rescue us. No sooner had the helicopter arrived than we threw on our bergens and we flew off with orders to abandon the radio kit for collection at a later date. On arrival back at Echelon we were relieved to be alive and in the warn. The comments started flying, 'Oh well, if you lost the tent, you could always build a 'snow-hole.'

THE NORWEGIAN JEIGER COMPANY - by LCpl Bury

I deployed to Norway on 30 January initially to the south. Once the Squadron had completed the arctic warfare training, we moved up to Storsteines in the north to take part in Exercise Adventure Express. This is where the fun began. The moment we got off the plane it was blowing a gale and the temperature was hideously low. I was less than impressed as I was expecting palm trees and white beaches. After sitting around at Storsteines for about four days a job came along. I could see the Yeoman, Foreman and SSgt Allan looking my way and smirking. I could read their lips, 'Buzz will do it.' Unfortunately, I was the only bloke there and I was going on an unusual task. The Yeoman asked if I wanted to deploy with the Norwegian Special Forces on Skidoos (Snow-bikes). I immediately said no, but off I went anyway. I was to provide secure HF Comm back to AMF(L) Headquarters from the back of a Skidoo, not quite in my job description. Fitting out an FFR Snow bike, nice one YofS.

After a short while it was time to deploy and I was to rendezvous at a bridge at 0900hrs. I turned up at 0850hrs and saw a bunch of lunatics flying about on snow bikes and was horrified at the thought of being a passenger. Soon enough I found out I was to be attached to the Jeiger Company and was introduced to the Company Commander, the Second-in-Command and the Reece Officer. They were all extremely friendly and spoke excellent English. The plan was to load sixty-seven snow-bikes and move them into enemy territory. As we carried the scheme out it started to look a little cowboy-ish. However, when we got onto the area, I could see why these people were a little more than the average infantry company. Their fire power, observation and riding skills told me they were something special. Riding on the back was quite a different experience. If you don't put your body weight in the right place at the right time you are off the back and in the snow. Getting back on with a PRC320, spare batteries, webbing, and weapon on you is not easy in deep now. The speed we were to travel at was faster than fast. I'd never seen anything like it and thought I was going to die on several occasions. At 70 miles per hour through trees and at night is slightly mad but normal for these blokes. The temperature was -25 standing still as the 'Huey' Helicopters flew over us. Luckily, they didn't spot the company and we were soon doing 80mph across a frozen lake. The cold was unbearable at that speed, but I realised that I was wrapped up in kit better than that of my hosts. During the next couple of days, we attacked ten targets causing mass mayhem amongst the enemy. The experience I had with the Jeiger was excellent and we worked so well together that we will be doing cross training in the future.

MANPACK REBRO - by Sig Galtress

In Northern Norway in a moment of infinite wisdom, 249 Sig Sqn decided that it would be a good idea to deploy a man pack rebro, just to see if it could be done. What an excellent idea. I was woken up at 2300hrs and told I was deploying at 0600hrs with the RRB. I got up and started to pack my Bergen, then I unpacked my Bergen and proceeded to refill up my Bergen with radio kit. By the time I'd finished it weighed about the same as I do. I finally got to bed at 0200hrs, then back up at 0500hrs ready to deploy, as planned, at 0600hrs. In total four of us deployed, Lt 'The Boss' Preston, LCpl 'Fruity' Fielding, Sig 'Shminka' Johnstone, Sig 'Az' Galtress. The journey to our drop-off point was via another detachment to collect some kit. Then it was off on our skis up the mountain. The ski up the mountain itself was not actually that hard apart from the weight. Lt Preston was pulling a pulk as well as carrying kit in his Bergen and 'Fruity' was doing the usual thing required of an airborne soldier, carrying a ridiculous amount of weight.

Once we arrived there, we had the task of digging in the tent and setting up. We set about this straight away, but during the non-tactical phase there was no great rush. A couple of hours later we had dug a pit big enough for a house and we could get the kit working. Once we were in and set up, we established communication and had to wait until we were told to make the rebro, so obviously we had to find something to occupy ourselves. That something was food.

As if by perfect timing the moment we had finished our food we were told to ‘make’ the RRB. The task was made more difficult by a weak HF Sigs Eng Net link and a broken trailer Rebro not far away. However, we proved that a man-pack rebro can be operated in North Norway. Once 'made' the RRB operated until we run out of battery power, which was about 24 hours and nine batteries later. Having finished, it was time to arrange our pick up at the bottom of the mountain. We had plenty of time, so we had yet more food then proceeded to pack up. Sig 'Tent Rhino' Johnston with his amazing tent admin packed up first, before being kind enough to let the rest of us do so. Once he had packed it was time to ski down, which I have to say was a lot more leisurely than skiing up. When we were finally picked up it was back to HQ Admin Area and then I was off again on my det after two hours. In summary, the man pack RRB was a success and it was proved it could be done. I think everybody on the RRB enjoyed it and gained valuable experience from it.

The Wire – August 2000

249 Signal Squadron (AMF(L)) Bulford

EXERCISE ARDENT GROUND 2000 - by Lt Mark Stoter

Another month and another arduous exercise for the Arctic warriors of 249 Sig Sqn (AMF(L)); this time, three testing weeks providing CNR comms for a Force Artillery exercise in Hungary. Twenty-three men from the Squadron deployed to the dust bowl that formerly served as an assembly area for the 3rd Shock Army as well as being an active chemical warfare training area. 'Just make sure your men stick to the tracks,' we were told, 'We did a sweep yesterday and found one tonne of unexploded ordnance. Oh, and there was a chemical incident a couple of year ago, so don't pick up anything that looks unusual.'

Before the work started, we were fortunate to have some time to ourselves while the Log Bn took their time setting up the camp. Sig Gallagher and LCpl Boyle quickly sniffed out the more dubious establishment in town; quite how LCpl Boyle managed to spend more than his debit cards daily limit in the pace of an evening remains a mystery. The comms plan was executed simply, with the deployment of two Rebros on a large feature that was at least a couple of metres out of the MLR danger zone. Danger close? The Exercise continued in the usual AMF(L) vein, with the Americans forgetting to tum up on the first day, the Spanish flying into the impact area during firing and the Hungarians landing rounds outside an impact area measuring 2km by 2km. Collective security? Multinational deterrent force? Cpl Ansell's naked shower in the middle of the day probably achieved the latter.

For the first NATO exercise in Hungary, we were warmly received by both the Host Nation Support unit and locals alike. Cultural trips to Budapest were particularly cultural; the East Europeans manage to do the most fascinating things with snakes. Cpl Howe certainly did his bit for cementing local relations, while Sig Wood and Sig Clark found the locals particularly accommodating in their kind loan of national flags. Sgt Allan and Sgt Jackson still seem a bit twitchy when they pass a parking attendant, though ... A final note to any

American readers: if you want your Gerbers, Leatherman, watch, rations, or anything else you may have mislaid, do contact LCpl Vallance (tall chap, seems to have lost all his berets).

The Wire – February 2001

249 Signal Squadron (AMF(L)) Bulford

EXERCISE ADVENTURE EXCHANGE 2000 - GREECE

by Lt Mark Stater

Ex Adventure Exchange 2000 saw a marked shift away from the Squadron's usual CNR role and a move towards CIS management and increased use of SATCOM as the AMF(L) continues its trial of the IRTF(L) concept - a command and control system based on a theatre-wide tactical WAN.

The deployment went smoothly, and we arrived in the dustbowl of Greece in the middle of the night. Sig 'Crypto Kid' De-Gernier confirmed everyone's fears of snakes when he leapt out of his sleeping bag at 3am screaming about being bitten. His intrepid Tp Comd investigated, hunting the beast with a stick and torch, only to discover that the 'snake' was in fact a trouser twist. The RRBs deployed to two large features and seemed to be re-supplied by the Padre more often than the re-sup team. Cpl 'Firestarter' Clifton, easing back into life as a Det Comd, caused a scare with a NO PLAY message that a fire was advancing toward his location. A team of would-be fire fighters, led by SSM Marsh, rushed to the scene only to find the inferno at least 2km away on the other side of the valley.

Then there was the snake ...

Other dangers were found closer to home. Requiring relief one morning, Lt 'Big Boy' Fayers ventured to the port-a-loo and left looking rather pale. As Mr Fayers commenced business, a hungry spider noticed something dangle into his territory and took a bite - a big bite. A special mention must also go to Cpl 'Peeping Tom' Walsh for ensuring the safety of RRB South every night, vigilantly patrolling the area and investigating the bouncing cars that turned up every night. Why he needed binos remains a mystery. Sgt 'Wacko' Jackson found himself as IC R&R and put together a superb three-day package at the beach for all those who wanted to go. Local relations were cemented and the squadron particularly thanks Sig 'Willie' Whitelaw for improving Anglo-Russian affairs.

MY FIRST EXERCISE WITH 249 SIG SQN (AM F(L)) - by Sig Taylor

I deployed on Exercise Adventure Exchange to Greece during September, flying from the UK to Thessaloniki. We were then transported to the port where we entertained ourselves unloading the boat in the blistering heat. Just as our MT Sergeant had pulled out the remainder of his hair, we began our 8-hour, 80-vehicle convoy trip to our exercise location Kozani, setting up the Ech CP complex in the dark was fun! I spent the duration of the exercise on wheels, re-supplying all of the Squadron detachments in the surrounding countryside, enjoying the scenery as I drove. A well-earned R & R package at the end of the exercise was spent in a three-star hotel 100m from the beach where we all sipped cocktails and bathed in the sun, great fun.

The Wire – February 2001

21 Signal Regiment (AS)

244 Signal Squadron - A TROOP

This year started with deployment on Ex Hardfall based in Southern Norway. The Troop ran three consecutive Novice Survival Courses for the Light Dragoons while new members of the Troop were experiencing the delights of the Cold Weather Environment, previously known as the 'Arctic' care of the Royal Marines and 249 Sig Sqn. The course covered topics such as 'Skiing', 'Survival in the cold weather (-30)', 'Teddy Throwing', jumping in frozen lakes and low-level infantry tactics. As well as offering quality training, the deployment also gave us the opportunity to welcome new members of the Troop and say farewells to LCpl Jez 'My rovers in 3-wheel drive' Skelhorn on his way to 101 Log Bde. With Norway out of the way for another year the Troop is looking forward to Ex Ardent Ground in Poland in April.

Sig Melanie Hall didn't see the hole in the frozen lake during his NSSC

Members of A Troop Skijoring behind a BV206 Snowcat

Alpha Troop hierarchy Voss, SSgt Jack Hawkins, Capt Bill Holbrook, SSgt Phil 'offender' Render - Capt Holbrook is the one in the middle

The Wire – April 2001

249 Signal Squadron (AMF(L)) Bulford

EXERCISE HARDFALL 2001 - NORWAY

by Lt Mike Fayers - OC Owl Troop

The Squadron deployed on its annual pilgrimage to Norway in early January to an alarmingly green Norway, with the usual seamless transition into war with a six-hour trip actually taking 20 hours. On arrival the squadron was introduced to its new friends, some members of Alpha Troop, 21 Sig Regt, some movers from 50 MM Sqn and a Squadron worth of Light Dragoons. It wasn't long until our new friends were also bonding well with the Quartermaster's Department, testing QM Steve 'Cough cough' Morgan and RQ Andy 'Scrumpy' Slack and their merry men's generosity to issue shiny white kit. Eventually, we were all ready for our Novice Ski and Survival Course and some good old-fashioned clean fun ....or so we thought!

The first morning was a quick orientation to our pocket contents, which was soon to become the bane of our lives, but the cornerstone of our fitness programme. Everyone was amazed just how many pairs of gloves, chocolate bars, para cord, ski wax, hats and other bits of kit you would never see again could actually be spring loaded into our four pockets.

However, our introduction into kit inspection, artic style, was soon over and we were on the slopes under our MSIs for our first morning of falling over with Army Planks on. I had left the UK quietly confident having skied before, but unfortunately my planks and I had a slight personality clash: That is to say we had differing opinions on what direction we thought we should be heading in, usually resulting in high speed followed by a sudden halt. By the end of the first day most had come accustomed with their special skis and legs relationship.

The rest of Week One was a mixture of skiing, falling over, tent routine and cries of ‘front support place', 'show me your (insert any item of kit, usually that item most difficult to get to)' not to forget lots of practice of our new found friend the snow plough. Most of this was under the careful eye of our attached Royal Marine Mountain Leader, Sgt 'The Moose Hunter' Renny who kept the course amused trying to work out exactly what he meant by his RM tongue. The finale to week one was a night ski that practised our snowplough to the exhaustion of our thighs followed by the feared ice breaking drills. This was run by the Sgt 'Formally known as Jacko' Jackson and Cpl 'Warm kit on' Witham and was actually quite enjoyable. No one had any major dramas though some did seem to spend longer in the pond than expected!

After a relaxing weekend absorbing the breath-taking sight of Voss everyone was ready for the Survival and transition into tactics phase. Most of the course turned up for the first stand 'survival' wearing every bit of warmest kit they possessed and with strange limps, however, these were soon removed. After a brief tour of improvised shelter, it was time to perform the dastardly deed on the chicken. Nobody was to upset, as these particular chickens virtually jumped onto our knifes as they were that sad.

After some helpful hints such as the wind direction we set about making our designer homes for the night. For some this did not only involve borrowing some design hints from the DS but the floor, ceiling, and the front door.

The night was cold, but bearable thanks to our raging infernos and burning gaiters. Unfortunately, the snow conditions did not allow snow holes, and despite being threatened with a night in a Quincy, the course was spared the ordeal. With our NSSC qualification in the bag after a few gentle bergen moves and helium pulks; all that was left was a week of tactical training, which proved to be equally as demanding and just as enjoyable when falling over.

Artic Warfare phase - All the gear - no idea!

Survival Night - Lt Fayers and Cpl O'Donell go about making a home for the night

MOUNTAJN LEADERS DICTIONARY

Saying	All that good stuff
Definition	A bit of beautiful and pucker mixed together with the finest ML planning.
Saying	Beautiful
Definition	Just how I would have liked to have planned it
Saying	The soldier formally Known as airborne
Definition	One that has been swayed to the dark side of the MLs training methods
Saying	Front Support Place
Definition	The press up position.
Saying	Hot Wet
Definition	A cup of tea, white one or NATO to the rest of the Army.

Saying	Lack of Moral Fibre
Definition	People who have an injury.
Saying	Nutty
Definition	Chocolate, biscuits, boilies, jelly babies and all that good stuff
Saying	Pucker
Definition	That which the Marines do
Saying	Obviously
Definition	Anyone who has also spent most of his or her life gaining the ML qualification would understand
Saying	Dragoon slayer
Definition	ML
Saying	These people are in way over their head
Definition	Their Training has obviously been insufficient
Saying	Threader
Definition	I'm rather tired of today's activities and working with amateurs
Saying	Top of the hill-Go!
Definition	Haven't planned the next phase, needs 10 minutes - pass me my fag packet
Saying	Wobble
Definition	Response to female emotions.

The Wire – June 2001

249 Signal Squadron (AMF(L)) Bulford

EXERCISE HARDFALL 2001 - BLUE PETER HOST

by Capt Teri Downer

The Squadron was fortunate enough to host 'Matt Baker' from Blue Peter for two days during Ex Hardfall 2001 in Norway. The aim was to allow him to experience some of the harshness of Norwegian weather and hopefully toughen him up a bit, but more importantly get 249 on prime-time BBC. (This included WO2 (SSM) Ken Marsh showing his best side during a BV sketch – 'Oh look SSM my breath freezes when it touches the window of the BV. Why is that?). Mat was kitted out in some of the Army' best Arctic kit and taken up into the hills surrounding Voss. He did not take a liking to the itchy Extreme Cold Weather hat and when asked why he insisted on wearing a bright red woolie hat he replied, 'A top hat for a top bloke,' - this received a few hidden sniggers from the hardy men around him at the time! He was teamed up with LCpl 'Mess tins' Sustins ("why do they call you mess tins - oh you eat from them in the Army don't you) and began to dig a snow hole. Many hours later they settled down for some gorgeous scoff 'Lancashire hot pot' and a wet (brew). After a few hours Mat was up again on candle watch (just because he is a civilian, he does not get away with stag)! He then emerged from the now hole to a fine morning and was transported down to the lake for a quick dip - ice-breaking drill. This was something he really didn't like; he would not smile on exiting the water or even stop far a chat before going into the warming tent! Obviously not toughened him up enough yet. The footage taken was screened during March just gone - if you missed it we have a few copies in the Squadron!

Mat from Blue Peter - just a little wet and unhappy

The Wire – April 2002

21 Signal Regiment (AS)

244 Signal Squadron - A TROOP

On returning from Ex Adventure Exchange in Turkey, Alpha Tp commenced preparation for the coming winter deployment. The annual build up exercise, Ex Dryshod, in Okehampton, Devon is the initial training phase for Norway. Along with 249 Sig Sqn, Alpha Tp Cold Weather Warfare Instructors (CWWI's) and Demo team produced a 10-day training package. The aim of the exercise was to teach the students the key skills of working in a cold weather environment and how to survive in an emergency in such harsh conditions. The exercise is broken into two phases; the first two days are classroom based with demo's showing everything from constructing a shelter to Helicopter handling in the arctic. For the second phase, the students deploy onto Dartmoor training area, where the weather is very unforgiving, for a 3-day field exercise. During the three days, the students cover various tasks, including navigation, tent group routine and a helper sledge race (simulating evacuating a casualty on snow, but in this case without the snow) where there is an expressed necessity for physical fitness. Anyone who has attended Ex DRYSHOD will say how much they enjoyed the gentle jogs over the Dartmoor Tors!

November also saw SSgt (YofS) 'Hutch' Hutchinson and LCpl Jamie Smith (then Sig) attending Ex Pre-Hardfall, along with Sgt 'Bish' Bishop completing the CWWI's course, spending five weeks in Norway only to be back again three weeks later. This hectic period also saw the Regiment put on standby for Afghanistan, and with all the Troop heads sheds away, SSgt Phil Render was left stepping in to the shoes of both OC Alpha Tp and YofS Alpha Tp and struggling to get into the Sqn Ops Room.

As always, December's silly season was upon us again, with 244 Sig Sqn leading the way with an altogether different theme - with a Scouse Christmas function, organised by Cpl Chris Alston. The night proved highly entertaining and successful, with some classy fancy dress outfits. Prizes for best turned out went to LCpl Rachel Goodall and Sig Micky Young. All the proceeds were donated to Alder hay Children's Hospital in Liverpool. Everyone had a good time with some harsh hangovers the next day. Capt Pete Brunton, 0C Alpha Tp decided he'd had enough of the late drunken nights and wild single life, and happily tied the knot with Tracy in the Lake District. Reality soon hit home with Alpha Tp back in work for the 3 January 2002. Christmas leave was definitely over as we found ourselves on a Hercules, heading north for Norway. Alpha Tp advance party did an excellent job of preparing the way for the remainder of the Troop, clocking up some serious mileage in the new Troop support vehicle (a Nissan Sunny hire care from Avis). Once Alpha Tp arrived in theatre, the Troop was dissected, with half of the Troop going to Brandseth camp to complete the emotional 4-week Cold Weather Warfare Course (CWWC), which involves some excellent skiing opportunities (if you can ski). LCpl Chloe Cowen, LCpl Sid Reynolds and Sig Andy Weekes have been putting their newly acquired skills as Military Ski Instructors (MSI's) to good use, teaching members of the Troop and other units how to ski on 'Army planks', along with Cpl Chris Alston acting as one of the CWWI's. The remainder of the Troop occupied the Rong hostel, with SSgt (YofS) 'Hutch' Hutchinson. SSgt Phil Render and Sgt 'Bish' Bishop running four 6-day Novice Survival Courses (NSC's) for various members of the UK Element of the AMF(L). To date, two courses have been completed. Cpl Tom Woodall has shown great potential of becoming an SQMS in the future, with his great one liner 'No I haven't got it - stores are for storing, now get lost'. The highlight of both the CWWC and the NSC is the ice breaking drills, which involve skiing into a hole cut in the ice, wrestling your bergen out of the water, dunking your head under the water and then dragging yourself out using your ski poles as spikes. This proved highly entertaining during a visit by the Norwegian Minister of Defence and the press, with Sig Lindsay Scott making page three of the local newspaper.

Disappointingly, Capt Pete Brunton, OC Alpha Tp, has so far managed to avoid his dunking, claiming to have injured his ankle and therefore could not ski! All of the Troops are eagerly awaiting the dunking of the Boss. Most of the Troop have taken opportunities to hone up their skiing skills on Voss ski slopes at the weekends, especially Cpl Fiona Murphy, who after forking out a small fortune on her own new set of skis, still can't get out of the car park! One of the highlights of the exercise so far, has to be when SSgt (YofS) 'Hutch' Hutchinson and SSgt Phil Render returned from a recce in a Puma, which on landing was mistaken for a VIP visit. Both jumped out to be greeted by various Staff Officers from the UK Element AMF(L) wondering what had happened to the Norwegian Minister of Defence.

Looking forward, the Troop will be moving north to the Trondheim area of Norway during the middle of February, to get down to some serious Comms business. By this time, it is hoped newly promoted LCpl Jamie Smith will have cured his fear of extracting himself out of hi BV to take his head torch off (which must have been a Christmas present from his Mum), and Sig John Leach will have got over the habit of every time a female is in sight, running to the mirror to gel his hair. By the time the Troop returns to UK, 2 months will have been spent in some seriously harsh weather conditions, and everyone will be keen to chill out and go on some well-deserved leave.

LCpl Dave 'Frostbite' Walker emerging from the lake having successfully kept his hair dry, but sadly lost his pipe in the process.

The Wire – June 2002

249 Signal Squadron (AMF(L)) Bulford

Currently in Norway, 249 Sig Sqn AMF(L) are in their element. Since the last issue, everyone disappeared on leave - much needed after the extremely hectic final week. Shaking off the Xmas blues and pies the Squadron reassembled on 3 January ready to rock and roll. Immediately into deployment mode, the vehicles were taken down to the boat and loaded and then the flights for Bergen started rolling out of RAF Lyneham and RAF Brize Norton. By 10 January all Squadron personnel and attachees were in theatre. The Squadron established itself comfortably into two different camps - Hagatun and Brandseth near Voss.

This year's Norway deployment included Ex Hardfall 2002 - the Cold Weather Warfare Training followed by Ex Adventure Express 2002 a full AMF(L) manoeuvre exercise in northern Norway. The Squadron has trained 90 odd on the Cold Weather Warfare Course (CWWC), which includes two troops of QDG and other attached personnel. A Tp, 244 Sig Sqn ran the Cold Weather Course (CWC) – (known as the snow shoe course), which is one week long and mainly for those individuals not likely to deploy up on top of mountains, for example Chefs, Clerks, Supply Specialists. Following all the training the Squadron deploys north to the Trondheim region of Norway for the AMF(L} exercise - more fun to come.

DIARY OF A COLD WEATHER WARFARE STUDENT

by LCpl Richie Hewitt

249 Sig Sqn arrived in Norway on 10 January 2002 to partake in Ex Hardfall 2002. Everyone on the course was a little apprehensive; the horror stories of years gone by had filtered down and scared the lot of us!! After the initial move in, the course began in earnest. The first week encompassed many aspects of survival in cold conditions, with lectures on clothing, cold weather injuries, mountain weather and the fitting/adjusting of skis. When not in lectures we were out practising our skiing in our ability groups, Group I for ski gods and Group 7 for the hapless or screaming eagles. The first week was

capped off with a one-night stay in a 10-man Norwegian tent and day and night skiing. Group 4 soon found thar Sig 'Firestarter' Sloan was highly proficient at lighting peak stoves and himself simultaneously! This was the introduction week - worse was to come. Everyone knew week two was to be more challenging than the first week. More time was spent in 10-man tents and 4-man tents, finishing with the dreaded ice breaking drills on the Friday.

The final day of reckoning arrived and after an hour's drive we arrived at Bømoen camp for ice breaking drills. We lined up one by one, each as anxious as the next about their plunge into the icy lake water. The day went well, and everyone had a good laugh taking the micky out of their mates struggling to get their name out and drag themselves from the ice.

Week three was the survival phase and this sorted the wheat from the chaff! Again, more time in 4-man tents. with the introduction of more weight on skis, causing problem for those who had not mastered the skiing yet. It was then time to spend a night in a snow hole and a brushwood shelter. My group's snow hole took seven hours to dig whilst groups digging 'Quincy's' or 'snow mounds' were digging for up to 11 hours! We were all surprised at the warmth that the snow holes provided.

The following day we spent 24 hours in a brush wood shelter or bivouac that we had built ourselves. Food that evening was two chickens (still alive) and some fresh vegetables. Those culinary experts amongst us produced some mean chicken broth. Fortunately, the weather was kind to us, but the cold night seemed like eternity, our smokey fire was our only comfort. Looking back the only funny part was Sig Absolum fainting whilst watching the butcher kill a sheep!

The final week was upon us. The first two day were quite relaxed with zeroing on the range, section attack drills and a ski test that everyone successfully passed. We deployed into the field on Tuesday evening. The drop off point to our first harbour location was a steady climb and approx 800m. This climb took five hours! By the time we got to our objective for the evening everyone was tired of carrying their 80lb bergens, almost farcical. W pulled pole (to the novice cold weather people out there, that means packing all kit away - tentage and personal kit in a record time of 15mins from the word 'go') next morning to begin another nightmare ski to our next harbour that we reached a little after last light. The next couple of days were taken up with recce patrols, CTRs on enemy locations and lying-in wait in horrid conditions – there was little time for sleep. The weather worsened and we were all cold and wet, morale was starting to wane. The Troop attack lasted about 40 minutes: we won and lived to tell the tale later at the fantastic thespian kit night back in camp where huge quantities of alcohol were consumed.

EXERCISE ADVENTURE EXPRESS 2002 - NORWAY

Probably, the best Exercise in Norway this year. Exercise is a little of a misnomer for many of the soldiers of the Squadron, especially if you happen to be stuck on a RRB on top of what seems to be the highest peak in the world, which happens to have only one track up (and down) for access, and the visibility is about 5m in daylight due to the horizontal snow. Or the Echelon troops, who although greatly under-appreciated, spend seemingly every hour trying to get around these RRBs and other outstations in order to re-supply them or fix the knackered generator/charging system or whatever. Or the TOC Main element, trying to co-ordinate everything else and plan for the next move that the 'Exercise' will bring. One thing that Norway brings home. especially in the really, really harsh weather that began this year's Adventure Express, is that almost everything is for real, less the ammunition that the Jaeger Battalion is firing at you. As the Arctic Warrior veterans around the Corps will know, the environment is ideal for bringing the best out of every asset the Squadron has, bringing it all together and making it work well. This year was no exception. The best was certainly brought out of Cpl 'The General' Griffiths, who found his remarks on how to fight the battle (made whilst showering) were greatly appreciated by Gen Holmes himself, who just happened to be drying off in the next room. Is it a coincidence that the battle plan changed pretty drastically over night?

Amongst fixing numerous radios that just happen to go duff, there is always apparently time to fix the nicer things in life ... Thanks go to technician LCpl Andy Weight for blowing up the Forman's Tele and totally destroying the OC's phone charger. It is comforting to know that the soldiers of the Squadron are always adaptable, and ready for the unexpected. Cpl Lee Dyson, technician by trade, Italian infantry LO/tactics adviser/personal councillor as required, thoroughly enjoyed leading his merry band of like-traded amigos on an Airborne assault...

Right up until collection time when Sig Gaz Ward managed to bog one of the recovery Landrovers in one foot of snow on a perfectly straight track. Interesting, you just can't teach that. Also worthy of mention are LCpl Richie Maybank and Sig Jim Walker who managed to fight off a sustained attack by a Jaeger Battalion skidoo section from their RRB Det for a full afternoon - without the support of the Det Comdr, LCPL Lee 'Shrek' James who was busy at Ech, tending the rear ...

From the ISIS former head honcho Sgt Matt 'Choppers are me' Tones, a special thanks goes out to the German power section for providing us with a pre-World War 2 generator that seemed to find it funny to turn itself off at 3:00am every morning. Not to forget the intelligent officers running the battle from their computers. but always finding trouble remembering their password. We must have been in good hands with them, 2nd Lt Tim (YTS) Sambrook. Welcome to AMF, Norway and ISIS. All in all, there were many magic moments on Ex Adventure Express, too many to list here, but the whole thing was a resounding success from all elements of the Squadron who really pulled it out of the bag again. The biggest magic moment, however, was the publication of the Flight Manifest back to UK. No matter how good an Exercise is, three months is a long, long time to be about it. Now, next year. ...

COMMANDER AMF(L) CUP CHALLENGE 2002 - by LCpl Cooke

Having already been in Norway for eight weeks and successfully completed the Cold Weather Warfare Course, I thought all the hard work was over. How wrong could I be? I somehow managed to get selected for the Commander AMF(L) Challenge Cup team, representing 249 Sig Sqn in a Ski and shoot competition over 10km of harsh terrain along with ten others. The competition is usually held on every AMF(L) deployment, normally consisting of a march and then a shoot. However, being Norway, it was deemed a good idea to ski as the snow was over a foot deep. 15 teams from seven nations within the AMF(L) took part, unfortunately we managed to draw the first start time and along with that, the privilege of cutting the track.

The team itself was made up of people with various abilities and fitness. Luckily, we had a couple of Military Ski Instructors, Sig Jim Woodhead and LCpl Jaffa Jefferson, who did most of the track cutting making it a bit easier for the remainder. Another form of support was received from the OC, Maj Hill and SSM Dewar at various stages along the way; cries of 'keep up with us' came from their Landrover window! Some of the nation's chose to use snowshoes for the race and some even competed on foot with no aids at all. With the use of skis and at various points skins, we managed to cross the finish line in a respectable 3hr 39mins, which gave us third place after the march.

There was a quick pose for the camera then straight onto the shoot. Five rounds each from the prone position at target placed at 100m and 300m. Some members of the team were new to the Squadron and hadn't zeroed their weapons properly and we had iron sights whilst most of the other nations carried SUSAT or equivalent. After considering the facts 2Lt Steve Cadywould decided that we would only shoot at the 100m targets and those who hadn't zeroed properly would position themselves close to someone who had so they could give them their ammunition. Lady luck must have been with us through that shoot guiding us onto a very pleasing second place. Overall, the competition went well, The Squadron doing itself proud against good competition once again. We were awarded first place overall in the minor unit's competition. Well done to 2Lt Steve CadywouJd and SSgt Jace 'But it's my last Norway' Raybould who managed to lead us round unscathed.

The Wire – August 2002

21 Signal Regiment (AS) - 244 Signal Squadron - A TROOP

Things are currently unsure for Alpha Tp, as the UK has decided not to participate in any AMF(L) exercises for the foreseeable future. While work goes on at all levels to determine what happens next, the Troop continues with equipment care and have begun training for future deployments with the Support Helicopter Force HQs rather than the AMF(L) role.

The Wire – August 2002

249 Signal Squadron (AMF(L)) Bulford

The Squadron is experiencing a period of uncertainty as this goes to press. In early May we learned that funding for our AMF(L) commitment was to be withdrawn thereby rendering us 'Signal Squadron without portfolio'. 249 Sig Sqn has become the epicentre of rumour control since then, as everyone seems to have their own theories of what is to become of us. It now seems likely that we will wind the Squadron down in the early part of next year and then go job hunting. With that said, we are yet to hear if winter training is to be cancelled so it may yet all change. Watch this space ....

Despite the above, we are keeping very busy al 249 Sig Sqn. Ex Clear Voice is once again reinforcing old friendships as we play host to 25 NATO Officers and Soldiers for a week of training. Concurrently battle camp is ongoing for the lucky few who are running around the Plain discovering once again that 'the rain on the plain falls mainly during ambushes'. In the near future we have a deployment to the Ukraine to look forward to as well as a number of exercises including Raynard's Chase in November when we will be providing support to the Reece Bde.

The Wire – October 2002

249 Signal Squadron (AMF(L)) Bulford

Despite the impending draw down and the continued uncertainty surrounding our collective futures, June and July have been exceptionally busy for 249 Sig Sqn. We have been involved in all manner of activities from support to training with 14 Sig Regt, our own Battle Camp and the annual exercise for training representatives from AMF(L) units in Comms procedures and VP.

The Wire – December 2002

21 Signal Regiment (AS) - 244 Signal Squadron - A TROOP

After the news that UK force are pulling out of the AMF in October, the Troop has been busy re-rolling the vehicle for Regimental deployments. It was a stressful time. Swapping our volleyball nets for cam cream and skiing kit for webbing and helmet was not easy, but with some gentle persuasion we eventually gave it all up. The Troop is looking forward to our final AMF exercise in the Ukraine and an official de-badging parade in October where the Troop will have a final bash to say goodbye to the AMF. As this is the final A Tp AMF party all units are warned that if any flags go missing on this night, the Troop take no responsibility.

The Wire – December 2002

249 Signal Squadron (AMF(L)) Bulford

Once again this has been an exceptionally busy period for the Squadron. We returned from leave and immediately began preparing for a full Squadron deployment to Otterburn. Despite the very real prospect that this may be the la t time the Squadron, as we know it, has a chance to exercise, spirits remained high throughout. Remarkably this was also the case during the Escape and Evasion phase that many found extremely testing but also thoroughly rewarding.

Following the recovery (in more ways than one!) our attentions turned to our uncertain collective futures. Armed with a briefcase full of preference posting proformas, the OC, 2IC and FofS boldly entered the labyrinth that is MCM Div with a view to securing postings for as many of our soldiers as possible. It transpires that the horror stories are an exaggerated (if enduring) urban myth. The desk officers couldn't have been more helpful, and we returned from Glasgow with postings agreed for virtually all the soldiers. Clad in Kevlar, the 2IC announced them after the MCM Div road show and was greeted with a much smaller than anticipated deluge of complaints. In the vast majority of cases, soldiers were given their first or second choices, so we don't appear to have done too badly.

The Kiwi trophy was run for the last time by 249 Sig Sqn (AMF(L)) on Salisbury Plain on 19 September 2002. As has become tradition, the day began with a ceremony in Tidworth Military Cemetery attended by the New Zealand High Commissioner, the New Zealand Defence Adviser, a number of staff from the High Commission and representatives from the Squadron.

Following a short but emotive service of remembrance we escorted our guests onto the training area to observe the competitors as they tackled the gruelling course. The Prize giving took place in the XL club later the same day, when the Hon Russell Marshall presented SSgt Oliver with the Kiwi Trophy, for the fastest overall individual time. The SOinC(A) then presented Sig Rockett with the Barry trophy and Sig Weaver with the Lang Memorial Trophy. Next year, ties with the New Zealand High Commission and the running of the Kiwi Trophy will be transferred to 1 Mech Bde Sig Sqn. We are certain they will fiercely contest the competition and wish them all the best for the future.

SSgt Oliver enroute to victory

The Wire – February 2003

21 Signal Regiment (AS) - 244 Signal Squadron - A TROOP

EX CO-OPERATIVE ADVENTURE EXCHANGE 2002 - UKRAINE

On a cold Sunday morning, 29 September, six members of A Tp started their journey on what was to be the final AMF (L) exercise, in the Ukraine. Eventually we arrived in the Yavoriv training area. After the initial formalities, we were fortunate enough to enjoy a cultural tour of L'viv. This was followed by our very own cultural tour in the evening!

When the exercise began, the MAOTs were busy providing comms for para drops, gun moves, para drops and even more para drops. On one occasion a Ukrainian para became rather too attached to one of our vehicles when he stacked into the side of it! The exercise ended with an R&R package in L'viv which was a great success. The end of the final AMF (L) exercise was celebrated by a rather early Xmas bash, held by 249 (AMF (L)) Sig Sqn, and to which all BRITFOR personnel were invited. However, the six-day journey back to the UK was not so good, with the movers proving their worth once again?? Alpha Tp now looks forward to exercising in some slightly less exotic locations e.g., Salisbury Plain.

The Wire – February 2003

249 Signal Squadron (AMF(L)) Bulford

THE UKRAINE ADVENTURE by SSgt (YofS) Holden

October saw 50 members of the Sqn deploying to North Ukraine, in support of EX CO-OPERATIVE ADVENTURE EXCHANGE 02, billed as the final nail in the AMF(L) exercise coffin. In addition to our task of providing ISIS and SATCOM to the AMF(L), the Sqn was also given the task of providing life support to all other deployed UK elements (some 100 individuals). This allowed Maj Alan Hill, OC Sqn to use the 'self-styled' grand title of Force Commander United Kingdom, or

FCUK for short. This extra logistical commitment played heavy on the support elements of the Sqn, with the QM, Capt Chris Laycock and W02 (RQMS) Robinson often having to retire to the sanctuary of log base to issue socks and swap war stories.

The deployment set the scene for the whole exercise, with the Sqn using a combination of road, ferry, train and luck to get into theatre. Fortunately, prior to our 68-hour train trip to the Ukraine, via Germany, Poland and numerous sidings, the Sqn was accommodated at Elmpt Station overnight. This stop allowed us to get a final hot meal, shower and gave Sig Patterson the chance to display his geographical knowledge by creating a very life like map of Africa on the QM's camp bed (fortunately the OM was not in it at the time). Border crossings and customs checks became the norm while we travelled through Europe, with SSgt (YofS) Holden getting numerous headaches from corrupt border guards and officials.

Once in location, life continued at a fast pace, with ISIS Troop and the sleepy SATCOM crews providing a first-rate service to the staff. SYSCON was run by LCpl King and his merry band, under the usual multi-national philosophy that when things go well, the G6 staff have worked well and when things go bad the screams of YofS and FofS ring around the HQ.

During the ex, the troops were kept fed and happy by Sgt Gray and hls chefs (they are not cooks!) who produced excellent results with food from dubious sources. One of these was a local gent who spent much of his day attempting to sell the good Sgt local mushrooms and a wide selection of fresh hedgehog. Each member of the Sqn was allowed to spend some down time in the local city of L'Viv, the cultural centre of the Ukraine on a little Rand R, staying in the overpriced 'Sputnik' Hotel (a cross between a Holiday Inn and Salvation Army hostel) for the princely sum of USO 18 per night. A good time was had by all, with special credit going to one of the Sqn augmentees from 12 Mech Bde Sig Sqn, Sig Soppitt, who showed outstanding teamwork throughout the exercise, but especially during R and R.

The return journey was much the same as the outbound, with the addition of an extra 12 hours on the train, no electricity or heating in the carriages and the ERV being stranded on the German/Polish border due to it having 'grown' during the deployment, making it too tall to return on the train! Always operating within the law, the OC and YofS had to 'persuade' (bribe is a bad a word!) the Ukraine Customs to let us out of the country with a selection of UK and USA ration packs.

All in all, the exercise was a success, mostly due to the hard work and long hours put in by all members of the Sqn, ensuring the AMF(L) swansong went with a bang!

AMF(L) DISBANDMENT PARADE - by LCpl 'Rob' Drabwell

It started (as things usually do in this Sqn) at 04.00hrs on a wet October morning as a mixed contingent of R Sigs, RLC, RA and one member of the RMP prepared to deploy on the AMF(L) disbandment parade. Things went from bad to worse when we laid eyes on our transport, a battle bus that we were to spend the next 14 hours in. After driving through every country in northern Europe we arrived in Heidelberg, the HQ for the AMF(L). We were soon taken to our accommodation, which was a 5-star hangar type with ensuite ablutions (well they were only a 20-minute bus journey away) and after a quick 'squaddie shower' we made our way into town to sample the local nightlife.

On our first morning in Heidelberg, we thought we'd set ourselves up for the long day ahead with a trip to the American consolidated dining facility. We soon discovered that the Americans have funny ideas about a fry up - only one meat product allowed, but you can have as much syrup as you like on it. Cpl Fielding managed to get around the only one meat product rule by convincing the chefs that he required more meat on medical grounds. The rest of the day was taken up with drill practice.

Some of the old and bolder members of the Sqn had to be given some guidance by the younger lads on some of the more technical drill movements like the present arms. Clearly all the drill we do at 249 had finally come in useful! The other contingents on the parade managed to entertain the Brits by performing some bizarre drill movements, especially the Turks whose drill resembled a step aerobics class! On the actual day Comd AMF(L) and Comd NATO Forces Europe were in attendance and both seemed suitably impressed with those who took part in the parade and conveyed their thanks to all involved. After the parade, everyone retired to the beer tent were the British contingent managed to dazzle all the other nations with their beer-drinking prowess. We then retired for a good night's sleep before setting off for the long uncomfortable journey back to Bulford.

The Wire – April 2003

249 Signal Squadron (AMF(L)) Bulford

9 January 2003 was a day that the Sqn and a good percentage of the Corps hoped would never come. Ever since the official news was received in April 2002 confirming that because of changes in the NATO force structure, 249 Sig Sqn (AMF(L)) was to disband in early 2003, most of us prayed that some reprieve would be given. Unfortunately, no such stay of execution was forthcoming and so 249 Sig Sqn disappeared from the Corps Orbat at the start of the year.

To ensure that the Sqn finished its current life in a correct and fitting manner, the OC, Maj Alan Hill and SSM W02 (SSM) Shean Dewar devised a cunning plan, involving drill, service dress, drill, bayonets, swords and some more drill. Oh, and a pennant. The task of forging the remaining members of the Sqn into some sort of drill-compliant unit fell to SSgt Dean Wilson, who could often be seen mumbling to himself and sprinkling holy water on the parade square after a particularly bad drill practice (of which there were a few). Slowly the troops made the painful transition from trekking with skis and tabbing with bergens to marching in a formed body in a semi-uniformed manner - and even starting to look pretty good at it! However, getting the OC to realise that slow march is not in fact done at warp factor 6 took somewhat longer.

Practice for the disbandment parade, combined with the drawdown of the Sqn took up the majority of the lead up to Christmas period, with all depts returning stores and throwing out strange items that had been lying around the Sqn lines for a number of years. Sgt Paul Binns had to be rescued from the skip a number of times during this hectic period.

Post-Christmas, with the parade just around the corner, and a good percentage of the Sqn deployed on operations and others being posted early to their new units, numbers became a problem. It came close to the point where there were more guests than people marching. Things became so dire that there was a rumour that SSgt (YofS) Mark Holden had been seen practising drill moves and dusting off his No2 dress in the silent hours ... come the day of the parade, everything came together nicely, with the SSM carrying off a very good parade - and we are sure no-one really noticed the OC's 'deliberate' mistakes! The salute was taken by the SOinC(A) Brig D McDowall MBE ADC and accompanying him on the inspection was Comd UK Element AMF(L) Brig CMG Elcomb OBE (late LI). Both were ably hosted for the day by the QM, Capt Chris Laycock.

A surprising turn came about when the spectators started clapping during the march-off, more than a few felt a lump in the throat and a tear in the eye whilst marching out of the compound gates for the last time. Around 100 veterans of 249 Sqn came to watch the marching and drink some beer afterwards. A special mention must go out to the 18 veterans of 249 in its FARELF days, who had seen service during the '60s and '70s in the Far East! Thank you to Graham Jolly for pulling your guys together and for the rendition of 'Happy Squadron' which entertained all present. Now, it is all over bar the MFO. The OC has departed to a cushy desk job in Northwood, the 2IC to 102 Log Bde Sig Sqn in Germany, and others have departed to places too numerous to mention. Best wishes go to all wherever you go. May you live long ... (and prosper!).

At the end of 26 years, 249 Sig Sqn is now no more. All that remains to say is to those Sqn members who are even now deployed on ops in far-off places, the remainder of us did not and have not forgotten about your being part of the Sqn in the final days of its current guise in AMF(L). To you and the Corps as a whole: keep the standards, keep the pride and keep looking forward to when 249 will, phoenix-like, rise once more.

SOinC(A) inspects the parade.

NATO Press Release on Dissolution of AMF(L)

NATO
OTAN

Online library
North Atlantic Treaty Organization

Updated: 12-Aug-2002 NATO Press Releases

Press Release (2002)098

12 August 2002

Allied Command Europe Mobile Force Land Headquarters to be dissolved in Autumn 2002

On 19 July 2002, based upon the recommendation of NATO's Military Authorities, the Defence Planning Committee has approved the disbandment of Allied Command Europe Mobile Force Land (LAND) (AMF (L)). The decision reflects the progress made on the implementation of NATO's new force structure concept and its continuing adaptation to the strategic environment. The concept of rapid deployment and flexible multinational forces, which was characteristic for AMF, is being incorporated into NATO's new concept of graduated readiness forces. Therefore the command and control structure of AMF(L) can be dissolved; its earmarked forces, however, will remain available for NATO's restructured force pool.

The AMF(L) is an immediate reaction force available to the Supreme Allied Commander Europe (SACEUR). It was created in 1960 as a small multinational force that could be sent on short notice to any part of Allied Command Europe under threat. AMF(L)'s mission was to demonstrate the solidarity of the Alliance and its ability and determination to resist all forms of aggression against any member of the Alliance.

The AMF(L) is a multinational brigade-sized formation, consisting of a Headquarters at Heidelberg (Germany), combat, combat support and combat service support units assigned to it by 14 NATO nations. For over four decades AMF(L) has supported a wide variety of NATO exercises. Elements of the AMF(L) deployed to Albania in support of operation ALLIED HARBOR to assist in the relief of refugees from April 1999 till September 1999. Its aerial counterpart, ACE Mobile Force Air deployed some of its elements to Southeast Turkey during the Gulf War from January 1991 to March 1991.

A dissolution ceremony is scheduled at the AMF(L) Headquarters in Heidelberg on 30 October 2002.

Tel:	+32 (0)2 707 50 41	B-1110	http://www.nato.int
Fax:	+32 (0)2 707 50 57	Brussels/Bruxelles	press@hq.nato.int

SHORT ANECDOTES

Chris Cox - 1978 to 1980 - 249 Signal Squadron

Freezing Rebro

249 was my first posting after Sandhurst and Blandford. I was a 2nd Lt and served there for 3 years, which means that I did 3 Hardfall's.

'Somewhere in Norway' March 1979

One of my "fondest" memories is being sent out to a hill with a crew to just set up a rebro site on the top of some hill somewhere. It started badly for me when the loadmaster asked me to jump out 30ft or so above the snow "as the pilot needed a marker". So I did and went up to my neck in snow - the chopper landed about a foot from my head (while I was yelling abuse at the pilot). Of course, a rucksack would have served the same purpose but they thought it highly amusing to scare the shit out of me.

So, we set up camp and all being well I went to bed to leave the lads to fiddle with their knobs etc. However, at 3 am I was woken to hear that all the batteries were dead, WTF I asked has happened to the genies? Couldn't start them sir. (Yes, my fault for not thinking of that from the start). I got dressed and went to the genies to see that they were in the open and fuel lines frozen, (another lesson learnt). After a few futile attempts to start one I asked for a jerry can of petrol and said "you never saw me do this" as I poured a pint or so over it and then set it on fire. Fortunately, it didn't explode and then started quite easily.

On return to base Major Waldren enquired what had happened, I thought best not to explain what actually happened and just said it was I knack I had. In hindsight it was remiss of me not to pass on this experience so that others would not make the same mistake, or the genies could have been insulated by REME. Now you know -

keep your genies warm (we had 2 so the exhaust from 1 could have stopped the other freezing), and start one before it freezes!

Survival Training

I should also take the opportunity to mention the highs and lows of my "survival training" under the direction of the infamous Bernie Tenman.

It was a 5-night course out in the wild and to start with we were dropped off at the base of a hill and I was tasked to take us up to the first campsite. We set off and then I saw on the map that the road we were skiing up went very bendy and, on the map, there was a red path marked that basically cut out all the corners. A short cut (always one of my map-reading downfalls) so I set the lads off on that path and we preceded to climb an ever-inclining path in deep snow. I was tempted to turn back as it was becoming too much with pulling the pulks etc, but we were already half way up this now very steep hill. To be fair to the lads, there were no complaints or whinges they just hacked on through the snow until we made it to the top. Luckily, they must have thought it part of the exercise. If they had realised it was my cock up there would probably have been a mutiny! Bernie was surprised that we were an hour late and I had to confess I had made the mistake of trying to take a short cut.

I redeemed my myself later, on a night mission, where I had to lead the patrol to a random hill about 15km away. I set up 3 compasses with bearings needed to reach the hill and gave two of them to the lads. We set off and I had calculated the distances for each bearing and asked the lads to count their strides so I would know when the next bearing was needed. It worked perfectly, to the surprise of Bernie and our LO who said no one had done that before.

The funny thing was that having reached the summit, I skied down and fell into a ditch at the bottom of the hill, which was like a round hill fort. I yelled back at the next soldier "mind the ditch at the bottom", but after the fifth lad "snotted" in the ditch I gave up and just watched with amusement. Getting back was easy of course as we just followed our own tracks.

One of the best things about being out at night was the sky - most people have never seen the sky so full of stars it was breath-taking compared to what we are used to in the UK.

Don't get me started on the snow trench we had to sleep in - the coldest I have ever been at -40C.

Terence Walton - 1980 to 1983 - 249 Signal Squadron

Unorthodox Recovery

Eddy Alan Gardner, Myself and Keith Goddard were together in a Volvo, without the radiators in the back, on an umpiring exercise for Prince of Wales Own and Royal Marines in 1983. We had been picked by Frank McAleer to stay behind after Ex Hardfall along with Colin Burnett and a handful of others. It was the middle of the night edging around a lake when the snowcat in front partially submerged soaking the Para Captain who'd flown out from the UK all squeaky clean... and keen!! POW Own Infantry NCO's set about stroking their chins and scratching their heads whilst a Norwegian Liaison officer suggested calling out a Chinook for recovery purposes. Whilst a discussion took place amongst them, Keith and I set about attaching a steel tow rope to the two vehicles and suggested towing out towards the centre of the lake. We were met with blank stares but finally got our way. Hurrah! Success! Our motivation had been that we would have had to walk to the next RV if nothing had been done and we'd already had a belly full of that thank you very much.

Joyriding

Cpl Pete Charles was detachment commander of a rebro sited on a hilltop overlooking a ski lift. The sort of ski lift with a couple of seats and somewhere to rest your feet. I believe he jumped on and was having a little "joyride" when the lift came to a halt. From his high up position, he could see the staff member for the ski lift locking up and leaving the site. He was left swaying to and fro in the breeze wondering how he was going to get down. Ultimately, he had to climb down the framework of his seat and dangle from the foot rest until he had the confidence to let go and crash down into the snow.

Skijoring

The skijoring incident was most likely Hardfall 1983 because I was quite competent on what was my 3rd Hardfall. There were a few rookies on the towing line and “snotting” was frequent. I can’t remember the name of the bloke who was supposed to be pressing the alarm buzzer but he’d ducked into the rear of the Volvo Snow cat for a fag just after yet another break due to falls. I hadn’t noticed that as I came to a stop, one of my NATO plank ski tips had slid into a coil from the slack rope. For whatever reason, the driver suddenly set off again and I was whipped to the ground and dragged on my back for some distance before ‘buzzer bloke’ emerged from his smoke cloud and sounded the alarm. I was concussed and evacuated back to one of the hotels for treatment from the squadron medic. I had insisted that I was OK to carry on but on alighting from the transport to prove my point I collapsed in a heap. After being “triaged” by the medic I was sent off to make my own way to my accommodation. This was by road which as is usual at the time of year was compacted with snow. The side walls of snow came up to the bottom of bus stop street furniture signs so I was committed to walking in the carriageway. It was dark by now but with my trusty reflective disc from the local bank I felt confident any motorist would be able to see me. What I didn’t count on was a dirty great snow plough coming down the road with lights blazing and the “blade” filling the entire width of the road. I had to literally leap and scramble up the snow wall to evade being scooped up.

Rob Peita-Read - 1984 to 1987 - 249 Signal Squadron

I arrived in Bulford in around November 1984 as a young Signaller straight from training. I was picked up from Salisbury Railway station by the duty driver and put into transit accommodation, a room on the bottom floor of the 'singlies' accommodation, with Jock O'Neil, Mo Morris and Ronnie Gault. My first week consisted of drawing kit for Norway and Troop and Sqn photo's.

I had only arrived a few weeks prior to this photo and I recall being asked 'where's you scarf??' (A piece of green towel used as a Sqn Scarf). Yep, apparently with 249 you wore a piece of green towel around your neck when in uniform!

Snow cat BV202 driving course with Paddy Lynch, Terry Petherbridge instructors and Moose Bruce with myself

We carried out BV driver training over in Tidworth around Nov/Dec 84. Lots to learn and a great way to pass time. We never managed to get it to climb the wall!

Norway Rebro Zulu, Rebro Xray passing the time with a beer and a game of risk played for hours. Being the youngest there meant a big learning curve from 'old sweats' Nobby Neville, Rigsby Richards and Geordie Hogg

Working on Rebro's was my first job. Being the sprog amongst the old sweats, I was easily led and had to get used to playing Games of Risk in the quieter times and being the focus of many wind ups on the det. For some reason I always drew the short straw for night shift on set, and yep, Cpl Nobby Neville would catch me many times checking the inside of my eyelids out during my shift. A steep learning curve which gave me a good start. Good times and great memories.

During my time with AMF(L) I became winter warfare trained through attending E usx Hardfall's in Norway. In total I completed 3 Norway deployments, 2 Turkey deployments and 1 Italy deployment. I also took part in 3 Lanyard Trophies; I think 3 Kiwi Trophies and was part of the Sqn cross country team where we were South West District runners up.

Kiwi Trophy. Some 29 years after leaving AMF(L) I had the honour to come back and take part in the Kiwi trophy again, this time as a Veteran, still doing the fitness at 50 years old.

Public duties Tower of London 1986. I was also part of 249 Sig Sqn when it was nominated to carry out Public Duties in London in 1986. It was a great honour to be part this

Reformation of 249 Sig Sqn. This photo was taken when 249 Sig Sqn was reformed in 2019 as a new Queens Gurkha Signals unit. As a Veteran of 249 Sig Sqn AMF(L), I once looked after the Chalk Kiwi monument in Bulford and married a Kiwi who is of Maori Origin. Being part of The London Māori Club (Ngati Ranana), we performed a Haka in font of Princess Anne, serving soldiers and veterans of 249 Sig Sqn. It was such an honour and privilege to be part of this club and be there on that memorable day, with some veterans I had not seen since 1987.

Steve Westlake - 1991 To 1994 - 249 Signal Squadron

"Never fall asleep on Candle Watch!!"

I was in Norway in 1993 at Stalheim and we were on snow Hole night. I was on stag going round all the snow holes in the middle of the night checking that there were no problems in each snow hole.

I skidded down one of the entrance tunnels and up the other side to pop my head up and check this snow hole. Everyone asleep. "Who's on candle watch I shouted" and one of the lads woke up and said drowsily that it was him. I didn't have to say a word I just pointed at a fire that had ignited in the hole. The candle had fallen down and set light to a day sack. "Fire Fire" he screeched in a nervous high-pitched voice when he saw it and tried to pat it out with his bare hands burning himself. Everyone woke up and joined in and eventually they extinguished the fire smothering it with whatever they used. Once the fire was out, I slid out and left them to contemplate the incident which I reported to staff.

That daysack was melted into an unrecognisable mess and I believe it was used by staff in future years as to "This is what happens if you fall asleep on candle watch"

Thank God I was on stag and more importantly actually doing it rather than skiving as some may have done.

ARCTIC KIT

Arctic kit issued in late 60's and early 70's was pretty rudimentary as you can see in the following photos. This kit was issued to early AMF(L) units. In later years the kit developed and improved

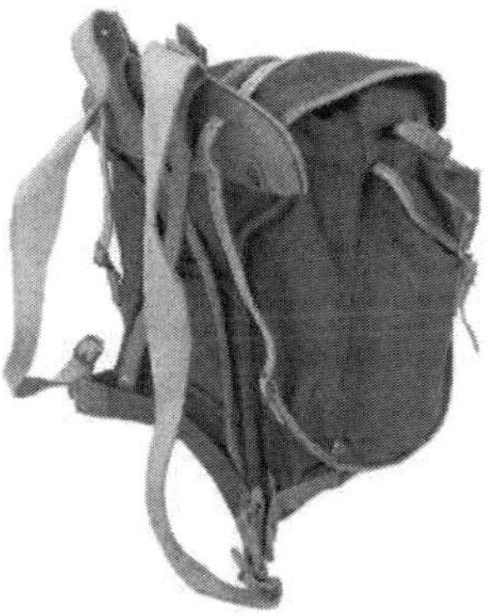	**Original Norwegian 'Bergen'** which replaced issued 58 pattern large pack. This was a major improvement over the issued webbing which froze easily. They were comfortable to wear and could carry a lot of kit. The leather straps did tend to freeze at times though and could be difficult to fasten when wearing gloves
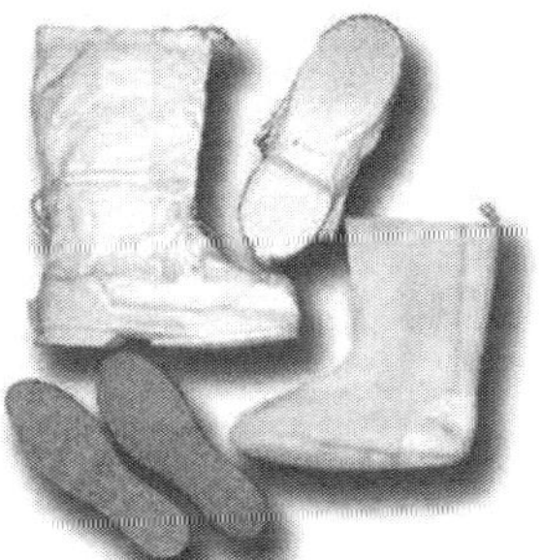	**Canadian Mukluk boots** with felt inners and felt soles. This boot was great in powder snow temperatures such as those found in Canada. In Norway the boot let in water from melting snow which made them very difficult to dry and so were next to useless.
	**Rubber Overboots** which fitted over issued DMS boots. These boots worked wonders in wet snow conditions in Norway.

	**Leather ski boots**. Comfortable when broken in and treated with dubbin. Norwegian. These were pre-worn and issued each year so you had to make the best of the pair you had.
	**Flask protector**. Used to carry a normal thermos flask to prevent damage and heat loss. This worked reasonably well if you didn't bang it about too much! Covered a standard 'Thermos' flask
	**Canadian Mittens** - made of soft leather, well insulated with lambswool pads on the back of the hands. Left one was for wiping your nose and the right was for warming up cold areas of the face. Made a mess if you mixed them up! Great piece of kit
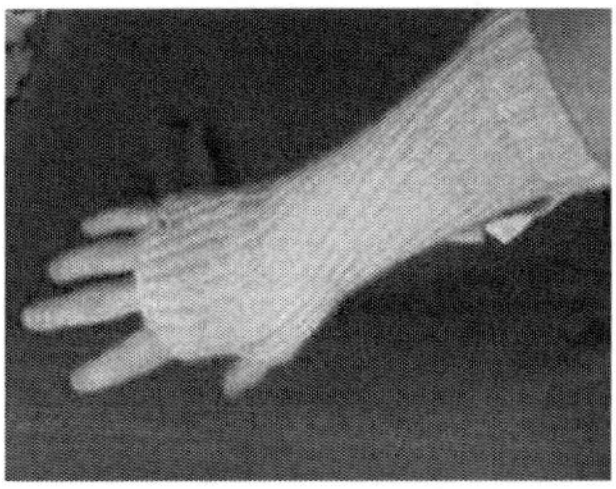	**Woollen Wristlets** - Fingerless knitted woollen wristlets designed to stop the wrist getting cold from any gap between glove and jacket. Once it got wet it was very hard to dry so wasn't very useful.
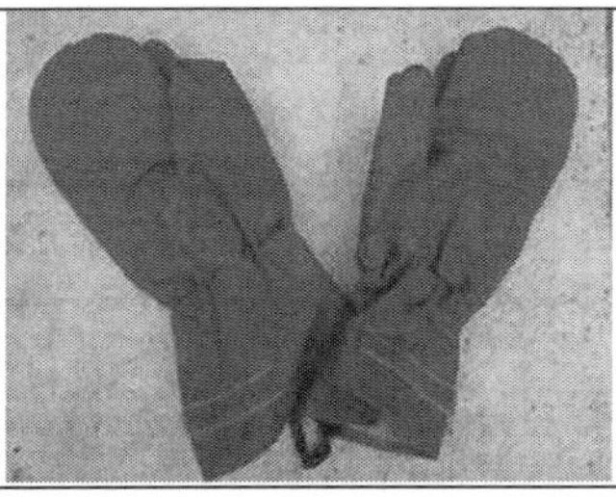	**Waterproof over mitts** - Used when conditions didn't allow the use of the Canadian Mittens. Very practical but could be easily lost.

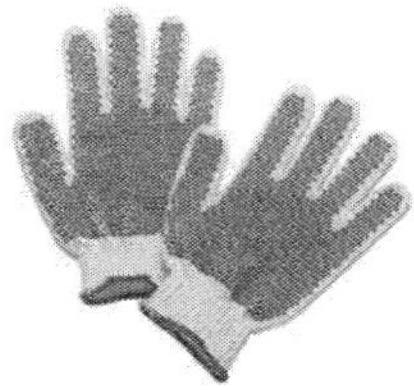	**Cotton Contact gloves** - Great gloves used for working on vehicles and equipment. Palms and fingers had black plastic dots on to aid gripping. If you didn't use these your hands would freeze to metal almost instantly!
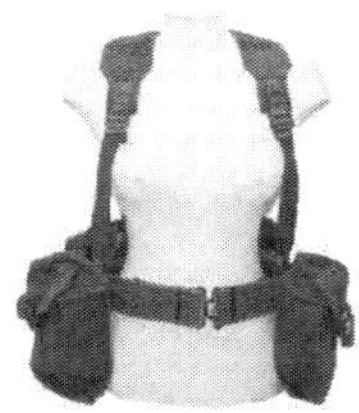	**58 Pattern Light Marching Order**. Still used in the Arctic for carrying ammunition and magazines. Used without kidney pouches so that Bergen could be worn. Easily froze when wet. Sometimes worn without the yolk.
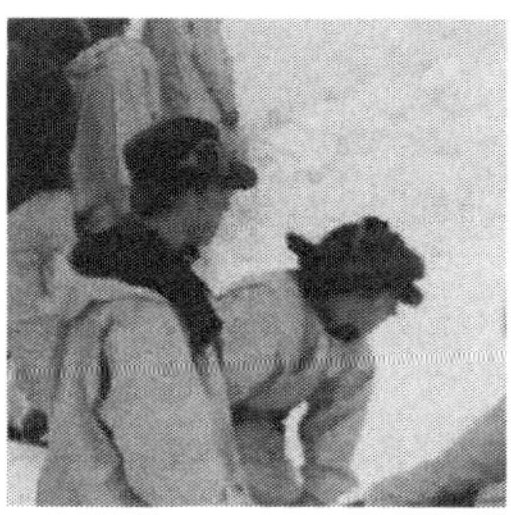	**Peaked Norwegian Hat and Snow Goggles** - Standard issue hat in the early days and used extensively. Snow goggles useful in 'White-outs'
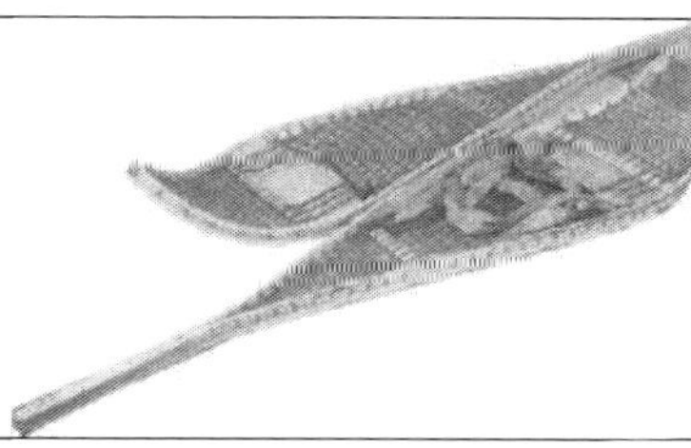	**Canadian snow shoes**. Made of aluminium with cotton webbing strap bindings. These worked well once you had learned to tie the binding on correctly and got used to the 'duck walk'
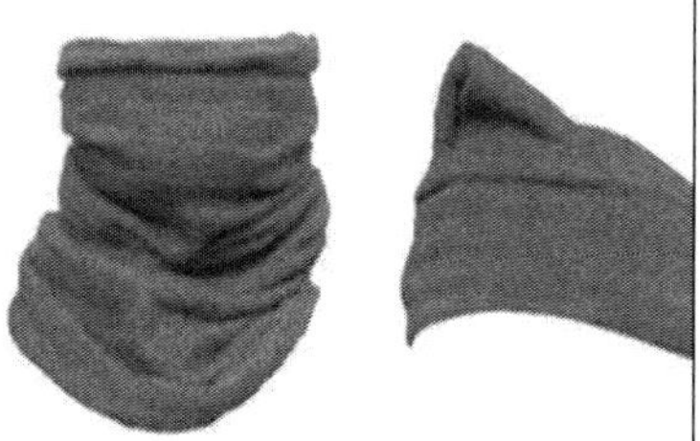	**Headover**. Light knitted tube which you could use as a neck funnel or up and over your ears to keep the cold out. Another great piece of kit which was well used

	**British Shirt KF** - Standard issue woollen work shirt used daily. KF stands for Khaki Flannel. Like wearing knitted Brillo pads! Hated by everyone. Eventually replaced with the Norge Shirt in the 80's
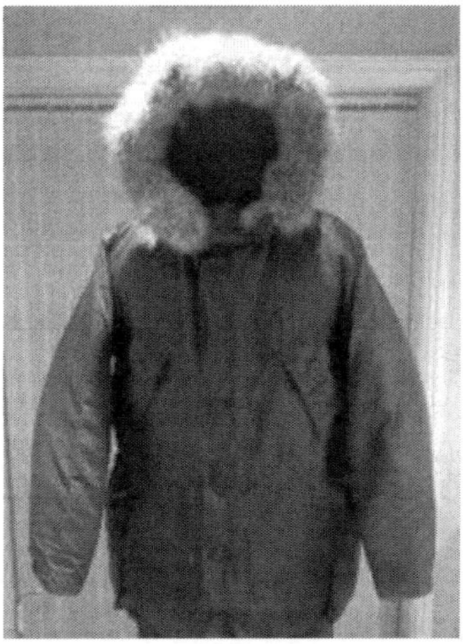	**Canadian Parka** – Very hard wearing, windproof and warm with a great fur edged hood. Well used and very much liked.
	**Canadian Over trousers** - Very hard wearing, windproof and warm. Well used and very much liked. Not a 'fashion item'!

	**Canadian Airbed (Lilo)** - the original Canadian sleep mat was a rubberised black airbed. You couldn't blow this up by mouth as your breath would freeze inside and cause cracking and the layers to freeze together. It was fitted with a 'bellows pouch' at the bottom which you filled with air and then rolled up to slowly inflate the airbed. This could take a while! A common mistake was to over inflate your lilo and have the hardest night's sleep you could imagine. Used correctly it provided good insulation from the frozen ground and was light enough to carry.
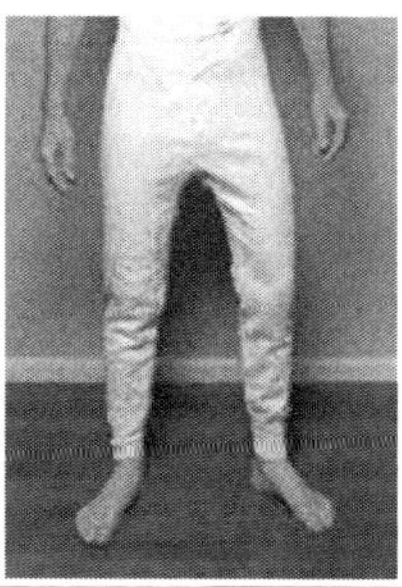	**Canadian Long Johns** - Made of white honey comb pattern thermal cotton. Great to keep warm when you were static but a nightmare if you were doing any physical work. You would often see some wearing only their long johns under their white cam jacket and trousers to keep cool while digging snow holes.
	**Woollen Socks** - Almost impossible to keep 'white' especially when the dye from a new pair of boots got to them. Froze at night if you didn't put them into your sleeping bag.
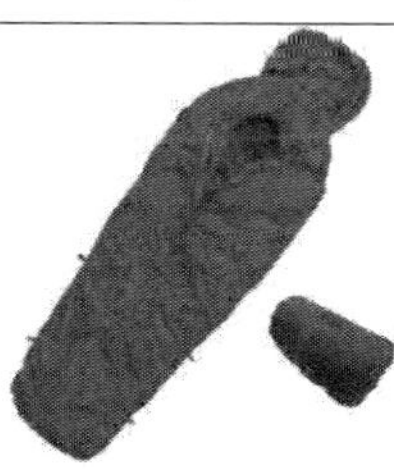	**British Army sleeping bag** - At the start we were issued with GS sleeping bags which weren't very warm in the arctic. It wasn't long before we were issued with 2 sleeping bags to be used one inside the other. This resulted in a heavy and bulky item of kit to carry and wasn't very popular.

	**Canvas Snow Gaiters** – Norwegian issue and worked well with their issued ski boots. Leather straps could freeze up but they did stop the snow getting into the top of your boot
	**Lightweight Nylon Arctic Camouflage Jacket and Trousers**. Could be used separately or together. In or below the tree line – jacket or trousers only. Above the treeline – both jacket and trousers. Soon replaced with 'reversible' Green/White jacket and trousers which were waterproof.
	**British Army issue Goloc (Machette)** Used for chopping branches etc and also used for cutting snow blocks for making an igloo. Also issued for use in the jungle!
	**Reversible Lightweight Green/White Winter Camouflage Jacket and Trousers** – Very useful in wet snow conditions and well liked. The 'white' tended to discolour easily.
	**Jersey Heavy Wool** – Standard issue British jumper. Great as long as you kept it dry. Well-liked by other NATO soldiers so became a good bargaining tool!

<table>
<tr><td></td><td>Coleman Twin burner cooker adapted to run on Naphthalene fuel which had a very low freezing point and didn't give off noxious fumes when burning</td></tr>
<tr><td></td><td>Pressure Cooker – this was the standard domestic 'Prestige' pressure cooker and was great for use in the Arctic. We rarely cooked food directly in the cooker but heated up the tins in hot water which we then used for drinks or washing etc.</td></tr>
<tr><td></td><td>Issued military ski's, known as 'NATO Planks'. They were made of wood with hard wood edges which wore down over time and were difficult to keep sharp. These were heavy and cumbersome compared with civilian cross country, Langlauf skis, but they needed to withstand heavy use in all terrains and conditions. The leather bindings tended to freeze up if they were left outside. In later years the binding was replaced by a more efficient binding.</td></tr>
</table>

	**Ski Wax** – Applying the right wax to your ski for the right conditions was more of a mystical art than a science. Trial and error and more practice usually paid off. You certainly knew when you had the wrong wax on! You also took advice from others selectively!
	**Canadian Pulk** Nightmare to pull either on snow shoes or skis but essential to carry tentage, rations and kit when on foot.
	**Larkspur C11/R210 and C42 radio installation** Fitted in FFR Land Rovers and BV202 Snowcats. Force Radio Troop used C11 SSB

From the late 1970's onwards, new items of kit were added when on issue and older items removed. Here are some of these items. It should be noted that during the Falklands campaign, winter kit was redeployed to troops in the Falklands for the duration of the war.

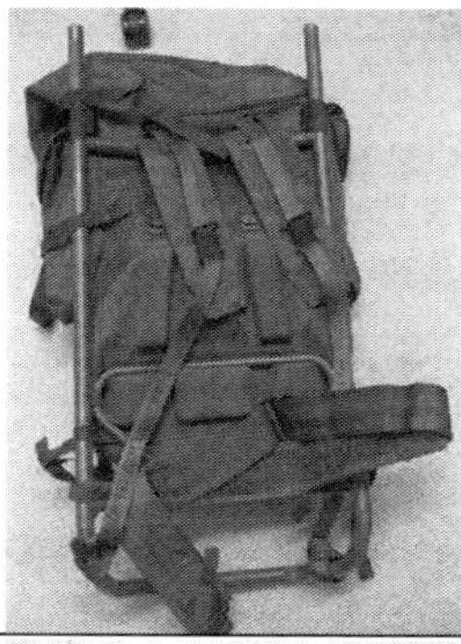	**1944 pattern British Army rucksack and carry frame** Not very comfortable or popular with users. This was soon replaced. Used in the late 1970's.
	**British Army rucksack with carry frame** With some well-placed padding it could be very comfortable. Used in the late 1970's.
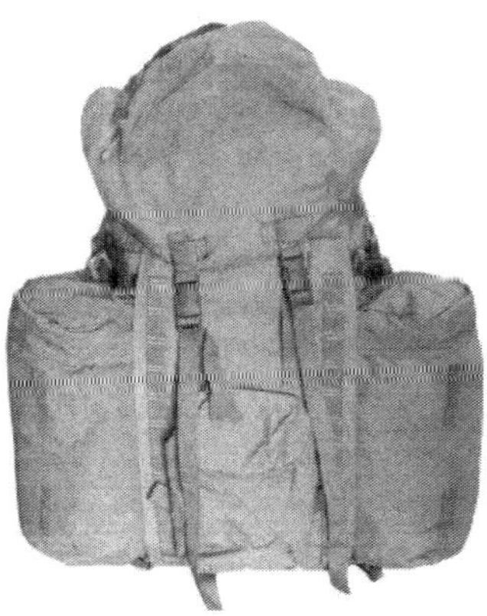	**British Army issue green PLCE Bergen** Came into service late 1980's early 1990's. Pure comfort. The only downside is that it fit snugly to the back causing too much sweating.

	**British Army issue Woodland DPM PLCE Bergen** Came into service mid 1990's and was well liked.
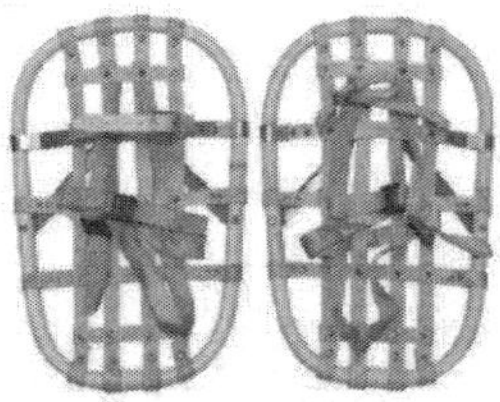	**Snow Shoes** Well-made and lighter than the older Canadian model. Came into service around 1982
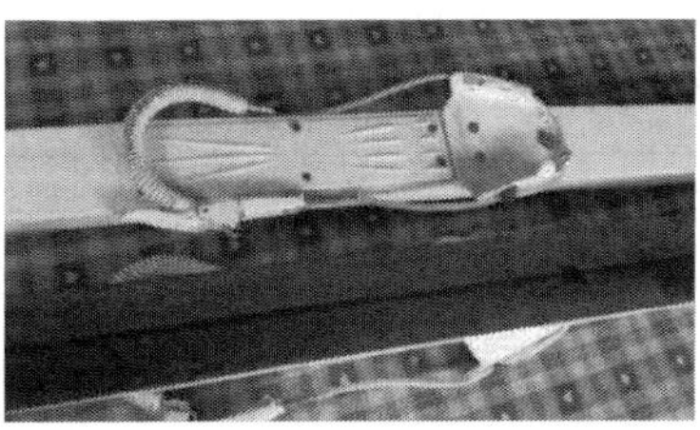	**Upgraded NATO Planks** issued skis that had a much-improved binding and construction.
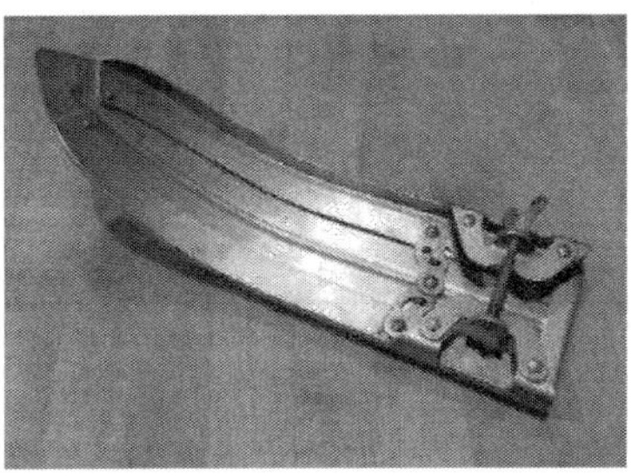	**Ski Tip**. For emergency repair of a broken ski

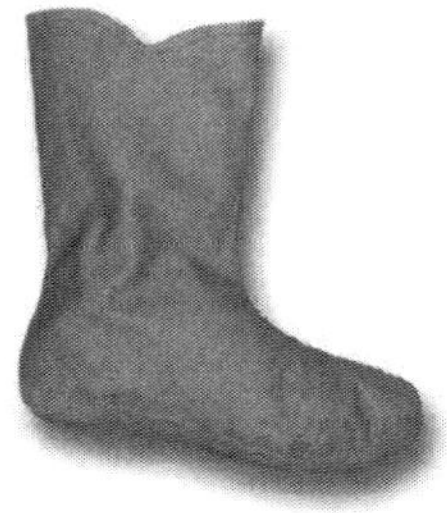	**Gortex Socks** Too bulky to wear in boots, too flimsy to wear as an overboot so little used.
	**Overboots or Mukluks** Of little use unless in very dry cold conditions such as Canada or arctic Norway
	**Ski March boots** Big improvement on the original all-leather ski boots. Came into service in 1996.
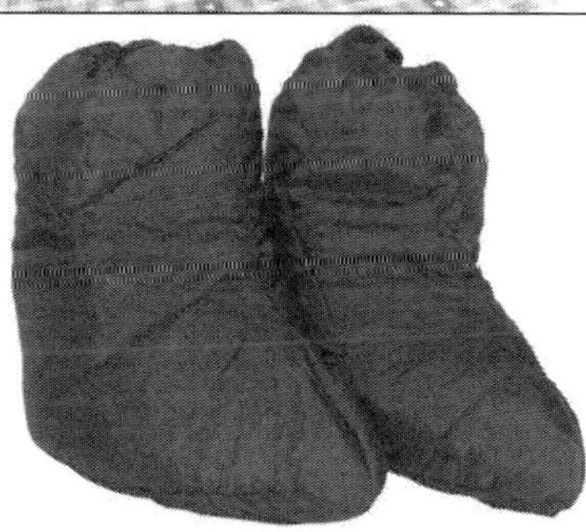	**Sleeping Bag Socks** Very warm and stuffed with man-made fibres so they retained the heat even when damp. Pity they didn't put a light sole on them as it was like skating on ice!
	**Cloth Cap Badge** Worn in the late 1970's early 1980's

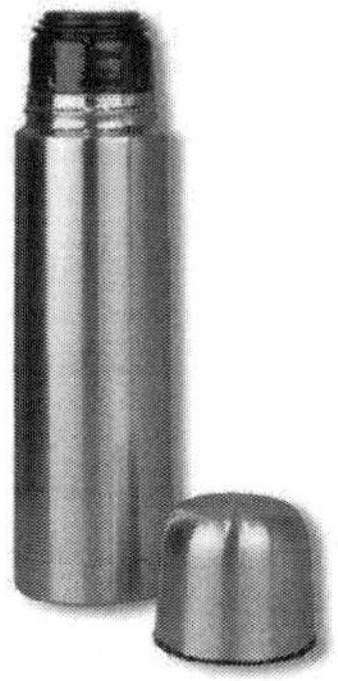	**Stainless Steel Flask** Finally, a flask that wasn't easy to break. A great improvement on the glass Thermos flask.
	**Gortex Gaiters** Far superior to the old Norwegian canvas ones. Came into service around 1984.
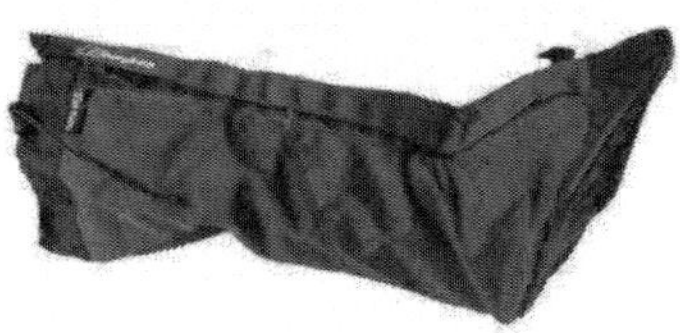	**Berghaus Yeti full leg Gaiter** Seen in use on the last Norway in 2002.
	**Ski Mittens** An improvement on the previous style. They tended to wear out quickly
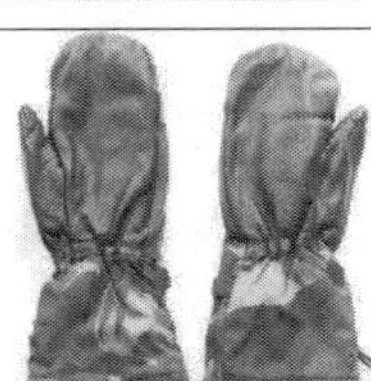	**Ski Mittens** An even bigger improvement on the previous style

	**Gore Tex Bivvi Bag** Eventually it became general issue in the early 2000's. A bit clumsy to get into, but quality made, robust and roomy
	**Roll Mat** OK for temperate climates but not much use in winter snow conditions.
	**Arctic Sleeping Bag** Faultless piece of equipment. Great when used with the Gore-Tex bivvy bag.
	**Norge Hat** Well insulated and well-liked hat. Issued in the mid 1970's
	**Peaked Hat** This was general issue and was pretty much perfect for most the physical work we did. Let the flaps down and it was good to keep the ears warm. Replaced the previous Norge Hat

	**Trousers Lightweight** Standard issue working trousers which were used for almost any activity. Dried quickly when wet and were hard wearing.
	**Norge Shirt** Became general issue in the 1980's. Prior to that you had to buy your own or trade!
	**DPM Hooded Smock** Excellent piece of kit and liked by all. Issued with matching DPM trousers that weren't used very often.

	**Parka** Great coat with a thick lining. Not good for any physical activity but ideal when static. Not general issues but most people 'acquired' one.
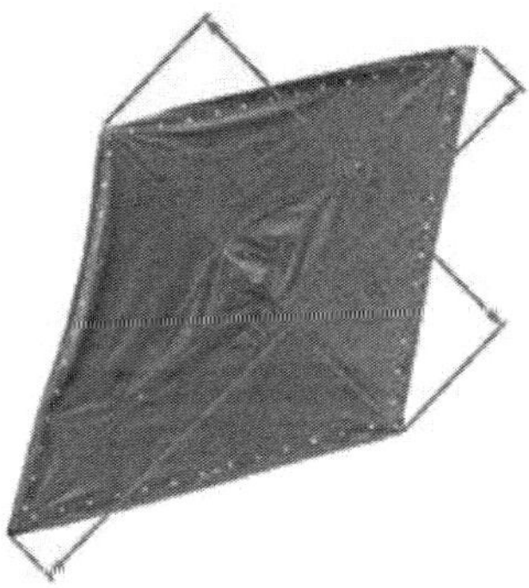	**Norge Tent Sheet** When combined with other tent sheets you could make a useable shelter.
	**Paracord** Essential item for all.

	**Poly Whites** Lightweight and essential. The fabric would keep snow from sticking to your clothes. Many a snow-cave has been dug in poly-whites and underpants! Oh, they were 'ok' camouflage too!
	**Pressure Cooker** Upgraded version of the original domestic one. More heavy duty and larger capacity.
	**Canadian Pulk** Nightmare to pull either on snow shoes or skis but essential to carry tentage, rations and kit when on foot.
	**Quilted Suit** Often referred to as the 'Ninja Suit'. Worn more during static phases, like comms exercises etc. It came with matching trousers that had a long zip down each leg.

	**Stove – Optimus 80** They needed some pampering, but burnt like demons. Often used to warm up cold chalets.
	**Stove – Optimus 111** Very good stove if treated well and looked after.
	**Stove – Peake Multi Fuel** Great bit of kit. Could run off all fuel known to man (almost) and fit in a water bottle pouch.
	**Clansman Radio** Predominantly the VRC 353 VHF set and VRC 321 HF set. Also used in the Rebro mode.

The Volvo Bandvagn 202 or BV 202

In 1969 Battalion Troop took delivery of its first BV 202 Snowcats. These were FFR versions

One of the first BV202 issued to Battalion Troop in 1969

The Bandvagn 202 or BV 202 articulated all-terrain tracked carrier was developed by Bolinder-Munktell for the Swedish Army. Production commenced in 1964 and ceased in 1981. This all-terrain carrier was purchased by Sweden, Canada, Finland, the Netherlands, Norway, and the United Kingdom. It is also referred to as the Snowcat. The BV 202 was employed in the Arctic, and Antarctica as well as Middle East.

This articulated all-terrain tracked carrier was designed to transport troops, cargo and equipment through difficult terrain, snow and boglands in the northern parts of Sweden. This twin-unit articulated tracked vehicle can carry 10 troops or 1000 kg of cargo. The front unit is fully enclosed, while the rear unit is covered with metal hoops and canvas cover.

The front unit contains the engine and gearbox. The initial version Mk.1, was powered by a Volvo B18 1.8-liter petrol engine, developing 82 hp. A later version, Mk.2 was fitted with a more powerful Volvo B20 2.0-liter petrol engine, developing 97 hp. These were standard car engines. Both engines are coupled with manual gearboxes and power is provided both to the front and rear unit tracks. The front unit accommodates the driver and commander.

The rear unit is connected via an articulated joint which is also used for steering. It gives great flexibility in all axles and extremely good manoeuvrability. It has bench seats and carries 8 troops or cargo. It can also be adapted for other applications. The BV 202 has incredible mobility over rough terrain. The vehicle uses wide tracks and has less ground pressure than a skier, which allows it to go over snow and marshes. This all-terrain tracked carrier is fully amphibious without preparation. On water it is propelled by its tracks. Production of the Volvo BV 202 ceased in 1981 and was succeeded by the Hägglunds BV 206.

Specifications:

Country of origin	Sweden
Entered service	1964
Configuration	Tracked
Cab seating	2 + 8 men
Dimensions and weight	
Weight (empty)	3.2 t
Payload capacity	1 t
Length	6.18 m
Width	1.76 m
Height	2.21 m
Mobility	
Engine	Volvo B18 petrol
Engine power	82 hp
Maximum road speed	39 km/h
Amphibious speed on water	6.5 km/h
Range	200 km
Manoeuvrability	
Gradient	60%
Side slope	40%
Vertical step	1.1 m
Trench	3.6 m
Fording	Amphibious

Winterised LWB FFR Landrover

Winterised FFR landrover deployed in Norway.

The Winterised LWB FFR Landrover was the AMF(L) 'workhorse' vehicle for temperate and sub arctic areas and was commonly used in deployments to Southern Norway, Germany, Denmark and Turkey. Winterised LWB (FFR) Landrover included insulated hard top, upgraded batteries, battery compartment heater, extra internal insulation, uprated heater/defroster and uprated cooling system. Different grade engine oil and greases were also used in cold climates. The Winterised Landrover was based on the Landrover Series III model.

The Hägglunds Bandvagn 206 or BV 206

Production of the Volvo BV 202 ceased in 1981 and was succeeded by the Hägglunds BV 206.

Bandvagn 206 or BV 206 is a tracked articulated, all-terrain carrier developed by Hägglunds for the Swedish Army. It consists of two units, with all four tracks powered. It can carry up to 17 people (6 in the front compartment, 11 in the rear), and the trailer unit can be adapted for different uses.

Hägglunds Bandvagn 206 or BV 206

The BV 206 was designed to carry troops and equipment through harsh terrain, snow, and marsh-lands in Sweden. The low ground pressure enables the BV 206 to cope with a wide range of difficult conditions and is widely acknowledged as an environmentally green machine because it does not tear up the terrain it is crossing despite being on tracks, this is because unlike a tank, the BV206 uses an articulated steering system as opposed to a brake and slew system.

In most forms it is also fully amphibious, powered by its tracks it can attain a speed in still water of up to 4.7 km/h. Over 11,000 units have been produced and they are used in more than 37 countries. The total payload capacity is 2,250 kg and a trailer of up to 2,500 kg gross weight can also be towed behind the second compartment. The BV 206 originally utilised a robust Ford V6 petrol power plant which was later joined by a 5-cylinder and 6-cylinder Mercedes Benz diesel engine.

Specifications

	Front Car*	Rear Car**	Total
Curb weight	2710 kg	1620 kg	4330 kg
Payload	580 kg	1670 kg	2250 kg
Gross weight	3290 kg	3290 kg	6580 kg
Passengers	5 (6)	11	16 (17)
Cargo space	2.5 m3 (88 ft3)	5.5 m3 (194 ft3)	8 m3 (283 ft3)

Weights
* Driver 70 kg (154 lbs) included in payload **Maximum 200 kg (441 lbs) of the payload can be carried on the roof rack
Maximum trailer weight 2500 kg (5500 lbs) Specific ground pressure Front/Rear car 11.6/13.6 kPa (1.68/1.97 PSI) 0.2/0.05 m sinkage
Dimensions
Length 6.9m Width 1.87m Height 2.4m GVW 6580kg Ground bearing pressure 140kPa (0.14kp/cm2)
Performance
Max. speed, on roads 55 km/h (34 mph) in water 3 km/h (2 mph) Grade, hard surface 60% (31°) deep snow 30% (17°) Range on roads 300 km (186 miles) Minimum operating temperature -52°C (-61.6°F)
Engine
Industrial Ford V6 Gasoline 136 hp Mercedes-Benz 5 cyl. Turbo Diesel 125 hp

Mercedes-Benz 6 cyl. Turbo Diesel 136 hp Ford 4 cyl. Turbo Diesel 136 hp
Gearbox
Daimler-Benz W 4A 040 Automatic 4-step forward, 1 reverse Transfer gearbox manufacturer: Hägglunds Vehicle AB Gear ratios: High 1.28:1, Low 2.11:1
Steering System
Hydrostatic, articulated (Centre Point Articulation) Turning radius 8m (26 ft) Emergency steering Standard
Tracks
Moulded rubber with cord Width 620 mm (24.4 in) Four track drive
Electrical System
Voltage 24V DC Alternator 55A Batteries 105 Ah, 2×12 V

COMMAND AND CONTROL IN A MULTINATIONAL FORCE

Extract from the Royal Signals Journal 1990 which describes the way comms were provided at that time and the difficulties of providing comms for a multi-national force. It also introduces the later Mobile Satellite Ground Terminal system of communications that were coming into use.

Communications for the ACE Mobile Force (Land)

BY MAJOR P B NEALE MA, MSc ROYAL SIGNALS

Editor's note

> *Major Peter Neale commands 249 Signal Squadron which provides the radio component for the Allied Command Europe Mobile Force (Land) or AMF(L) as it is more conveniently titled. The article provides an interesting insight into the way that a multinational force operates.*

Introduction

THE Allied Command Europe Mobile Force (AMF) is a multi-national, conventional force, which can be deployed to any of the countries which are part of the NATO alliance and which may be threatened by a hostile power. It consists of Air and Land Components which can be used together or separately. The purpose of the force, formed in the nineteen sixties, is to make it clear to any potential aggressor that an attack against one nation of the Alliance would constitute an attack against all. The presence of soldiers from a number of nations in the area of potential conflict is intended to demonstrate Alliance solidarity in concrete terms.

The major concentration of NATO forces in the Central Region leaves both the Northern and Southern flanks relatively thinly defended and, perhaps of greater significance, defended only by the forces of a single nation. Thus, the AMF concentrates in its planning and exercises on the areas of North Norway, Denmark,

Northern Italy, Greece and Turkey. Current exercise areas are shown below. Whilst the primary mission of the AMF is to deter aggression by its demonstration of NATO's determination and solidarity, it is fully equipped and trained to fight alongside the local forces, should this become necessary.

The AMF is one of a small number of multinational forces, such as the United Nations Force in Cyprus (UNFICYP) or the United Kingdom/Netherlands Amphibious Force. With the emphasis on deterrence, rather than on fighting in a major conflict, the AMF may provide a pattern for forces of the future, where strategic mobility may also be essential, in order to make optimum use of smaller forces.

The demographic trough and the possibility of the reduction of Conventional Forces in Europe (CFE) will both have an impact on NATO's capability to deter a potential enemy; the ability to insert rapidly a small coherent force may bring dividends out of all proportion to the force size. This article will concentrate on the command-and-control communications provided for the AMF (Land Component) (AMF(I)), of which the author has personal experience.

Orbat

The outline Orbat of the AMF(L) Is shown below. Whilst this is applicable to any deployment of the Force, the exact composition of the AMF(L) varies from one contingency area to another. In particular, individual infantry battalions are normally committed to either Northern or Southern areas, but not both. However, we are concerned here with the characteristics of the command-and-control problems and with the communication systems provided to assist in

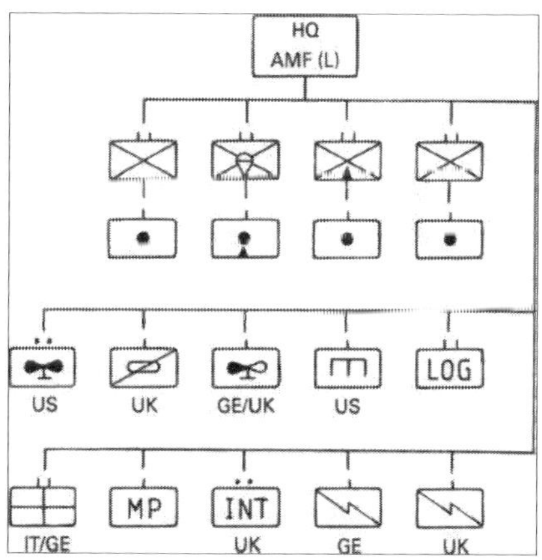

Orbat of the AMF(L)

their solution and so the minor differences in detail will be ignored. The headquarters of the AMF(L), based in Heidelberg in the Federal Republic of Germany, is staffed by officers and NCOs from all the countries which contribute to the Force.

Concept of Operations

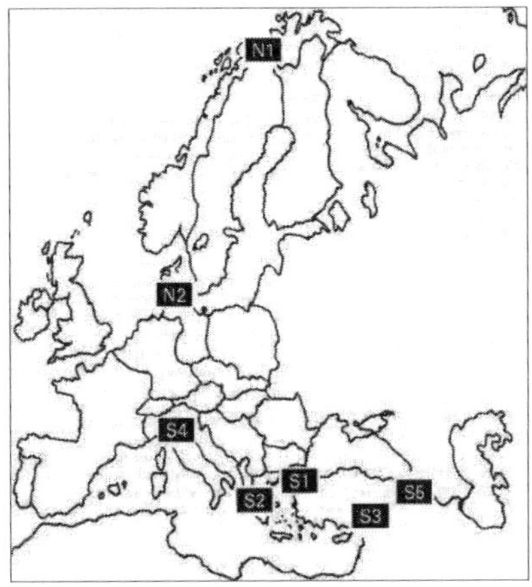

AMF(L) Deployment Areas

Deployment. Most units of the AMF(L) are based in peacetime in their home countries and their training is a national responsibility. Therefore, the first major activity of any deployment is the move into the designated area. On arrival, units occupy an overt Staging Area, where personnel and equipment can be married up and local training can take place. Communications in this phase must be established as quickly as possible and must demand the minimum of management.

Deterrent Operations. Deterrent patrolling starts as soon as possible with a reinforced company from each battalion carrying out overt patrols over a wide area. "Patrols" in this context can include football matches against the local clubs, taking tea with the Mayor and giving lectures to schools and societies. These companies, known as Key Companies, are commanded directly from Force Headquarters, posing a major communication challenge.

Combat Operations. It is to be hoped, of course, that the Deterrent operations will have their effect and that no aggression against NATO will take place. However, should enemy forces cross the border, the AMF(L) is prepared to stand and fight alongside the local forces.

Key/Command Net. This VHF voice net is used during deterrent operations to link the Key Companies and certain force-level units to Headquarters AMF(L). Because the Key Companies are usually widely spread, several rebroadcast stations are normally required. Because experience in any one of the deployment areas is limited, it may often take some time to find suitable sites for these stations and so this net may take some time to establish and may not be available at the start of deterrent operations. In combat operations, it is used as a conventional command net, linking the infantry battalions to the Main Force HQ. Distances are likely to be much shorter than in the deterrent phase so fewer rebroadcast stations are normally required.

HF Guard Net. In order to provide a service before the Key/Command Net is established, or when equipment failures at rebroadcast stations temporarily prevent its use, an HF Guard Net is provided. This net also works in voice mode, but its inferior sound quality and the lack of a squelch facility mean that the VHF net is much preferred by the users.

General Purpose/Medical/Logistic Net. A second VHF voice net is established to carry administrative and logistic traffic. During deter rent operations, it is known as the General-Purpose Net and links the battalions (less their Key Companies) to the Force Headquarters. As they are concentrated in the Staging Area, ranges are normally short, and few rebroadcast stations are required. During combat operations, the net is known as the Medical/Logistic Net and links the B Echelons of the battalions to the Force Rear Headquarters, to the Logistic Support Battalion and its sub-units and to the Field Hospital. Ranges may now increase considerably, requiring the use of several more rebroadcast stations.

Host Nation Support

The term "Host Nation Support" normally brings to mind the provision of transport and the supply of food and fuels. There is also, however, a considerable requirement for host nation communications to support any mobile force, such as the AMF(L).

The detail of what is provided varies from one contingency area to another, but would typically consist of:

- Access to the host nation's field trunk communication system.
- Liaison officers from higher and neighbouring formations, each with his own communications.
- Access to static NATO communication systems at a convenient point within the host nation's territory.
- Provision of circuits over static military communication systems.
- Provision, on repayment, of civil telephone lines and instruments.

Level of Communications Support

With, normally, three or four infantry battalions under command, the AMF(L) is comparable in size to a UK brigade in BAOR and readers may, therefore, be surprised to learn that it has two communication sub-units to support it. This surprise may turn to amazement, or even envy, when they learn that there is also a Headquarter Company, provided by the US Army, to administer the Headquarters in the field. Here, then, are three sub-units, each commanded by a Major, carrying out the functions which would be carried out by a Brigade Headquarters and Signal Squadron when in the field in BAOR. There are reasons for this:

First, the staff is much larger than that of a UK brigade. The Force is commanded by a Major General and each branch is headed by a Lieutenant Colonel. In peace, it has to plan for several different deployment options in widely differing theatres. During an exercise or operation, it has to coordinate the activities of the Force with those of the Host Nation and receives much less detailed direction from above than would the staff of a UK brigade.

Secondly, particularly during deterrence operations, the Force covers a much larger geographical area than a UK brigade and so requires more communication support.

Thirdly, the Force has to be largely self-sufficient for communications. The German Wire Company has to provide all its own relay stations and its own Nodal Site. The Force Radio Squadron has to provide a total of eighteen rear link detachments to the infantry battalions and to other force units, such as the Force Helicopter Unit and the Field Hospital. Both have to be largely self-sufficient for resupply and repair in the field. Thus, the communication task is considerably larger than in a UK brigade.

Communication Systems Provided

The AMF(L) usually follows the conventional wisdom of providing a telephone and telegraph service within the headquarter elements and rearwards, whilst using net radio to provide the communication to and within the units under command. The wide geographical dispersion of the Key Companies during deterrent operations and of the headquarter elements and logistic units during combat operations often make reliable communications difficult to achieve, but a combination of civilian and military communication systems is used to provide a fall-back service wherever possible.

The division of responsibility between trunk systems and net radio is a sensible one and allows each unit to train separately before meeting on AMF(L) exercises.

The provision of rear link detachments by the Force Radio Squadron is essential, as it provides compatible equipment at each station and avoids language problems on the net. It also allows those operators to train together and ensures that, even in difficult operating conditions, the user is always offered the best service that is technically possible.

Organization

The main challenge to the command and control of the AMF(L) arises during the transition from deterrent operations to combat operations. At this time of increasing international tension and with the outbreak of cross-border hostilities possible and perhaps imminent, the Force has to re-organize almost completely. The Key

Companies are withdrawn from their patrol areas and re-join their parent battalions, whilst those same battalions move from the overt staging area to concealed combat positions. The Force Headquarters also moves, and radio silence is normally imposed on radio users who change their functions and identities as this is done.

The change from deterrence, which must be overt, to combat, where concealment is essential until contact is made, presents difficulties in the way of a major re-organization and perhaps considerable movement. Only by frequent practice on exercise can the procedures become familiar to all participants and only if the Force Commander gives clear, concise orders, based on thorough preparation by his staff, can this most difficult operation be carried out successfully. Tight control of both the trunk system and the radio nets by their appropriate managers is essential, as is a good and free exchange of information between those managers and the staff. Given this, errors can be corrected, new unit locations can be confirmed, and communications can be provided as soon as they are required, and the emission control policy allows.

New Developments

In order to supplement the rather long and tenuous links to SHAPE via the existing static NATO systems, the AMF(L) will shortly bring into service a new satellite communication system. This will be provided jointly by the Force Radio Squadron and the German Wire Company, straddling the current division of roles of these units and necessitating even closer cooperation than in the past.

The Force Radio Squadron holds two UK/VSC 501 Mobile Satellite Ground Terminals (MSGT), each mounted in a winterized Landrover 110. These provide the bearer circuit between AMF(L) Headquarters in the field and a static ground station in Belgium, from where the individual voice and telegraph circuits are extended to SHAPE. Within Main Headquarters AMF(L), a modem in the MSGT separates the individual speech and telegraph circuits, all of which remain in digital form at this point. The German Wire Company provides a cable and links the MSGT to its Communication

Centre Vehicle, which houses the terminal equipment for both voice and telegraph circuits.

The new system is still being evaluated. Experience so far shows that the inability of either unit to train on this system without the cooperation of the other is a serious disadvantage when they are stationed in different countries and meet only during major exercises. This is becoming less serious as experience is gained and a plan has now been formulated to allow training to take place with both units in their peacetime barracks, connected by a second satellite link in place of the cable used in the field.

The other major concern regarding this system is that it has been assumed until now that it will always be possible to locate the MSGT at AMF(L) Main Headquarters, close enough to be linked by cable to the communication centre vehicle. Some difficulty has already been experienced with this in some of the wooded locations of Denmark, where except in a few selected places, trees prevent a clear view of the sky. During an operational deployment some trees might be felled in order to allow the station to work from the desired location, but this is not acceptable during training. Reconnaissance in North Norway suggests that the mountainous terrain may not allow a clear view of the satellite which, at such high latitudes, is very low in the sky. If this turns out to be the case, we may have to consider modifying the system in some way to allow the MSGT to be connected at another node of the trunk system, or to provide dedicated terrestrial radio relay to replace the field cable and thus extend the allowable separation between the MSGT and the Main Headquarters.

Conclusion

Despite its unusual role, the communications provided for the AMF(L) are broadly similar to those provided for a brigade or division in BAOR. The peculiar problems of command and control in a multinational force are overcome, partly by the provision of rear link detachments from a single unit and partly by training on regular exercises.

TIMELINE AND EVENTS

Date	Event	Description
1960 January	AMF(L) formed	The Allied Command Europe Mobile Force - Land (ACE Mobile Force-Land or AMF(L)) a small NATO quick reaction force, headquartered at Heidelberg, Germany, is formed
1967 November	AMF(L) Troop formed	AMF(L) UK Battalion Signal Troop, 30 Signal Regiment is formed to provide HF and VHF comms for the UK Infantry Battalion.
1968 February	Norway	AMF(L) Battalion Signal Troop first arctic survival training in Norway on Exercise Hardfall II in Tvildemoen, Voss followed by Summer Exercise in Tromso in July.
1968	Greece	
1968 November	New Troop	AMF(L) Force Radio Troop of 80 men is formed under the Command of Captain Ian Crouch. It is to serve HQ AMF(L) using the latest SSB Radios and Winterised 3/4 Ton Land Rovers
1969		244 Sig Sqn (AS) based at RAF Tangmere
1969 January	Norway	AMF(L) Battalion Signal Troop deploys 20 men to Voss on Exercise Hardfall 3. Equipped with Volvo BV202 Snowcats and arctic kit from Canada and Norway. There are no buildings to live in, just 2 large Swedish tents with wood burning stoves!
1969	Turkey	Ex Olympic Express
1970 January	Norway	Ex Hardfall IV. Bn Signal Troop fly to Bergen and Force Radio Tp sail to Oslo to stay with the Norwegian School of Signals
1970 April	3 Sqn formed	AMF(L) Force Radio Troop and AMF(L) Battalion Signal Troop amalgamate to form 3 Squadron 30 Signal Regiment, Blandford, under the Command of Captain Ian Crouch.

1970 June	Visit of Princess Anne	The AMF(L) Battalion Signal Troop put on a display for Princess Anne during her visit to Blandford.
1970 September	Visit	Comd AMF(L) visit the Sqn in the field at Blandford 10 September
1970 September	Germany	Ex Deep Heat a CPX exercise
1970 October	Turkey	Ex Deep Express. Deploy by air and sea for Turkey. Some elements joined direct from Germany.
1971		244 Sig Sqn (AS) move to RAF Benson
1971 January	Norway	Ex Hardfall. A smooth LSL crossing followed by NO snow!! The Sqn is based in Ulven and snow is eventually found in Kvamskogen. Training commences from a Ski hut and Swedish tents! The end of ski training is celebrated with the locals in the Village Hall.
1971 July	VIP Visit	AMF(L) Battalion Signal Troop put on a display for Under Secretary of State for Defence - Sir Geoffrey Johnson-Smith
1971 September	Greece	Ex Hellenic Express. Deploy by air and sea
1972 September	Germany-Norway	Ex Fjord Test in Germany followed by a flight to Norway for Ex Strong Express. Force Radio Tp win the NATO Challenge cup
1973 January	Norway	Ex Hardfall Mjolfjell Camp near Voss
1973 September	Denmark	Ex Absalon Express. Queen Margerethe of Denmark visits the Sqn in the field.
1974 January	Norway	Ex Hardfall 74 Voss
1974 May	Norway	Ex Argus Express in Arctic Norway. Returned by LSL Sir Geraint
1974 September	Germany	Ex Autumn Test in Southern Germany.

1975 February	Norway	Ex Hardfall 75. Arrived in Trondheim by LSL Sir Lancelot. 244 Sig Sqn train at Bomen Camp in Voss
1975 June	Old Sarum	Ex Clear Voice. A Joint Voice Procedure exercise held Old Sarum.
1975 September	Turkey	Ex Deep Express. Deploy by sea to Saros Bay in Turkey
1976		244 Sig Sqn (AS) move to RAF Brize Norton
1976 February	Norway	Ex Hardfall 76 near Voss and Ex Atlas Express in the Arctic. Training at the youth hostel at Mjolfjell. 244 Sig Sqn join the training
1976 July	249 Formed	The role out grows its original home of 3 Sqn, 30 Signal Regiment, Blandford Camp. 249 Signal Squadron is brought back into the orbat and moves to Old Sarum Camp just outside Salisbury. Authority has been given by MOD(ASD) for the forming of 249 Sig Sqn (AMF(L))
1976 September	Sardinia	Ex Augustus Exchange 19 Sep - 18 October. A full deployment moving in three convoys across Europe passing through Calais, Douie, Chaumont, Orange, Savona, Genoa, Gagliari
1977 January	Norway	Ex Hardfall 77. 249 Sig Sqn billeted in the Dalane Hostel Voss.
1977 April	Sardinia	Ex Allegro Express
1977 September	Denmark	Ex Arrow Express in Denmark
1977 November	Salisbury Plain	Ex Avon Express.
1978 January	Norway	Ex Hardfall. 249 Sig Sqn billeted in Flatlandsmo Camping Site which consists of 12 chalets. Second camp is Espland and has 10 chalets.

		Ex Arctic Express held in Arctic Norway. A Tp, 244 Sig Sqn train in Norway
1978 May	Northern Ireland	249 Det serving with 51 Fd Sqn (Const) RE in Armagh
1979 January	Norway	Ex Hardfall 79. 4th Jan - 12 Feb. The first Norway when helicopters were used extensively. A Tp, 244 Sqn undergo training with 249 Sqn
1979 March	249 Sig Sqn renamed	249 Signal Squadron is renamed to 249 Signal Squadron (AMF(L)) and moves to Bulford Camp
1979 June	Denmark	Ex Agate Exchange. 6 Jun 79 - 17 Jun 79
1980 January	Norway	Ex Hardfall 80. Followed by Ex Anorak Express in Arctic Norway in May
1980 September	Turkey	18 Sep - 2 Oct. Arrived in Turkey 1 week after the Military Coup.
1981 February	Norway	Ex Hardfall 81. 7 Feb 81 - 5 Mar 81. A Tp, 244 Sqn Join 249 Sqn for training
1981 May	Italy	AMF(L) CPX. 4 May 81 - 15 May 81
1981 July	Denmark	Ex Amber Express. 249 win NATO Challenge Cup. 244 Sqn involved in the Ex
1982 January March	Norway	Ex Hardfall 82. Voss area. 249 and A Tp, 244 Sqn Ex Alloy Express. Arctic Norway. 249 Sqn win NATO Challenge Cup
1983 January	Norway	Ex Hardfall 83. Based at Stalheim Hotel. 249 Sqn joined by A Tp, 244 Sqn Ex Eagles Return - FTX
1983 June	Turkey	Ex Adventure Express.
1983 September	Denmark	AMF(L) CPX. 249 Sqn matches 1 Paras time on the march and wins the NATO Challenge Cup for the 3rd year

1984 January	Norway	Ex Hardfall 84. Based at the Stalheim Hotel. 249 are joined by A Tp, 244 Sqn. This year a third of 249 Sqn formed D Company. The final assault against 1 Para consisted of: Heli lifts to a frozen lake, 4-mile ski then a final assault on snow-shoes
1984 March	Norway	Ex Avalanche Express. Bardufoss area of Arctic Norway
1984 September	Denmark	Ex Bold Gannet. 249 Sqn provide communications and control for the Umpire Organisation of the Ex.
1985 January	Norway	Ex Hardfall 85. Stalheim Hotel, Voss area. 249 Sqn joined by A Top, 244 Sqn
1985 March	Norway	Ex Cold Winter. Bardufoss. Part of 249 Sqn take part in an Ex with 1 Para and RM.
1985 April	Portugal	Ex Ardent Ground. A Tp, 244 Sqn provide Air Support comms for the Annual live firing ex for Artillery and Offensive Support Aircraft of AMF(L) and AMF(A)
1985 June	Denmark	Ex Albatross Exchange
1985 September	Turkey	Ex Archway Express.
1986 January	Norway	Ex Hardfall 86. Brakanes Hotel, Ulvik. 249 Sqn joined by A Tp, 244 Sqn
1986 February	Norway	Ex Anchor Express. Bardufoss, Arctic Norway
1986 November	Italy	Ex Allegro Exchange. North East Italy
1987 January	Norway	Ex Hardfall 87. Brakanes Hotel, Ulvik. 249 Sqn joined by A Tp, 244 Sqn
1987 May	Turkey	Ex Aurora Express in the mountains of Erzurum Kars.
1987 September	Denmark	Ex Accord Express. 249 Sqn wins the NATO Challenge Cup

1988 January	Norway	Ex Hardfall
1988 March	Norway	Ex Arrowhead Express in Arctic Norway
1988 September	Turkey	Ex Alley Express. 249 Sqn deploy with their newly acquired SA80's and SATCOM. D Tp, 244 Sqn deploy two MAOT's
1989 January	Norway	Ex Hardfall 89
1989 May	Italy	Ex Armanda Exchange
1989 September	Denmark	Ex Action Express. 249 Sqn retain the Minor Units NATO Challenge Cup
1990 January	Norway	Ex Hardfall 90.
1990 May	Norway	Ex Array Encounter 90
1991 January	Norway	Ex Hardfall 91
1991 September	Denmark	Ex Action Express 91. The NATO Challenge Cup (Biathlon) is won by 249 Sig Sqn
1992 January	Norway	Ex Hardfall 92. 249 Sqn joined by A Tp, 244 Sqn
1992 July	UK	Ex Allegiance Express. AMF(L) CPX held in Otterburn Training Area
1992 August	UK	Ex Ardent Ground. Field firing Ex in Sennybridge
1992		244 Sig Sqn (AS) amalgamated with 21 Sig Regt
1992 September	Turkey	Ex Alley Express ???
1993 January	Norway	Ex Hardfall 93. Stalheim Hotel, Ulvik.

1993 September	Denmark	Ex Action Express. 249 Sqn wins The NATO Challenge Cup
1993	Italy	Ex Arena Exchange
1994 January	Norway	Ex Hardfall 94
1994 March	Norway	Ex Arctic Express in Badufoss, Arctic Norway
1994	Turkey	Ex Arrow Exchange
1995 January	Norway	Ex Hardfall 95
1995 March	Norway	Ex Strong Resolve. NATO FTX held West of Trondheim in Norway to practise the deployment and operation of a Combined Joint Task Force (CJTF)
1996 January	Norway	Ex Hardfall 96
1996 September	Turkey	Ex Dynamic Mix. First AMF(L) deployment for 18 months
1997 January	Norway	Ex Hardfall 97
1997 March	Norway	Ex Adventure Express in Northern Norway
1997 July	Turkey	Ex Ardent Ground. AMF(L) Field Firing Ex supported by 244 Sqn
1998 January	Norway	Winter Warfare Training
1998 March	Norway	Ex Strong Resolve. Arctic Norway
1998 November	Slovenia	Ex Cooperative Adventure Exchange.
1999 January	Norway	Ex Snowhole. Winter Warfare Training for UK AMF(L) Units.
1999 March	Italy	Ex Adventure Exchange. Based in north-east Italy in the regions of the Camil Alps and

		Friuli Venezia Giulia. The Exercise itself was part FTX and part CPX and involved five battalions including NATO's newest members, the Hungarians, Polish and Czechs
2000 January	Norway	Ex Hardfall 2000. Central Winter Warfare training based at Mjolfjell Camp near Voss
2000 March	Norway	Ex Adventure Express. Arctic Norway
2000 June	Hungary	Ex Ardent Ground. Force Artillery Ex.
2000 September	Greece	Ex Adventure Exchange. A marked shift away from 249 Sqn usual CNR role and a move towards CIS management and increased use of SATCOM as the AMF(L) continues its trial of the IRTF(L) concept - a command and control system based on a theatre-wide tactical WAN.
2001 January	Norway	Ex Hardfall 2001. 249 Sqn host Blue Peter host Matt Baker
2001	Turkey	Ex Adventure Exchange
2002 January	Norway	Ex Hardfall 2002.
2002 March	Norway	Ex Adventure Express. Tondheim area, Northern Norway.
2002 September	Ukraine	Ex Cooperative Adventure Exchange. Final AMF(L) exercise for 249 Sqn and 244 Sqn
2002 October	Heidelberg Germany	AMF(L) Disbandment Parade.
2002 October	AMF(L) Disbanded	30th October AMF(L) is disbanded. 249 Sqn forms part of the disbandment parade in Heidelberg.
2003 January	Bulford	249 Signal Squadron AMF(L) Disbandment Parade

ABREVIATIONS AND MILITARY SLANG

Word or Phrase	Meaning
1 PWO	1st Battalion Prince of Wales Own Regiment
110	Model of Landrover (long wheel base)
2i/c	Second in command
9x9	Framed tent or shelter measuring 9ft by 9ft
AMF(L)	Allied Command Europe Mobile Force (Land)
AP	Associated Press
AS	Air Support
asap	As soon as possible
AWI	Arctic Warfare Instructor
AWT	Arctic Warfare Training
Baby's heads	Tinned Steak and Kidney pudding from ration packs
Basher	Simple tent sheet or shelter
BASO	Brigade Air Support Operations
Beasting	Being pushed physically to your limits
BID	Secure communications equipment
Blancoing	Blanco came in round cake form and was used as a cleaning and colouring compound for a soldiers webbing. It produced a standard 'buff' colour that allowed all soldiers webbing to look the same.
Bull	Putting a high polish on Parade Boots and other uniform parts
Bumpering	Polishing barrack room floors with a bumper
Cam net	Camouflage netting
Capt	Captain
Casevac/Casevaced	Abbreviation for Casualty Evacuation
CFB	Canadian Forces Base
Chalk Commander	Senior person responsible for a named group of military air passengers
Chin-strapped	Tired or worn out physically
civpop	Abbreviation for Civilian Population
Civvies	Civilian clothing or civilians in general
Comms	Communications
Compo	Ration packs
Cpl	Corporal
Cyalume	Tactical chemical light stick
Det	Detachment

Word or Phrase	Meaning
DS	Directing Staff
Ech	Echelon. A subdivision of a headquarters, i.e., forward echelon, rear echelon
End Ex	Every soldier's favourite words. Means the exercise or event is over and you can start to pack up ready to return to base and relax
Ex	Exercise
FAC	Forward Air Control
FANY	First Aid Nursing Yeomanry
FHU	Force Helicopter Unit
FLOT	Forward Line of Troops
FofS	Foreman of Signals
Full Screw	The term 'Full Screw' is British Army slang used to describe someone holding the rank of Corporal
Galley	Ship's kitchen and dining area
GS	General Service
Hardfall	Winter Warfare training exercise in Norway
Heads	Toilets on board a ship
Imbiss	Imbiss is a general German term for a small food stand or street food stall, usually tiny and locally run (often a family operation).
Kip	Sleep or rest
Lance Jack	Lance Corporal
LSL	Landing Ship Logistic
Lt	Lieutenant
MAOT	Mobile Air Operations Team
Married pads	Term for married soldiers who lived in married quarters
Medevac	Medical Evacuation – usually by helicopter
MSI	Mountain Ski Instructor
MSR	Main Supply Route
NAAFI	Navy Army and Airforce Institute. A welfare organisation for forces personnel providing canteens and leisure facilities
Nause	Nauseous or 'a bother'
NCO	Non-Commissioned Officer. Lance Corporal or Full Corporal
O Group	Orders Group or meeting of senior staff
OP	Observation Post

Word or Phrase	Meaning
Pongo's	Naval term for soldiers
QM	Quartermaster – Officer responsible for all stores and supplies in a unit
Quinzee	a type of shelter originally used by North American Indians, consisting of a mound of snow with a domed chamber dug into it.
RAF	Royal Air Force
RaTT	Radio automatic Tele Type
RCP	Regimental Command Post
RE	Royal Engineers
Rebro	Rebroadcast station
Recce	Reconnaissance
Scoff	Food
Singlies	Single persons. Usually used for single persons accommodation
SLR	Self-Loading Rifle
SMG	Sub Machine Gun
SNCO	Senior non-commissioned officer – Sergeant or Staff Sergeant
Snotting	Falling off your ski's – usually violently!
SQMS	Squadron Quarter Master Sergeant – an appointment in the rank of Staff Sergeant
Sqn	Squadron
Squaddie	Colloquial name for a soldier in the UK
SSB	Single Side Band
SSgt	Staff Sergeant
SSM	Squadron Sergeant Major
Stagging On or On Stag	A period on Duty or Guard
Stoppages	Money deducted from a soldier's pay ("stopped") as a punishment or fine or to pay for loss of kit
Tabbing	Tactical Advance to Battle: typically marching in full kit and carrying your weapon
Tacevalled	Tactical Evaluation
TACP	Tactical Air Control Party
YMCA	Young Men's Christian Association
YofS	Yeoman of Signals

Printed in Great Britain
by Amazon

60074042R00270